The Elements of Friendly Software Design

Praise for the First Edition of
The Elements of
Friendly Software Design

*And Praise for
the Second Edition of*

The Elements of Friendly Software Design

The Elements of
Friendly Software Design

Computer users are not all alike.
Neither are SYBEX books.

We know our customers have a variety of needs. They've told us so. And because we've listened, we've developed several distinct types of books to meet the needs of each of our customers. What are you looking for in computer help?

If you're looking for the basics, try the **ABC's** series, or for a more visual approach, select **Teach Yourself**.

Mastering and **Understanding** titles offer you a step-by-step introduction, plus an in-depth examination of intermediate-level features, to use as you progress.

Our **Up & Running** series is designed for computer-literate consumers who want a no-nonsense overview of new programs. Just 20 basic lessons, and you're on your way.

SYBEX **Encyclopedias** provide a *comprehensive reference* and explanation of all of the commands, features and functions of the subject software.

Sometimes a subject requires a special treatment that our standard series doesn't provide. So you'll find we have titles like **Advanced Techniques, Handbooks, Tips & Tricks**, and others that are specifically tailored to satisfy a unique need.

You'll find SYBEX publishes a variety of books on every popular software package. Looking for computer help? Help Yourself to SYBEX.

For a complete catalog of our publications:

SYBEX Inc.
2021 Challenger Drive, Alameda, CA 94501
Tel: (415) 523-8233/(800) 227-2346 Telex: 336311
SYBEX Fax: (415) 523-2373

The Elements of Friendly Software Design

The New Edition

Paul Heckel

SYBEX®

San Francisco   Paris   Düsseldof   Soest

Acquisitions Editor: Dianne King
Editor: Savitha Pichai
Word Processors: Lisa Mitchell, Ann Dunn, Deborah Maizels, Scott Campbell
Book Design and Layout: Charlotte Carter
Technical Art: Delia Brown
Screen Graphics: Cuong Le
Desktop Publishing Production: Dan Brodnitz
Proofreaders: R.M. Holmes, Dina F. Quan
Indexer: Anne Leach
Cover Designer: Ingalls + Associates
Cover Photographer: Mark Johann

Apple, Macintosh, and HyperCard are registered trademarks of Apple Computer, Inc.

VisiCalc is a registered trademark of Lotus Development Corporation.

Zoomracks and HyperRacks are registered trademarks of Quickview Systems, Inc. and HyperRacks, Inc.

SYBEX is a registered trademark of SYBEX, Inc.

TRADEMARKS: SYBEX has attempted throughout this book to distinguish proprietary trademarks from descriptive terms by following the capitalization style used by the manufacturer.

SYBEX is not affiliated with any manufacturer.

Every effort has been made to supply complete and accurate information. However, SYBEX assumes no responsibility for its use, nor for any infringement of the intellectual property rights of third parties which would result from such use.

Library of Congress Card Number: 90-72075
ISBN: 0-7821-1538-1

Manufactured in the United States of America
10 9 8 7 6 5 4 3 2

Dedicated to the Memory of My Father, Charles Heckel

singing each morning out of each night
my father moved through depths of height
e e cummings

And to My Mother, Elizabeth Heckel

Everything goes by the board: honor, pride,
decency…to get the book written. If a writer
has to rob his mother, he will not hesitate; the
"Ode on a Grecian Urn" is worth any number
of old ladies.
William Faulkner

Table of Contents

xvi

commu-
-nication

Each chapter in this book begins with an illustration of a different communications craft. Calligraphy is one such craft, and Scott Kim shows what can be done if the communicator understands and can manipulate the factors affecting his audience's perception.

Copyright © 1981 Scott Kim.

Please turn the page upside down.

Introduction

Writing and rewriting are the constant search for what one is saying.

John Updike

W hile I have been writing computer programs for twenty years, my major interests for the last ten years have been in developing software that will be used by people who are not computer professionals and thus need programs that are easy to use. I knew a few techniques, but I didn't understand how to make a program easy to use on a fundamental level. As far as I could see, few other people did, either.

Almost everyone wants his software to be easy to use, or "friendly." Unfortunately, the term *friendly* does not seem to have any objective meaning. Too frequently, it is a term a vendor uses to describe a software product, the same way a soap manufacturer uses the phrase *new and improved.* It communicates positive associations to the customer more than real substance. I hope that this book will help provide some useful meaning to the term *friendly software,* both for the customer, who should know what to expect, and for the software designer who wants to make his software friendly but is unsure of how to go about it.

In 1982, I wrote an essay to crystallize my thoughts on what made software easy to use. The essay expanded into a series of articles in *Infoworld,* an all-day seminar (with several other speakers), and finally into this book. What I discovered on that long and interesting journey is that writing friendly software is a *communications* task, and to do it effectively you must apply the techniques of effective communication; techniques that are little different from those developed by writers, filmmakers— virtually anyone who has attempted to communicate an idea over the past decades, centuries, even in some cases millennia. It is the use— consciously or unconsciously— of these techniques that makes software successful in the marketplace.

In short, the software designer must learn to think like a communicator and to practice an artistic craft as well as an engineering one.

I have tried to support my premises with several examples, both from computer software design and from other communications crafts. Few of the concepts presented here will be new to professional communicators. What is new is the application of these principles to designing friendly software, and a look at how certain very successful software designs, such as VisiCalc®, have used these principles.

What I say may also be of interest to a more general audience— people interested in computers or the techniques of effective communication. The general reader need not be afraid that this book is too technical. Indeed, such a reader has a distinct advantage over the computer experts in that he has less to unlearn.

Except for a few brief excursions, I have spent my professional life developing software. After receiving an undergraduate degree in electrical engineering, I became a programmer and joined a project to develop a time-shared computer. During the sixties, I was fortunate to work with several sharp technical people on a succession of technically interesting projects, none of which became a commercial success.

The pieces from the last of these, a startup called Berkeley Computer Corporation, were dispersed throughout Silicon Valley. One group of eight formed an important part of the nucleus of Xerox PARC, the laboratory where so much interesting work originated: Smalltalk, the Dynabook concept, Alto (the first high-quality desktop computer), Xerox Star, and Ethernet. These and other Xerox PARC ideas have already worked themselves into Apple's Lisa, VisiCalc's Visi-on, and many other products.

I worked for Xerox PARC part-time for two years while going to business school to get an M.B.A. (Berkeley Computer's failure was due to a lack of business savvy.) During the last few years, I have been an independent consultant doing microprocessor software product design. My typical client has been an entrepreneurial company in Silicon Valley.

I specialized in products that were to be used by the general public, rather than by computer specialists, and this focused my attention on the problem of ease of use. Along the way, I published two technical papers in the *Communications of the Association of Computing Machinery* and spent a year selling time-sharing services. Several threads from the sales experience are woven into the fabric of this book. But when I reflect on the experience, I am reminded of the old Japanese adage, "A man is a fool if he does not climb Mount Fuji, or if he climbs Mount Fuji more than once."

It is always difficult to credit everyone who contributes to a book. But I will do my best.

Larry Tesler, who headed the design of the user interface for Apple's Lisa, read the essay on which this book is based and encouraged its publication. Without that encouragement, I might never have completed this book. Dave Smith, the major designer of the Xerox Star user interface; Chuck Clanton, my associate at QuickView Systems; and John Zussman provided important suggestions at various stages in the manuscript's development.

Bob Frankston of Software Arts, who (with Dan Bricklin) developed VisiCalc, and Rob Barnaby, who developed WordStar, both gave me their time to describe their experience in those projects. (I owe Rob a second thanks since I used WordStar to write this book.)

Several of my clients during 1980 and 1981 provided work that stimulated many of the ideas in this book: John Jones (formerly of Atari), John Peters of Integrated Office Systems, Thijs Moes (formerly of Descor), and Bill Gates of Microsoft.

Whitfield Diffie, John Zussman, Gerald Tomanek, Quinn Yarbro, Mark Halpern, Esther Dysan, and Don and Shirley Hall all provided helpful suggestions, as did David Casci, a film director, who suggested I read *Disney Animation: The Illusion of Life*. While he did not contribute directly to the book, Tom Zimmer has done most of the programming for the Viewdex product described in Chapter 10.

Though they had no immediate effect on this book, two people had a strong indirect effect. It was through Butler Lampson's patience in editing my design documents at Berkeley Computer and later at Xerox that I first learned to write. And it was through my association with Alan Kay at Xerox PARC, and indirectly through his work (which is determining much of the direction in which computers will go), that many of my ideas were formed. Alan is one of the very few true visionaries in computers. Mary Fischer is a good friend with whom I had many discussions during the time I was writing this book. You will get an idea of her influence if I tell you she is a tester of software products, an Egyptologist, and a wild animal trainer.

An earlier version of this book was serialized in *Info-world,* where John Markoff provided encouragement and help, and Tom Shea, Eva Eangfeldt, and Patricia Sinervo copyedited my manuscript into English. Mary Fischer, Ruth Tubbs, Ron Biell, and Miki Pryor edited and typed portions of the manuscript.

I would like to thank two literary agents for the help they provided. Even though he had retired, Paul Reynolds read the manuscript and suggested I pursue publication. Second, John Brockman placed the work with a publisher who shared my vision of the book.

My editor, Reid Boates, has been most helpful in spotting weaknesses in the manuscript and making useful editorial suggestions, while at the same time supporting me in making my vision of this book work. Charles Riley checked the accuracy of my quotations, some of which were half-remembered quotes from unknown authors.

Finally, and very briefly, some people feel my writing is sexist, since I do such things as use the word "he" when referring to the designer or the user. I find that when I attempt to avoid such usage I am forced into longer phrases ("he or she" rather than "he"), less vivid images ("users" rather than "your user"), and the passive voice. I apologize for any offense my readers who are women may take, and ask each of you to picture in your mind whatever designer and user you desire and not let the specific pronouns I use get in the way of that image.

In these marvelous days of computers, I could quickly change all instances of "he" in my manuscript to "she," and similarly change "him" to "her." I asked my publisher to publish the book in His and Her editions, but he said it would be too expensive.

Introduction to the Second Edition

In the computer industry, technology and books tend to get obsolete rather quickly. However, by treating user-oriented software design as a communications craft, this book addresses the fundamentals, and the fundamentals change slowly. It is a pleasure to find people telling me that my message is just as relevant today as when I first wrote the book, so I was happy that SYBEX wanted to republish it. I have added two new chapters (actually, one new chapter and an epilogue) that, like the rest of the book, can be read in whatever order the reader prefers. The new Chapter 11, "Roses and Cabbages," describes our approach to computer metaphor in general, and the card and stack metaphor in particular. Some readers might find it too technical and wish to skip over parts of it.

By contrast, the new Epilogue, "The Wright Brothers and Software Invention," will appeal to the general reader and be of less interest to readers who are only interested in the issues of software design. While my experience as a software developer informed the first edition of this book, my more recent experience has been as an entrepreneur trying to put my ideas into practice. The Epilogue reflects that more recent experience. It gives an overview of the invention process from conception of the idea through litigation to get one's rights recognized. It tells not just of my experience, but the experience of many inventors— especially that of the Wright brothers.

Some people who read drafts of the Epilogue told me that while what I say should be said, it would be better if I did not say it, lest I antagonize some readers and get an undeserved reputation as someone difficult to deal with. I have considered their advice, but have decided to go ahead with the Epilogue. I don't want to sugar-coat the problems an entrepreneur and inventor faces or, by my silence, suggest that they do not exist. My sense of intellectual integrity does not let me say, "Write easy to use software," and not provide a fair warning of what is involved in protecting your intellectual property rights.

The fact that software patents are a much-discussed issue is another reason I feel I should speak. At a time when most discussion of software patents is hypothetical hogwash (if I may use a technical term) by people with no practical knowledge of patents, my experience stands as an exhibit of software patents in actual use and is a useful addition to the record for others to learn from. Since most articles have an anti-software patents bias, the Epilogue provides me a forum in which to present the patent holder's point of view and to educate people on some of the practical realities of patents and patent negotiation.

Whether it is IBM defending its Microchannel patents rights, Walt Disney defending its copyright on Mickey Mouse, or me defending my rights in the card and rack metaphor, if we want people to create things worth copying and seriously pursue their development and marketing, we have to respect their rights. By treating software design as communication, I tried to connect it to the mainstream of existing knowledge. By treating software as intellectual property, I am trying to connect it to the mainstream of jurisprudence. I realize that this stands in contrast to many in the software field, who prefer to reinvent things from scratch rather than search for what is proven to work.

The opening quotation to this Introduction to the Second Edition is both appropriate and inappropriate. Although my publisher will tell you that I extracted the customary pound of flesh (he kept the other nine), unlike Samuel Johnson, I am less interested in the money I make on sales of this book than in getting my message out. My primary work is as a software developer, and there, like Samuel Johnson, I do it for money. I expect my rights to be respected.

In preparing the new edition, we considered updating the text and illustrations. We could, for example, replace references to VisiCalc with references to Lotus 1-2-3 and references to WordStar with references to its modern version, WordStar 6.0, which— as you can see by the screen shot below— has advanced substantially over the pioneering version of Wordstar from the early 1980s described later in this book. I could also have replaced references to Lisa and Visi-on with references to the Macintosh. I did not make these changes for several reasons. First, the basic argument presented here is that what we should be bringing to software design is what we have learned about communicating during the last 2500 years. Using more recent examples would contradict my message that age-old techniques of communication are more important than the latest technology.

Second, it is too often the tragedy of pioneers to have their contributions forgotten as more modern products backed by bigger pocketbooks and more massive marketing

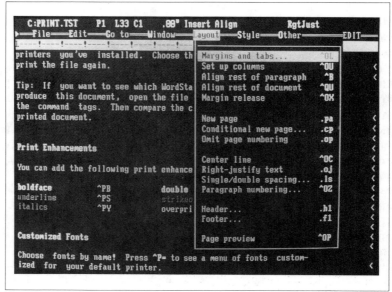

Used by permission of WordStar International Inc.

capability move to the forefront. I prefer to highlight, rather than obscure, the contributions the pioneers made. VisiCalc no longer exists, and WordStar, after some early problems where it lost market share, is once again an important word processor in its current version of WordStar 6.0. Third, one change begets another and I am reluctant to open Pandora's box, making first one change and then another until the whole book has been rewritten. Fourth, as anyone who has read *1984* or *Animal Farm* or who admires George Orwell knows, the greatest sin of intellectual integrity is to rewrite history. The record of what I said in early 1984 should stand unchanged.

Fifth, our Zoomracks patents make us controversial. Having settled with Apple for a substantial sum, we expect to be treated seriously, but many will still refuse to respect our rights. When you read this, you may know us as a cause célèbre and want to know whether what you are reading is the 1984 original or a 1991 rewrite. This edition includes everything that was in the original edition, complete and un-changed except for a few copyediting corrections and a few illustration changes that were caused by permissions matters. New material is confined to the new chapter, the Epilogue, and this new introduction.

I first came up with many of the ideas for Zoomracks in 1981 and, except for taking time to write this book, have developed them full time since then. Others have made a major contribution to developing this metaphor. Chuck Clanton worked on a consulting basis as a codesigner of Zoomracks from the founding of Quickview Systems in the summer of 1982 until the summer of 1986. Chuck also con-tributed to writing the "Roses and Cabbages" chapter, which describes our ideas behind Zoomracks. Tom Zimmer did most of the programming on Zoomracks. Even if it is hard to determine exactly who contributed what in a group effort, our respective roles are clear. I was the visionary and "producer-director." Chuck brought an academic knowledge of the software literature, along with much practical experience. While Chuck and I argued and theorized and designed, Tom wrote most of the code.

Chapter 10, "Works in Progress," was written in the summer of 1983 and reflects our plans at that time. Obviously, much has changed since then, and this is the one chapter that is in some sense dated. We did not develop Viewcheck beyond its description there. However, credit card transactions are moving in the direction I described. As I write this Introduction to the Second Edition, credit-card purchase receipts are frequently printed out on adding-machine size paper for the customer to sign, with the credit authorization and transaction completed over the phone lines. Clearly, a practical move in the direction of electronic funds transfer is taking place, and we are generally moving in the direction of hand-held computers described in Chapter 10.

The years since this book was first published in 1984 and particularly since Zoomracks was introduced in 1985 have been difficult. What kept me going were the support and encouragement of many people. The reasons I persisted through some dark times were the encouragement of hundreds of enthusiastic Zoomracks users and the variety of applications they developed—far beyond what I would have imagined. I would like to thank all the Zoomracks users, but particularly those who pushed the metaphor in their respective directions: Greg Alter, psychology office management; Marty Brown, employee benefits and project management; Jim Bumpas, law office management; Sal Chandon, innkeeping; Fred Choate, graduate research; Stan Farwig, horticulture and gardening; Gary Ferren, genealogy; Jerry Finzi, photography office management; Russell Fox, symphony conductor; Stephen Frye, project and home management; Dave Flory, police records; Dr. Robert Funke, medical records; Irwin Gemlich, manufacturing management; Hank Hattendorf, security systems sales management; Tom Howard, television station records and home management; Larry Jones, teaching; Dr. Mich Kabay, project management; Jack Kosiorek, home management; Cecil McGregor, personal records; John Mofield, archives of recipients for the Congressional Medal of Honor Society; Ken Murr, newsletter management; Cliff Panata, seminar and mailing list management; Ann Paull, home management; Steve Randall, telemarketing sales; Joanne Sattley, small business accounting; Mark Slomka, church management; Ray Soifer, security analysis; Jeff Stern, sales management; John Stout, wildlife management for the U.S. Fish and Wildlife Service; David Wade, novelist; Mark White, service support; and Madilon Wilson, writer of a Zoomracks column in *ST-XPRESS*, a magazine for Atari ST computer users. Each of these people developed several different applications with the card and rack metaphor within his field of interest. Without the support of these and thousands of other Zoomracks users, I would have given up and gotten an honest job long ago.

I would also like to thank Alan Kay, who recognized Zoomracks' rack metaphor as "an important new metaphor" back in 1985. Dan Shafer was one of the first people to publicly recognize my patent rights with respect to Hyper-Card. Ron Lesea, Jim Bidzos and Jeff Cherniss also gave helpful advice. Most of all, I want to thank my mother who was always there when things got really tough and I had to borrow a little more money to support my single-minded pursuit. Savitha Pichai, my editor, provided much useful criticism and suggested many improvements to the manuscript. I would like to thank Rudy Langer, Editor-in-Chief at SYBEX, one of the first publishers to specialize in computer books. Rudy wanted to publish this book in 1983, but at that time publishers with more money than sense were discovering that computer books were hot. When my first publisher offered me a sizable advance, Rudy was smart enough to pass. But slow and steady wins the race. My first publisher is no longer in the computer book business, but SYBEX is, and stronger than ever. While most people in this industry have wanted to get rich quick, I always wanted to get rich *slow*. And let me tell you something, I got the slow part down pat.

I would also like to thank a few lawyers (which might come as a surprise to those who read the Epilogue)— Hugh Finley, Steve Lundberg, Susan Nycum, Woody Higgins, Richard Silberman, and my uncle, Harold Herr— for the help and advice they gave me. The contribution of certain other lawyers is acknowledged in the Epilogue.

Finally, Quickview, the fox pictured in Chapter 10, is doing well. I had dinner at the owner's the other night and slipped her some fettucine with pesto sauce. Quickview is no longer a puppy and has grown older, as have I. I don't know whether in choosing an arctic fox, an animal that is particularly adept at surviving in harsh conditions, I was inviting harsh conditions to occur or protecting against them when they did occur. Nevertheless, the next time I start a business and my friend wants a pet named after my company, I will give her a lion cub.

Figure 1: Film. D. W. Griffith, by changing filmmaking from an engineering craft to an artistic one, invented the modern medium of movies. Computer software is undergoing a similar evolution from what is presented to how it is presented.

The Bettman Archive.

An Historical Perspective

If you cannot—in the long run—tell everyone what you have been doing, your doing has been worthless.

Erwin Schrödinger

It's not how good the technology is; but how it's presented to its users.

Don Valentine, venture capitalist

Although writing was two thousand years old when the printing press was invented, only an elite few could read, let alone write. The printing press made the written word plentiful and inexpensive, which in turn made the average person literate, and had an incalculable influence on civilization thereafter.

Today, many expect that the low cost of computers will make the average person "computer literate." It will. But there is a crucial difference between the environment of the printing press and that of the computer: the art and craft of the writer as a storyteller or communicator was in full swing long before the printing press was invented.

The printing press certainly gave writers new and larger audiences, and was responsible for changes in the craft—it spawned the invention of the modern novel, for example. Yet it did not fundamentally change the task of the writer, a task that was already well developed.

When personal computers were developed, the equivalent of writers did not exist. Some of us were *programmers;* our expertise was in communicating with computers, an

Writing	Painting	Film	Drama	Photography	Architecture	Music	Computers
3300 B.C. Egyptian hieroglyphics	20000 B.C. Cave paintings of Lascaux, France	1884 Thomas Edison demonstrates kinetoscope	600 B.C. First Greek amphitheatre built for festival of Dionysos	1839 Daguerre announces his photographic method	2700 B.C. Pyramids at Sakkara and Gizeh	2000 B.C. Invention of the Egyptian harp	450 B.C. First abacus
2300 B.C. Maxims of Ptahhotep	3000 B.C. Egyptian tomb paintings	1903 Edwin Porter's *The Great Train Robbery*	550 B.C. Introduction of the chorus in Greek plays	1861 Mathew Brady's Civil War photographs	400 B.C. Parthenon, Athens	1306 A.D. First pedal organ	1864 A.D. Charles Babbage's analytic engine
1500 B.C. Development of phonetic alphabet	1100 A.D. Invention of oil paints	1915 D. W. Griffith's *Birth of a Nation*	442 B.C. Sophocles' Antigone	1882 Eastman develops Kodak camera	1100 A.D. Development of flying buttress	1404 First clavichord	1955 First commercial mainframe computer
800 B.C. Library of Assyria founded	1497 Da Vinci's *Last Supper*	1927 First sound movie: *The Jazz Singer*	1580 A.D. Establishment of the first repertory companies	1902 Stieglitz's "Spring Showers"	1400 Completion of Chartres Cathedral	1520 First violin	1958 Fortran: First high level language
1440 A.D. Gutenberg's invention of moveable type	1654 Rembrandt's *Portrait of Jan Six*	1941 Orson Welles' *Citizen Kane*	1603 Shakespeare's *Hamlet*	1947 Ansel Adams' Yosemite photographs	1920 Invention of pre-stressed concrete	1602 Monteverdi's first opera, *Orfeo*	1975 First personal computer
1605 Cervantes' *Don Quixote*	1937 Picasso's *Guernica*				1936 Frank Lloyd Wright's "Falling Water"	1720 J. S. Bach: *The Well-Tempered Clavier*	1978 VisiCalc
1719 First modern novel: Defoe's *Robinson Crusoe*						1824 Beethoven's Ninth (Choral) Symphony	1979 WordStar

Figure 2: Most communications crafts started as inventions and evolved slowly in the direction of an art form. Software is a newcomer to the world of communications crafts.

ability substantially different from communicating with people. What we had yet to develop were the skills needed to get computers to communicate with users.

Many have recognized this shortcoming and have talked about making computers and software "friendly." Unfortunately, this too frequently has meant little more than editing some messages, turning, for example, an annoying "Syntax error" into the more "respectful" "Syntax error, Sir."

No programmer writes an unfriendly program on purpose. If some of us write unfriendly programs it is not because we want to; it is because we do not know how to do any better. While everyone has ideas on what makes software "friendly," we don't really *know* much about it.

The purpose of this book is to identify the skills of the communicator, to persuade you that they are the appropriate skills, and to help you on your way to mastering them.

The critical problem of making average people literate was to teach them to read— skilled writers already existed. But in the computer age the major problem is just the reverse— it is to make the software designer a skilled communicator, not to make the average person computer literate. As any writer knows, the primary task of any communication falls on the originator.

The point of view taken here is that "friendly" software is software that communicates well. It follows that the place to look for understanding how to make software friendly is in any number of communications crafts, such as:

Writing	Filmmaking
Acting	Sales
Advertising	Playwriting
Teaching	Journalism
Photography	Graphic art
Fine art	Musical composition
Magic	Set design

Even architecture and industrial design, crafts having to do with presenting physical things to people, use communication principles and will be referred to occasionally here.

THE BIRTH OF AN ART FORM

The task I'm trying to achieve is above all to make you see.
D. W. Griffith

Among all the art forms that can teach us about communication, the most appropriate is filmmaking. While the origins of most art forms are lost in antiquity, filmmaking began in this century, within the span of our own experience. It illustrates the transition from an engineering discipline to an art form—a transition we are seeing today in computer software. This transition is now so complete that we find it hard to think of filmmaking as an engineering discipline, yet that is what it was when it began.

For several years, Thomas Edison controlled filmmaking. He did not see the artistic possibilities of the medium and stubbornly fought against Edwin S. Porter, who wanted to make films that would tell stories. "Eight minutes on a single story," Edison objected, "it won't sell. People want variety. At least four or five subjects on every eight-minute reel."

Having worked for several engineers, I know how Porter must have felt.

Movies did not flourish until the engineers lost control to artists—or more precisely, to the communications craftsmen. The same thing is happening now with personal computers. Inexpensive computers have made it easier for software designers to come out from under the control of the engineers, and the result has been a proliferation of independent software companies and better software.

The earliest filmmakers did little more than point a camera at an interesting event and wind the crank. Films varied from the photographing of theater as seen from a prime orchestra seat to photographed sideshows. A movie was one long shot of continuous action taken by a stationary camera. It was Edwin Porter who first staged outdoor events that he would film. In 1903, he made *The Great Train Robbery*, the first film to purposely tell a story. This important film was a big success, but technically it consisted of a series of 30- to 60-second action shots.

If one person can be credited with inventing the film as art, it is D. W. Griffith. In 1914, Griffith made *Birth of a Nation*, an immediate artistic and commercial success. With this picture, filmmaking became what it is today—the art and craft of using film to communicate to an audience.

To do this, Griffith invented, or was the first to use in an important way, the basic techniques of filmmaking. These are the same techniques that are used today: the closeup, the moving shot, the fade, the cutaway, and the dissolve. (It is difficult to realize just how innovative these techniques were at the time: the first closeup caused panic when shown because the audience mistook it for a "severed head.")

Griffith's basic contribution was his use of editing (*montage* would be a more descriptive word)—the ordering of the various shots (long, medium, moving, closeup, panorama) into the finished film. He used crosscutting—alternating shots from different simultaneous action sequences—and he varied the lengths of his cuts for the psychological effect they would have on the audience. He slowly decreased the length of the average cut, for example, to slowly increase the audience's anxiety. In the concluding sequence of *Birth of a Nation,* he crosscut between scenes of the heroine besieged in the cabin and scenes of the rescuing riders several times, using twenty-six different cuts including long shots, medium shots, closeups, extreme closeups, and moving shots, all of this in only one minute of screen time. In doing this, Griffith not only communicated the action to the audience more effectively than had been done in the past, but he created interest, excitement, and tension. By today's standards the acting may be mediocre and the technical quality poor, but the editing is still first-rate.

Figure 3: This shot is typical of the shots in Porter's *The Great Train Robbery* (1903). It was a long shot of thirty to sixty seconds, and it, like all films of that time was cut only when the action moved elsewhere.

The Bettman Archive.

Before Griffith, the average film was one eight-minute-long reel. The films were made in less than a week—scripted on Monday, shot on Wednesday (with no rehearsal), and shipped on Saturday. They cost only a few hundred dollars to produce and were shown in nickelodeons to the lower classes; the middle and upper classes disdained such crude entertainment.

Birth of a Nation was two hours and thirty minutes long, took six months to make, and cost the enormous sum of more than $60,000. Millions of people of all classes paid

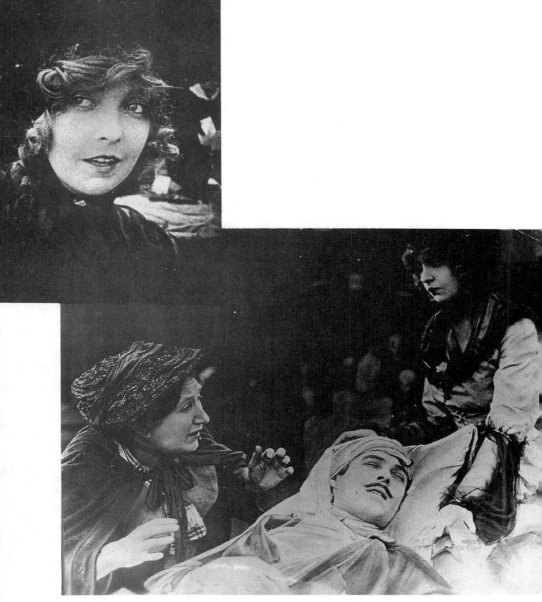

Figures 4 and 5: These stills taken from D.W. Griffith's *Birth of a Nation* vary substantially in their points of view. Griffith was the first to photograph diverse kinds of shots and compose a montage of them to make the movie.

The Bettman Archive.

CHAPTER ONE

the extraordinary price of two dollars to see it. It grossed fifteen million dollars and was the first film shown at the White House. (Woodrow Wilson said it was like writing history with lightning.)

The effect this film had on motion pictures— both as an art and as a business— was revolutionary. After Griffith's opus, serious films had to be at least an hour long and use Griffith's filmmaking techniques. Having worked for Griffith, even as an extra, was all one needed to get a job in motion pictures, and such people became the major source of directors and filmmakers during the twenties and thirties. Making a film was no longer a one-week affair; it was a major undertaking lasting for months.

Since Griffith and *Birth of a Nation,* we have seen many advances including sound, color, a more natural acting technique, and various special effects. Still, none of these techniques changed film fundamentally. Griffith wrote the bible on how to make films, and though the filmmakers who followed might have split into different schisms and interpreted his bible differently, none rejected it.

The fundamental change that Griffith brought to filmmaking was a shift in emphasis from *what* was being presented to *how* it was being presented— from an engineer's craft to an artist's. Filmmaking was never thought of in the same way again.

Significantly, some of the first people to recognize the possibilities of the new medium were communicators in other media. Henry Dreyfuss, a set designer, and Raymond Loewry, a graphic artist, became two of the earliest industrial designers. An important pre-Griffith filmmaker was a magician— Georges Méliès. This was not an accident. Two of the primary skills of a magician are communications skills: showmanship and the creating of illusions in the minds of the audience. Griffith, who admitted that he learned much from Méliès, was himself an actor who always wanted to be a novelist.

FRIENDLY SOFTWARE: A NEW COMMUNICATIONS MEDIUM

Friendly software design is in much the same state that filmmaking was at the time of *Birth of a Nation*. The existing audience has been limited until recently to programmers, specialists, or data entry clerks. But now the audience is becoming much broader.

To make our products useful to new audiences, we have to identify and develop the software equivalents of the filmmaker's techniques— closeup, moving shot, editing, and so on. We already have some of these techniques— menus and cursor control, for example— but just having them is not enough; many of Griffith's techniques were first used by others. Even more important, we have to learn how to use our techniques to communicate more effectively to our users. We can only do this by changing our perspective of software design from *what* the software does to *how* it does it— from an engineer's perspective to an artist's.

People use various terms to describe aspects of making software friendly: *human factors, ergonomics, user friendly, cognitive engineering,* and *user psychology,* to name a few. In earlier versions of this work, I used the phrase *intelligence design* because it was reminiscent of the term *industrial design,* which is the art or craft of making industrial products user-oriented. The unfortunate fact is that none of these terms works very well. So I will use the term "friendly software design."

The closest thing we have to a *Birth of a Nation* in designing friendly software is VisiCalc. Unlike *Birth of a Nation*, VisiCalc's main appeal is to a limited marketplace (generally people who do financial planning). But it has an important similarity to this seminal film: although other financial packages existed, VisiCalc became an instant and unexpected success. During the three years of Apple's strongest growth, 1979–1982, VisiCalc (at $100 to $250 a copy) was responsible for at least half of the Apple computers sold (at about $3,000 each). While VisiCalc no longer represents the state of the art, it was a significant advance in its time. Like *Birth of a Nation*, VisiCalc focuses our attention on the underlying principles rather than the latest techniques.

The reason that VisiCalc (and to a lesser extent Word-Star) has proved successful is that its design was "friendly" on a fundamental level. Things that are done well tend to be transparent and are not noticed, while things that are done badly intrude and are noticed. That is why a generation of designers have been able to improve VisiCalc, but few have been able to since make a quantum advance anything like it.

BEFORE   AFTER

Figures 6 and 7: Industrial Design. One of the first industrial designs was Raymond Loewry's 1929 redesign of the original Gestetner mimeograph machine. The gears are no longer in plain view where they can collect dust and catch peoples' hair and fingers, and the legs no longer stick out to trip the user.

Courtesy of the Gestetner Corporation.

CHAPTER TWO

Our Counter-
productive Instincts

*It's not the things we don't know that get us into trouble; it's
the things we do know that ain't so.*

Will Rogers

In business, it is a serious if not fatal mistake not to identify your real adversary. Pennsylvania Railroad saw its competitor as the Chesapeake and Ohio; in fact, it was the
airlines. Keuffel and Esser, the slide rule manufacturer,
thought it was Pickett, and Hewlett-Packard introduced the
HP-35 scientific calculator. General Motors thought it was
Ford, and Japan exported Datsuns and Toyotas. It is not a
question of underestimating your adversary, but of not
recognizing it.

Those of us who are engineers and scientists by training are used to an adversary that is logical, consistent, and
predictable, if also subtle. That adversary is nature, and when
we understand her laws, we construct bridges that span
wide rivers, buildings a quarter of a mile high, airplanes that
cross continents, and television systems that instantly transmit pictures around the world. We can send men to the
moon, and build computers that can do millions of calculations a second.

But, in writing friendly software, our real adversary is
the user's mind. We need very different techniques to do battle against this adversary. And it is not just that our natural
techniques and thought processes might not work; they can
actually be counterproductive.

We think logically, not visually.

As software engineers, we think of what works logically. But a good communicator will think about how things work visually.

Suppose we want to design a command in a word processor to search for a word. If the user starts the search in the middle of a document, and the word processor cannot find a match by the end of the document, should it resume the search at the beginning of the document, or should it stop and make the user go back to the beginning to restart the search? Among programmers such a question is usually worth at least a three-hour discussion and is usually argued in terms of what logically makes sense. Little if any time will be spent discussing how to communicate the results of that discussion to the user. Faced with the same question, a professional communicator would spend the same three hours discussing how to communicate the two possible solutions to the user and would probably select the solution he can communicate best, even if it is not logically best.

A user doesn't necessarily expect his programs always to do the right thing, but he does expect that they clearly communicate what they do.

We base our designs on our own knowledge rather than the user's.

We select computer functions and data structures according to how interesting the program we build will be. If we think of any user at all, we think of ourselves. Much of this is done subconsciously. Only as an afterthought, if at all, do we think about communicating our concepts to the user.

Because many of our products demand knowledge of their users that the designer already has, the products seem good to their designers. However, the user of a program will know little of file structures and computer algorithms in general, let alone the specifics of a program that are second nature to a designer who has lived with it for a year. Thus, the user of that product will have a knowledge base very different from the designer's and will likely find the product difficult to understand and use. The person who knows most about a product is often in the poorest position to evaluate its ease of use. It is as if we wrote a book in English and seemed surprised that a Frenchman could not understand it. The difference in the knowledge base among people who speak the same language can be just as big, even if it is not so obvious. A good communicator is constantly aware of the intended users and their knowledge base.

A user does not expect a program to make him understand computer terms and concepts, but to communicate in terms and concepts that are already familiar to him.

Our programs evaluate our user's actions.

Our natural inclination is to have our programs view input from the perspective of whether it is right or wrong according to what the program expects. For example, we give our user a message like "Illegal Command" when he enters something the program is not prepared to receive. The user finds this judgmental and becomes defensive. The effective communicator structures his communications to be descriptive of the problem involved.

A user expects that programs will not judge his use of them, but will help him overcome his problems in using them.

We make our programs take control.

We want a program we design to take control of a task, and in trying to control the task we end up trying to control the user. Our natural tendency is to design our programs so they do input and output for the user at the program's convenience without regard for the user's convenience.

A user expects to feel that he is in control of both the computer and the task.

We think in generalities, not specifics.

Our training as programmers and engineers leads us to develop general-purpose solutions. Programming languages are designed to solve general-purpose problems. The better our programming skills are, the more general-purpose are our designs. Yet most people are better at thinking in specifics rather than in generalities and would rather generalize *after* they've been given enough specifics.

A user expects to communicate in specific terms and with concrete examples, rather than in general terms and abstractions.

We structure for internal organization.

As programmers, we are concerned about the internal organization of our programs, their overall design, their data structures, and their subroutines.

A building has an internal organization: a framework of steel girders and a shaft that is used to distribute water, power, and telephone lines to specific floors. But it also has an external structure. This is the appearance as seen from the street, its entrance, and within the building: the arrangement of offices and corridors. Both are important, but as engineers, we tend to think mainly if not exclusively of the internal structure and ignore the external structure.

The communicator is primarily concerned with external structure perceived by the mind of the user, and that is the structure the user interface designer must concern himself with.

A user doesn't want the program's internal structure to intrude into the external interface.

We strive for
a program's internal simplicity.

We naturally look for simplicity of internal design and implementation. We like the simplicity of elegant equations like $F = ma$ or $E = mc^2$, but such an equation is simple only after a year or more of college physics. The effective communicator looks for simplicity as it will be perceived by his audience, and he will do complex things to achieve that simplicity.

A user expects that his programs be no more complicated to understand than the task they are doing for him.

Our knowledge constrains our vision.

As engineers, we know what we can and cannot do, and work outward from this knowledge to the product. We are uncomfortable working with something if we don't know how to handle all the implementation details.

A user is focused on the task he is trying to do, and not the mechanism for doing it.

If there is a common thread running through this list, it is that, as engineers, our primary consideration is how the program works, rather than the effect it achieves. If we are going to be successful designers, we must work backward from the effect we want our programs to achieve to how they work.

The skills of the software engineer are quite useful for solving the engineering problems in friendly software design. However, to be a good designer, you not only need to have know-how, but "know-when."

Figure 8: Writing. Like all communications media, writing is based on an invention. The hieroglyphics script was invented by the Egyptians about 3000 B.C.; the inscriptions shown here were chiseled on the Egyptian temple at Denderah.

The Bettmann Archive.

The Elements of Friendly Software Design

Chance favors only the prepared mind.

Louis Pasteur

Most of us like a formula that we can follow to get ensured results. Failing that, we like a well-defined problem whose solution we can optimize. This is particularly true for those of us who are engineers. we expect a problem's parameters to be given. We don't question them. In college, we learn Newton's laws and Maxwell's equations, and find that a few powerful formulas explain mechanics and electronics. In school, we are graded on how well we apply these laws; in industry, we use these and similar laws to solve a wide variety of problems. Once we have found the correct way to solve a type of problem, we rarely look at such problems in a different way.

Unfortunately, we tend to expect other things to be explained by unambiguous formulas or recipes— if only we can find the right ones. Following this approach, when we are faced with a complex problem we make simplifying assumptions to make the problems manageable. But having done that, we tend to forget the assumptions, casting the real problem adrift while we concentrate on solving the simplified one we created. All too often we get the right solution to the wrong problem.

When one deals with softer problems, like communicating with people, there is no right way to solve them. We must think in different ways and look at a problem from many different angles. Each new angle might eliminate some tentative solution, suggest a new one, or give fresh insight into the problem. Each angle adds something to the image that you are building in your mind. My intention here is to focus your attention on the important elements, or angles, of friendly design so you can recognize them and think about your designs more effectively. But I have no formula to offer.

I am not saying formulas don't exist. Many writers create them. Erle Stanley Gardner had a formula that he used to write Perry Mason stories. But any such formula is restricted to a specific use: Gardner's was useful for a particular type of detective story. Similarly, formulas exist for friendly software, but they are not universally applicable.

Many of the design elements below can be seen as variations of each other. Nevertheless, it is better to have too many perspectives on the design problem than too few. The technique of providing a variety of perspectives is none other than montage, the technique Griffith invented for the movies.

If this chapter cannot provide formulas, it will prepare your mind to recognize what is good and bad in a particular design approach. And, as Pasteur pointed out, having a prepared mind has its advantages.

1. KNOW YOUR SUBJECT.

A writer should know how to do research the same way that a driver should know how to shift gears.
James Michener

Before beginning to write, a writer researches a subject, generally spending as much time on research as on actual writing. The same is true of advertisers and filmmakers. In a similar way, to design a word processor, you need to understand typing, typesetting, hyphenation, how a secretary works, and related subjects. Neither can you write a general ledger system without understanding bookkeeping and accounting.

Figure 9: Leonardo da Vinci was a great artist, not just because he could communicate, but because he understood the details he was trying to communicate. He examined the human body in minute detail so he could better paint it.

The Bettmann Archive.

More than one programmer developed an accounting system only to find out later that an audit trail was needed.

One needs to learn the important issues and not get engulfed in the details. In designing a word processor, for example, it would be a mistake to focus on sophisticated hyphenation algorithms before the basic design is proven.

VisiCalc, the first of the spreadsheet programs, is a prime example of an innovative solution to a real problem resulting from its creators' knowledge of the subject. It was developed by Dan Bricklin and Bob Frankston. Dan Bricklin was an M.B.A. student struggling through cash flow homework assignments. He understood the subject and, as a computer science graduate, he understood the technology that would solve the problems. Because Bricklin and Frankston had immersed themselves (however accidentally) in both the software technology and the user's problem, they had the experience base they needed to come up with a creative solution.

Depth of knowledge in one area— either the user's problem area or software technology— is less important than some knowledge and experience in both areas.

Structured programming is a successful technique that has been used lately to develop better programs. However, one study shows that the quality of the customer interface is three times as important as structured programming to the success of a software project.

This explains why computer amateurs frequently develop effective software solutions to problems they know intimately, while the software professionals' solutions prove ineffective. The amateurs know their subject. Even if the programs they write are inelegant, unstructured, and have poor or nonexistent comments, these flawed programs are often more useful than technically perfect programs that solve the wrong problem.

I know a manufacturing control manager who, though he had never used a computer, subscribed to a five-dollar-an-hour time-sharing service. He wrote a simple BASIC program to control his inventory. In three or four years, he expanded his initial program into a manufacturing system of significant capability; it produced well over one hundred reports. It was so successful that he sold the system to several Silicon Valley startups. Interestingly, he knew so little about software that even while he had a dozen customers happily using his program, I was able to show him how he could replace his bubble sort with a simple ten-instruction Shell sort; it made his sorting go fifty times as fast and eliminated several five-minute delays. Anyone who used a bubble sort in that situation had to be ignorant of the most basic computer science techniques. Yet he was obviously intelligent or he would not have built such a successful system. He knew his subject—manufacturing—cold. And he knew his audience—manufacturing managers.

2. KNOW YOUR AUDIENCE.

If you are going to design for yourself, then you have to make sure you design deeply for yourself. Otherwise you are just designing for your eccentricities, and that can never be satisfying to anyone else.

Charles Eames

The most important difference between professional writers and amateurs is that the professionals have a clear picture of whom they are writing for. The first question a good writer asks is "Who are my readers?" followed by another series of questions: "What is important to them? How do they think? Why are they reading this? What do they know? What don't they know? What are their expectations?"

An architect will ask similar questions about the people who will use his buildings, and a salesman about his prospects. Alfred Hitchcock kept a picture of a typical user in his mind:

I always feel comfortable about a project when I can tell the story in a very simple way....I like to imagine a young woman who has been to see the movie and goes home very satisfied with what she has seen.

Her mother asks her, "What was it about?"

And the girl replies, "Well, it was about a young woman who so and so and so...."

I feel that before undertaking to shoot a movie, one should be able to do just that: To satisfy oneself that it can be narrated just as clearly, the whole cycle.

The Master's quote is a telling one. This is the image he calls to his mind when trying to evaluate some aspect of his work. Not only does he have a vivid picture of who he is communicating with, he imagines her explaining his film to someone else. If he were a software designer, I wonder if he would have said:

"I always feel comfortable about a project when I can describe the program in a simple way. I like to imagine a businessman who has just used it for the first time and is satisfied with it."

The most important thing to know regarding your user is that he is not interested in using your product. He is interested in doing his work, and your product must help him do it more easily. No one wants to use VisiCalc, but many people want to do cash flow analyses. No one wants to use a word processor, but many people want to write reports and books. If the job requires it, your user may have to use your product whether he likes it or not.

This will be less true in the future as the communicative products drive the less communicative ones from the market. Your program will be important to your users only if you make it important to them.

Some of the best marketing professionals I know have a somewhat cynical attitude about the customer. They see products as being used by a high school girl who is thinking about her boyfriend, or by a businessman who is continually interrupted by telephone calls and people walking into his office. Such pictures are useful to keep in mind as you design your product— if only because they have a sobering effect on you.

When I designed a hand-held language translator, I felt it was unrealistic to imagine someone using it to negotiate business deals. I pictured the typical user as an American tourist trying to impress an attractive stranger in a French bistro. Similarly, I designed an intelligent telephone while picturing its user as someone who had not used it in a month, had lost the instruction manual, and had just come back from a three-martini lunch.

There may be disagreements on who the typical user for a product is, but the best designs will be created by designers who have a clear picture of a realistic user.

Because every person knows what he likes, every person thinks he is an expert on user interfaces. However, much of this knowledge is misleading. For example, two groups of users were given different word processors to use. After a while, each group started using the other group's word processor. Later, when asked, each group said it preferred the one it learned first. We all have strong biases about what we like from our past experience with computers, but we are too quick to generalize from this experience to what a larger population wants. When we design something, this experience unconsciously influences our design decisions and, if we are not careful, we can easily design something that is just great for someone whose experience is similar to our own, but difficult for anyone else.

Rob Barnaby, WordStar's developer, designed it as a solid workhorse that could be used to do substantial jobs. From the earliest days of its development he used it to write the manual. He was constantly faced with the reality of how well WordStar worked in practice, and this gave him both the information and the stimulus he needed to make several improvements. But in designing WordStar to meet *his* word processing needs, he did not lose sight of his larger audience. He made WordStar a success not just by solving his personal word processing needs, but by designing deeply and presenting it well to a wider audience.

Every effective communicator thinks in two different worlds. The first is the media: words for a writer; wood, concrete, and steel for an architect; subroutines, data structures, and information flow for a software designer. The second world is the audience: its needs, expectations, concerns, thought processes, and knowledge. Only by melding a knowledge of both worlds can the communicator give his audience an effective performance.

3. MAINTAIN THE USER'S INTEREST.

The art of acting consists in keeping people from coughing.
Sir Ralph Richardson

The kind of reader (or readers) that a skilled writer imagines will depend, of course, on the occasion, the kind of piece he's writing, and other such factors. But whatever the occasion, he'll always imagine that the reader has many other interesting things to do with his time, is reading at a fast clip, and is just waiting for an excuse to tune out. The writer's challenge, then, is to avoid giving the reader his excuse. The supreme challenge, then, is to make the reader forget the other things he was going to do.
John R. Trimble

Effective writers know that people don't read boring books, so they try to maintain their readers' interest. The good salesman is something of a showman as well— the interested customer is more likely to buy than the bored customer. Audience interest is crucial to the filmmaker. The user's interest is crucial to effective communicative design. While a clerk *may* enter data into a dull program, the average consumer or business executive will not.

Faced with two programs, one boring and one interesting, people will prefer the interesting one— even if it is not as useful as the boring one. For example, computer games have no utility; people pay to use them because they are entertaining. While we will rarely be able to design software that is as appealing as a good computer game, we must try to make our designs as engaging as we can. When I design a product, I think of my program as giving a performance for its user.

The user's task is like an object that must be manipulated from the other side of a wall. Your program must enable the user to see through that wall. Fortunately, we have devices for seeing through walls; they are called windows. But a window, to be effective, must be transparent. Ideally, your software should be transparent; it should not get in the user's way.

George Orwell said that "good prose is like a windowpane." The best writing is so transparent that the reader does not see it as being there. Thoughts flow through the communication medium unclouded.

Whenever you enter a formula into a VisiCalc cell, the result of that sum appears immediately. Interest is stimulated when the user sees the effect of the calculation. The user might check the result for reasonableness, consciously or subconsciously. While entering formulas, the user is continuously stimulated. Similarly, when changing a number, the user is stimulated by the effect of the changes as they ripple through the spreadsheet.

Compare VisiCalc with a traditional financial modeling system where the user must enter all numbers and formulas before the results can be seen. The user will be bored with inputting data and easily diverted from the immediate task to subsidiary chores such as debugging.

A writer or filmmaker who feels that the audience's attention might be flagging will edit the work to regain their interest. Our users can also get bored, and their attention can wander while they wait for a computation to be completed. Depending on the situation, we might be able to decrease the waiting time, display something interesting and useful, start displaying results as they are computed— or we could restructure the interface to avoid the wait.

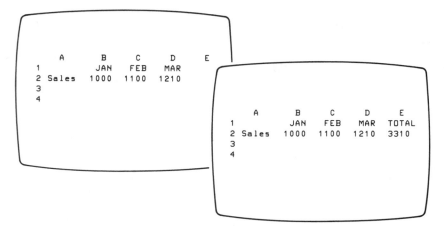

Figures 10 and 11: Here we see two VisiCalc screens. In the first screen, three numbers are entered. In the second, the user puts the formula B2 + C2 + D2 into cell E2. Immediately, the sum— 3310—appears in cell E2. This, the user finds interesting.

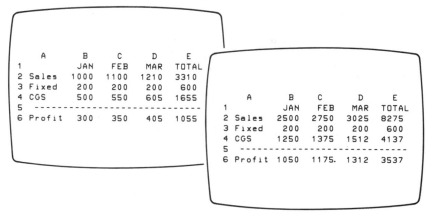

Figures 12 and 13: This example is more complex than the previous one. Only two numbers (2500 and 200) have been entered. All other entries are formulas. By changing a single number— in this case 2500 to 1000— the user changes the whole screen in a useful and interesting way.

4. COMMUNICATE VISUALLY.

A scrupulous writer, in every sentence that he writes, will ask himself: What image or idiom will make it clearer?

George Orwell

To make oneself understood to the people, one must first speak to their eyes.

Napoleon Bonaparte

Logic is a system whereby one may go wrong with confidence.

Charles Kettering

To me one of the cardinal sins for a scriptwriter, when he runs into some difficulty, is to say "We can cover that by a line of dialogue." Dialogue should be a sound among other sounds, just something that comes out of the mouth of people whose eyes tell the story in visual terms.

Alfred Hitchcock

Filmmaking, advertising, and industrial design are primarily visual media. Writing and sales, on the other hand, are primarily verbal— their basic elements are words. But words can be visual too.

Words convey both logical information to the left brain and images to the right brain. Words that convey the same logical information— for example, "determined," "stubborn," and "pigheaded"— can convey different images of the person being described. The good writer selects words carefully and uses them to create images and paint pictures in the minds of readers. Good writing is frequently a sequence of effective images disguised as logical exposition.

The effective salesman or writer communicates visually whenever possible, using pictures, photographs, drawings, charts, and diagrams to convey a message. Even when he uses words, he selects them to tell stories and create images in his audience's mind.

Filmmakers develop the skill of previsualization. This is the ability to visualize what the film will look like. The software designer must also develop this skill, to visualize how the user will experience the program. Filmmakers generally "storyboard" a film before going into production: They make a rough drawing for each shot (there may be hundreds) that will make up the film. This gives the film visual structure and provides a common basis of communication for the filmmakers. I have found a similar technique useful for designing software: a series of rough diagrams that show what is in the display during a user interaction. These help me to communicate my visualization of what the user will experience to others involved in the project.

Little communication is entirely verbal. The clothes you wear, the tone of your voice, your unconscious motions (body language), and your deliberate motions (such as pointing a finger) all communicate information. The visual form of communication has achieved the status of a profession; its practitioners are called actors— and some of them have been able to use these skills to achieve great success and high office!

An example of a good visual interface design is the Xerox Star. It uses different icons— small pictures— to visually represent documents, files, printers, in-baskets, out-baskets, and other devices. The user's work is spread out on the screen. Even the cursor takes on different shapes as it's used for different tasks.

The visual nature of the spreadsheet does much to explain the success of VisiCalc and other spreadsheet software. For a sales application, the user can list sales and profits in rows and monthly figures in columns. These present a visual picture that aids the thought process. The important image is that the third column is "March's figures" and the fourth row is the "expected sales in dollars," not that the third column is called "C" or the fourth row is called "4."

The important image is not the one on the screen, but the one in the user's mind. Spreadsheet programs, for example, only display a portion of the spreadsheet on the screen, but this helps paint the image of a much larger spreadsheet in the user's mind.

We have to use words in designing user interfaces, and their careful selection is important. However, I don't think that making computers communicate in English will significantly advance user interface design. The important advances will come from developing new, largely visual, communications forms, not from adding English to existing ones.

As an example of this, I suggest that if we had the technology to make a computer speak, listen to, and understand English, and used it to design an accountant's application that otherwise used pre-VisiCalc user design technology, the result would be inferior to VisiCalc. VisiCalc provides a better language for discussing financial spreadsheet problems than the ones that earlier financial analysis tools were able to provide. VisiCalc is successful largely because it is so visual.

When I talk about communicating visually, I do not mean to restrict communication only to that which the eye can see. Radio is a visual medium in the sense that it allows the painting of pictures in the minds of listeners. Sound is an important part of film and television and will become an important part of our programs.

This is one of those places I warned you about in Chapter 2: Our instincts and training as engineers encourage us to think logically instead of visually, and this is counterproductive to friendly design.

5. LEVER
THE USER'S KNOWLEDGE.

All communication consists in "making concessions" to the recipient's knowledge.

E. H. Gombrich

The filmmaker will lever his audience's knowledge. If the director wants to establish a character as a tough but good guy, he can hire an unknown actor, have a sequence written that establishes the character, and fold this sequence into the rest of the story. The sequence may show the character coming across an old man being robbed and helping the man get his money back. While the ostensible purpose of the scene is to show bandits robbing an old man, the real reason is to establish a character in the mind of the audience. The better the scene is done, the more subconscious the effect. Or the filmmaker might have hired John Wayne, in which case the scene above is no longer necessary: John Wayne's character is firmly established in the minds of audiences, and that perception can easily be leveraged by the director.

Should you design a user interface that presupposes that the user has knowledge that takes ten years to acquire? The obvious answer is no. The correct answer, however, may be yes: It takes ten years to learn English, and because most users already know English, you will probably take advantage of their knowledge in your designs.

Sometimes a designer is asked to design an application that assumes the user knows nothing. Not only is this unrealistic, it indicates a basic misunderstanding of the principles of effective communication. The good communicator finds out what knowledge the intended audience possesses and starts there, leveraging that knowledge to effect the communication. A writer can only use a word or image effectively if the reader has some familiarity with it.

How much knowledge we unconsciously take for granted is illustrated by something that happened to a friend of mine. His newspaper delivery boy rang the bell every time he delivered the paper. Annoyed, my friend put up a sign asking him not to ring the bell; the paper boy still rang it. My friend put the sign over the door bell. This time the paper boy pushed a hole through the sign to ring the door bell. My friend called the newspaper company to complain— only to find that the delivery boy could not read.

Should you assume, for example, that the user knows how to type? The answer depends on who the members of your projected audience are. Secretaries are proficient typists, and that knowledge can be leveraged. Most people can hunt and peck on a typewriter keyboard; even those who can't will find the typewriter a familiar object. This lesser amount of user knowledge is still useful and can be leveraged in designing the program. Similarly, a knowledge of bookkeeping can be leveraged when you wish to design an accounting application to be used by bookkeepers.

The communicator leverages his audience's knowledge in many ways, including speaking their language and using metaphors that they are familiar with. Many of us know that a good user interface design provides a consistent interface to its user. The reason this is useful is that it effectively leverages the knowledge the user gains in using the program.

6. SPEAK THE USER'S LANGUAGE.

In Paris they simply stared when I spoke to them in French; I never did succeed in making those idiots understand their language.

Mark Twain

Sales managers frequently hire ex-teachers to sell products to teachers, and ex-librarians to sell to librarians.

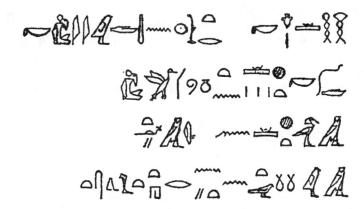

Figure 14: Ptahhotep, Vizier to Isesi, Fifth Egyptian Dynasty, 2300 B.C.

This enhances the sales process, partly because the prospect finds a salesman who comes from a similar background more credible than one who does not. But more important, the salesman and the prospect have a shared experience base; they tend to think alike and they speak the same language.

While we all speak standard English, we also speak different dialects. Doctors speak one dialect, policemen another, accountants a third, and software engineers a fourth. An important part of any dialect is its jargon— terms such as *contraindicated, modus operandi (M. 0.), budgeted variance,* and *core dump.* These specialized terms exist because they have precise meanings within their subcultures.

We can't design a good application if we don't understand the user's dialect and, more important, the meaning and knowledge that underlie the dialect. The designer who doesn't have this knowledge is at a disadvantage because he has much less knowledge to leverage, and less of a common base with the intended users.

Typical VisiCalc users know about spreadsheets. They can think in terms of columns and rows of numbers, and of adding them up. Even a passing familiarity is useful. The language of VisiCalc is a visual one: the row on the top of the page may be the "expected sales"; the third column may be the "data for March." The program communicates as much through the two-dimensional visual language of the accountant's spreadsheet as it does through words, numbers, and formulas. A major strength of spreadsheet programs is that they communicate in the user's language. By doing this, they even enhance their users' ability to think in that language.

A good interface with the user's knowledge is basic to a good design. If an interface is fundamentally flawed, you can rarely patch it up. While you can usually change the names of various commands late in the development cycle, you can rarely affect the fundamental communications form. The concept of the spreadsheet, for example, is deeply embedded in VisiCalc's design— the designer could not replace it without totally redesigning the program.

The words and phrases a program uses must be carefully selected. Jargon from the user's dialect can communicate precisely and effectively; jargon from the programmer's dialect, being unfamiliar to users, should be avoided. Much of the word selection can be done late in the project, but it must be done, and done carefully. Every word and sentence should leverage the user's knowledge and help him understand what is happening.

In my first job as a programmer, I heard a story about an IBM vice president who found out that when a tape drive wasn't running, an indicator that said *idle* lit up. The IBM vice president ordered field servicemen throughout the country to replace every *idle* light on IBM tape drives with a *ready* light. "IBM machines are never idle," he said, "they're ready." Even though they are identical technically, the concepts *idle* and *ready* are different to a user— particularly one who pays IBM rates. When I heard the story fifteen years ago, I thought, "How foolish." We grow too soon old, too late smart.

Another advantage of using jargon is that it makes the user feel comfortable. One mistake that some designers make, however, is to choose a jargon word from the user's vocabulary, but give it a slightly different meaning to suit the needs of the program. This has the advantage of making users feel comfortable at first, but when they find out that the word has a different meaning they will only get confused and frustrated. Any experienced communicator chooses words with precision. An experienced consumer marketeer like Proctor and Gamble always chooses a new name for a new product, instead of using an existing brand name that people are familiar with. It would never introduce a hand soap and call it Tide. The quick initial sales that result are not worth the fuzziness created in the minds of their consumers. Giving the same name to two different things only confuses the audience. If the audience is willing to pick up a new concept, it will be willing to pick up a new name for it; how else can it crystallize that concept?

Similarly, if there is no word in the user's dialect for what you want to say, it is probably better to invent a new word or get one from another context and attach your meaning to it. If you grab a familiar word and try to give it a slightly different definition, it will probably confuse the user.

The frustration that a user feels at not understanding your language is indicated by the frustration that you probably felt when you could not read the Egyptian hieroglyphics at the beginning of this section. What they say is relevant to making your software friendly, but those of you who do not read ancient Egyptian will have to wait a little while longer before finding out what the translation is.

7. COMMUNICATE WITH METAPHORS.

The sole aim of a metaphor is to call up a visual image.
Aristotle

All knowledge has its origins in our perceptions.
Leonardo da Vinci

Most of us know that much of our thought is based on logic. Few of us realize, however, how much of our thought and language is based on our experience. Most of the words in our language have an origin in a metaphor or some form of association. A computer, for example, was originally someone who used a mechanical calculator to compute. An electronic computer was a machine that did the same thing a person did. Now the prefix *electronic* has been dropped. Even prepositions communicate by analogy. *In* and *out* refer to the container metaphor: Something is in the container or out of the container. But we generalize by analogy and fall "in" love or fall "out" of love.

Read the works of a good writer— the works of George Orwell or Arthur Koestler, for example— or listen to a businessman who is an effective communicator, and you will be surprised at the frequency with which images and analogies appear. The best book on managing software development, Fred Brooks's *The Mythical Man-Month,* is filled with effective metaphors: a large programming project is like the dinosaurs stuck in the La Brea Tar Pits; a late programming project is like a partially cooked omelet; conceptual integrity of design is like a medieval cathedral. Not only do these images communicate effectively, they get the listener's attention, maintain interest, and appeal to audiences at many levels of sophistication. When asked to explain what it is like to direct a film, Francis Ford Coppola, the director of *The Godfather,* reached for a metaphor and said it was like running in front of an express train.

When we design something, we can always benefit by finding an effective metaphor that triggers the desired knowledge and experience in the minds of our audiences.

The visual nature of a spreadsheet is not its only value. It also brings to the user's mind his previous experience with spreadsheets and the things that he can and cannot do with them. These become the expectations the user starts out with when using VisiCalc.

By providing normal spreadsheet functions such as summation, VisiCalc reinforces the spreadsheet metaphor in the user's mind and thus reinforces the user's understanding of the software possibilities.

Many of our best user interfaces will be those that choose familiar metaphors to communicate with users. One good metaphor is *paper.* Everyone knows you can write on it, copy it, erase it, and cut and paste it. This paper metaphor is useful in designing word processors and other systems. But the software designer who wants to make this or any metaphor work must consider how well the details of the communicative design and implementation enhance or impair the metaphor. A system that communicates using the paper metaphor but has unpaperlike details can confuse and distract the user—just as a movie set in 1920 can distract the audience if one of its scenes shows TV antennas.

Xerox Star provides a good example of using a metaphor. The user is presented with a metaphorical office complete with files, documents, filing cabinets, and other devices. The user can call on his knowledge and experience of how real offices work to get a feeling for how the meta-phorical office works. Again, the designer has been able to leverage the users' knowledge to communicate with them.

For another example, consider a system that allows the user to delete files but does not really delete them. Files can be "undeleted" later if the user needs them. While this is a useful feature, there is a problem in communicating it effectively to the user. First, *delete* doesn't really erase the file, which is what the user's expectation of *delete* is; second, new commands *undelete* and *expunge* have to be explained.

A useful metaphor—wastebasket—will improve the situation. The command *wastebasket* suggests throwing

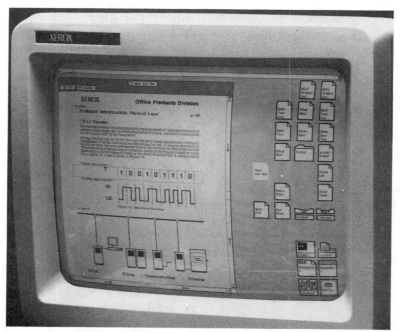

Figure 15: The Xerox Star was the first system to use the office as a metaphor for communicating with the user. Its interface is an extremely visual one. On the left is the page being worked on. On the right are icons for documents, folders, an in- and an out-basket, a printer, and even (in the lower-right hand corner) a file cabinet.

something away, but it also leaves open the possibility that things might still be available, and commands such as *search wastebasket* and *empty wastebasket* can naturally fit into the user's model. If you really want to delete the file, use a paper shredder as a metaphor.

The metaphors of writing, filmmaking, and other communications crafts have helped me structure and communicate my thoughts on user interfaces. As a result of my initial success in understanding friendly software design as communications design, I explored the techniques and thought processes of film, writing, and other communications crafts more fully and was able to recognize several other useful concepts.

This brings us back to our second counterproductive instinct. We think and design based on our own experience, implicitly assuming it is a microcosm of the experience of the rest of the world. We unconsciously use metaphors and knowledge based on computers, but these are different from those of our users. When we bring that knowledge to our consciousness, and start looking for knowledge and metaphors that have meaning to our users, we will be thinking like communicators.

8. FOCUS THE USER'S ATTENTION.

Words are like pointers that single out significant peaks from the unbroken contour line of a mountain range on the horizon. The peaks are not created by the pointers. They are given objectively; but the pointers fortify the observer's urge to discriminate them.

Rudolph Arnheim

Although we may think visually, we can only focus on one concept at a time. A writer is constrained by the nature of language to focus the reader's attention on one concept at a time. By ordering words, the writer focuses the reader's attention at a series of places. The essence of Griffith's contribution to film was to develop editing techniques that structured the focus of the viewer's attention.

The artist considers how a picture focuses the observer's attention. Through the choice of colors and shapes, and the use of other techniques, the artist controls the way a viewer's eyes move across the picture. Magicians use subtle pressures to direct the audience's attention. Selecting a volunteer from the audience, moving one hand slightly, having the magician (and his assistant) look at a particular point, all affect the audience's focus of attention. Stage actors use similar techniques.

VisiCalc focuses the user's attention on the current cell, the one selected by the cursor, but few other applications do a good job of focusing the user's attention. Too frequently the display is filled with more information than the user needs, and one has trouble identifying what is important.

WordStar provides a simple example of how a user's attention can be focused.

If you print a file, it asks you questions one at a time. The screen starts with a minimum of displayed information, and because it is uncluttered, you can focus your attention effectively. The first line says, "For default press RETURN for each question." If the user had initially been faced with the last screen, he would probably not notice the most useful line on the screen. (The message can be improved. Most people think a default is what happens when a loan is not repaid; in computerese, it means a standard selection the computer makes for you when you don't specify a choice. A better message would be: "If you press RETURN, WordStar will answer for you.")

9. ANTICIPATE PROBLEMS IN THE USER'S PERCEPTION.

If something can go wrong, it will.

Murphy's Law

Clear writers assume, with a pessimism born of experience, that whatever isn't plainly stated the reader will invariably misconstrue.

John R. Trimble

Most software managers know the realities of software development. Its folklore, Murphy's Law, has achieved the status of religion with the publication of Fred Brooks's *The Mythical Man-Month.* The problem of developing *real* software— bug-free, useful, working software— is that one must continually struggle with the things that can go wrong, will go wrong, or already have gone wrong. Good engineering is a fight against Murphy's Law. Every good engineer, software or otherwise, expects his designs to operate under worst-case conditions and designs accordingly.

When we design a user interface, we often forget Murphy's Law. We forget that our user interfaces will also be used in worst-case conditions. A good writer doesn't make this mistake. He strives to identify and defuse potential reader misunderstandings: he selects words to convey his meanings precisely and he searches for effective metaphors. He knows that if the reader misunderstands his message, it is not the reader's failure, but the writer's.

As communications designers, we should expect users to misunderstand how to use our products. Good design is a constant fight to anticipate and eliminate these misunderstandings.

One simple design technique is to have the program reinforce the *intent* of a command after the user uses that command. WordStar does this. It doesn't ask for a *file name,* it asks for the name of the *file to print,* the *file to delete,* or the *file to write marked text on,* depending on which command you entered. The user either gets a warm feeling that everything is going well and has his model of what the program does reinforced, or sees that something is wrong and aborts the command. This helps both novices who aren't sure of what they are doing and experts who inadvertently type an incorrect command.

There is only one way a writer can find out that his readers are not misconstruing what he says: he can give

```
^KP     B:ILLUS  PAGE 3 LINE 1 COL 37

NAME OF FILE TO PRINT?B:ILLUS

WARNING: You are printing the same file as you are editing.
The last saved version will be printed, not reflecting un-
saved changes. Furthermore, WordStar will not allow you to
save the file being edited while the print is in progress.
```

Figure 16: Note here how WordStar clearly communicates what it is doing to eliminate potential user misunderstandings.

Used by permission of WordStar International Inc.

his work to others (either editors or people from the intended audience) to read. Pretty soon, a sadder but wiser author has the necessary information to guide the task of rewriting.

Similarly, the test of a user interface is to get users to try it. The misunderstandings that the user has should spur the designer to change the user interface.

It is easy to fail to recognize a source of problems. For example, one program used a standard office filing system as a user interface metaphor. When a secretary used it, she destroyed a file she had just made by making another file and giving it the same name. "But," she explained, "in my office file I can have two files with the same name."

As the author of this book, I am looking out over time and into space and seeing you in my audience as you read this. I see some of you cringing, and some of you perplexed. Those of you who are cringing are obviously software engineers— systems are always designed so that no two things can have the same name. Those of you who are perplexed are obviously familiar with file cabinets and don't understand why anyone wouldn't be able to have two files with the same name.

The designer can frequently solve a problem such as this without abandoning his basic metaphor. The computer does not have to be an exact analog of the office system if the user is informed of the differences at critical points. For example, if you were to try to write information to an existing file in WordStar, you would get this message: "File XXX exists, Overwrite (Y/N)." Not only are you saved from a possible catastrophe, but you can revise your model of how the system works.

10. IF YOU CAN'T COMMUNICATE IT, DON'T DO IT.

Whereof one cannot speak, one must remain silent.
Ludwig Wittgenstein

The insufficient is better than the superfluous.
Tokugawa Ieyasu

It is better to remain silent and be thought a fool, than to open your mouth and remove all doubt.
Anonymous

A good writer will cut a passage he likes if it doesn't advance what he is trying to say. More than one filmmaker has cut a favorite scene for the same reason. The part must be sacrificed for the whole or else the total effect will be weakened.

Apple pie, vanilla ice cream, and chocolate sauce may all be good, but when it comes time to serve the dessert, a decision must be made to sacrifice either the apple pie or the chocolate sauce.

Most programmers don't think that way. They often defend their use of a software feature by saying: "You don't have to use it if you don't want to, so what harm can it do?" It can do a great deal of harm. The user might spend time trying to understand the feature, only to decide it isn't needed, or he may accidentally use the feature and not know what has happened or how to get out of the mistake.

If a feature is inconsistent with the rest of the user interface, the user might draw false conclusions about the other commands. The feature must be documented, which makes the user's manual thicker. The cumulative effect of many such features is to overwhelm the user and obscure communication with your program, like tea leaves clogging a sink's drain.

This approach reminds me of the combination hammer-screwdriver-monkey wrench-can opener-bottle cap remover I purchased and never used. The best that this approach can hope to do is to make the equivalent of a Swiss Army knife with its awkward-to-use features. The Swiss Army knife is better than nothing, but worse than the desired tool. Its virtue is that it is light and compact enough for people to carry with them, a useful tool when nothing better is available. But it is never as useful as the real hammer, screwdriver, or knife.

An example of what can happen with the hammer-screwdriver-monkey wrench-can opener-bottle cap remover approach is provided by an evaluation of personal computer word processors I did for one client. We tested five word processors. I prepared a list of twenty questions covering different aspects of the user interface and asked a novice user—an intelligent, literate, quick learner with little computer experience—to answer the questions. (She was a Ph.D. student in Egyptology at the University of California.) She and I both took the test. We each answered the twenty questions using the word processor being tested.

Both of us were motivated to finish the project as quickly as possible. We appreciated everything a word processor did to help, and disliked everything it did to hinder us. The questions and the interaction with the word processor stimulated our thinking, and the resulting evaluations were interesting, though sometimes unprintable.

Two of the word processors ran on a well-known personal computer. One program had limited capability and a few flaws, but did the basics right. It was perceived as being helpful.

The novice user's evaluation sheet of the other word processor began, "I hate it. I hate it. I hate it."

When I tried it, I could see why. Like the other word processors we evaluated, it ran on a system with a forty-character-wide screen. A full line had somehow to be broken up. After I typed in forty characters, the screen shifted from the left to the right half of the page. I continued to type and soon found the computer shrieking at me to tell me I was halfway into a word that wouldn't fit on the end of the line. (While we computer people don't seem to mind computers shrieking at us, it is only because we have gotten inured to the noise, like those people who live at the end of an airport runway.)

No problem, I thought. I erased the just-typed halfword, pressed the carriage return, and continued to type. But, having lost my train of thought in the confusion, I glanced back at what I had just typed in— only to find that the system had flipped back to the left screen, preventing me from reading the right half of the previous line. I looked through the manual but could not find anything about automatic word wraparound.

The funny part of the story is that after I was halfway through my evaluation, I accidentally typed something— to this day I don't know what— and the word processor magically went into the desired mode. The program stopped using left- and right-half pages and displayed the uninterrupted text on the screen. And now the program did word

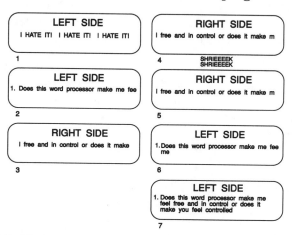

Figure 17: This is a sequence of screens presented to me by one word processor I tested. The last screen allowed me to see the whole text I typed in. But I have no idea as to how I got it to display that information.

wraparound—automatically taking the half-word typed at the end of a line and putting it at the beginning of the next line.

Now somewhere in the manual amidst a cornucopia of confusing features invoked by magic multikey sequences there was, I suspect, a description of the feature I had accidentally invoked. God knows I looked for it earlier to no avail.

What good are the features of this word processor? They only confuse users by hiding what little gold there is in a bucket of yellow sand. Our evaluations might seem unfair because we didn't understand how to use the system correctly and charged it with faults it did not have. However, in testing the word processors, we had several advantages over the typical user. We were more knowledgeable about computers, we were smarter, and we used the instruction manual.

Most things have to work in failure mode. Many drivers don't change the oil regularly, have tires that need air, and bring their cars in to be serviced only when something goes wrong. Automobiles are built to tolerate that kind of use, and software has to be built to stand analogous use. Most software is run by confused users acting on incorrect and incomplete information, doing things the designer never expected.

Application programs need not be limited to the barest minimum of capabilities—WordStar, for example, can be used by both novices and experienced users. But whatever programs do, they should do it well, and communicate it effectively.

11. REDUCE THE USER'S DEFENSIVENESS.

It's a poor tool that blames its workman.
Mike Fitzpatrick, computer user

Any salesman knows that the worst thing you can do is argue with a customer. It raises the customer's defensiveness and leads to closed minds.

But computer programs argue with users all the time. They say "Illegal Command" or shriek at the user with the lucidity and communicativeness of a two-month-old baby. This kind of treatment makes the user feel confused, helpless, frustrated, and angry.

Salesmen have a word for the feeling a prospect has: FUD. It stands for Fear, Uncertainty, and Doubt. It describes the state of mind a person has when he contemplates parting with his money. A salesman handles this problem by creating rapport and trust with his customers, by being aware of his customers' concerns, and by helping to allay their fears.

A user learning new computer programs also suffers from FUD. Most designers are blithely unaware of this problem. We don't see our programs the same way a new user sees them— as masses of indecipherable, complex, and intimidating commands that, if used incorrectly, could destroy the whole day's work.

In his essay "Defensive Communication," James Gibb points out three factors that reduce defensiveness in communication.

Make the communication descriptive instead of judgmental.

If someone criticizes a program we've designed, our natural inclination is to be defensive. All good salesmen would resist this impulse— first, because they would not argue with the customer, and second, because they know the reacting customer is the buying customer. Good salesmen welcome such criticism (they call it an objection) and respond to it in a positive way.

Software designers should look at such evaluative comments as useful raw material for improving their products. Remember that the complaining user wouldn't complain if he didn't value the program enough to use it in

48

CHAPTER THREE

the first place. The only person who never complains about a program is the person who never uses it.

If designers get defensive easily, the poor user gets defensive just as easily. A user who sees his keyed-in input request answered with an unhelpful, judgmental response such as "Illegal Command" feels stupid and frustrated. Our messages should describe the users' problems instead of evaluating his actions.

This is not always as simple as changing the wording of a message. The program should be designed so that, when an error occurs, the program has the information it needs to describe the problem to the user.

Communicate from empathy instead of superiority.

A good writer respects his reader, empathizes with his reader's situation, and becomes his reader's servant. You have to look at your work from the reader's perspective. You must see how he can get lost, lose interest, or misunderstand what you are saying. Writers who don't do this are perceived as arrogant and unconcerned. Their readers (if they have any) feel inferior, become defensive, and lose interest.

Designers should recognize that their products are frequently perceived by users as being arrogant and unconcerned. There is nothing like a 500-feature program with an unreadable instruction manual to create a feeling of inferiority and defensiveness in a user.

I am surprised at how the smallest thing a program does to help the user is appreciated. WordStar, for example, provides a great deal of helpful information. When it starts asking for the name of the file you intend to edit, it displays the information the user needs to know to type a valid file name. This is a trivial example, but WordStar is full of such trifles. Every time a user is helped this way, he becomes less defensive and more appreciative of your program.

Make your user's decisions provisional.

Gibb mentions a third factor: The more provisional and less certain the communication environment, the less defensive the user will be. Computer products that let the user browse and explore will be better accepted by users than those that force them to make decisions and then live with them.

In VisiCalc or WordStar, for example, typing a down arrow and going off the screen is a provisional action. If you don't like it, you can press up arrows to get back to where you were.

This brings us to our third counterproductive instinct: As software designers, we tend to evaluate the user's input according to how it corresponds with what our programs expect. This makes the user defensive.

Earlier I mentioned that I had hired a friend, a graduate student in Egyptology, to help me test word processors. After using word processors, she said she felt like Eliza Doolittle (the Cockney girl in *Pygmalion* who was taught proper English and introduced to the upper class). Before she tested the word processors, she was satisfied with her method of writing. After she had used them and had seen what the better ones could do, she didn't want to go back to her old method.

When we started the project she told me that she felt that, like many other people, she was going to be left out of the computer age. At the end, after finding one word processor to be an effective servant, she saw that technology could meet her halfway and that she would not be left out.

She didn't want to use the unfriendly word processors she had tested either— she found them confusing, controlling, and arrogant. "You programmers," she said, "must live with a high level of discomfort."

She also told me that the ancient Egyptians valued the ability to communicate and write well. One famous Egyptian, Ptahhotep, a vizier, or second in power to the

Pharaoh, lived in 2300 B.C., and many of his aphorisms about writing have been recorded; some principles of effective communication are indeed ancient. One aphorism was "Writing is harder than all other work." (It is still true 4,200 years later.)

My Egyptologist friend asked me to tell my readers what Ptahhotep said 4,200 years ago. The quotation appears at the beginning of element 6, in this chapter. It means: "Be careful when you speak so as to say things that count. I am going to give you this information and it is a profit for the one who will listen and a woe for the one who will not listen."

In the future when you design software for people, if you try hard to make it friendly (speak so as to communicate effectively), your having read the spell will help you write friendlier software. If you don't try hard to make your software friendly, it will be "a woe for one that will not listen." Personally, I am skeptical about Egyptian spells, but then again, the Earl of Carnarvon, who financed the expedition that found Tutankhamen, and several others who opened the tomb all died mysteriously shortly thereafter.

12. GIVE THE USER CONTROL.

Universities are designed for the convenience of the faculty, not for the convenience of the students.

Adam Smith

When I was a kid, my parents told me what to do. When I went to school, my teachers told me what to do. Now I'm married, and my husband tells me what to do. I'm not going to use a computer and let it tell me what to do.

The author's sister

When reading a book, you are in control because you can stop reading when you want to. But if the writer can keep you interested and continuing to read, the writer is, in a more subtle sense, in control.

Similarly, a good salesman controls a sales situation while letting the prospect feel in control. Instead of saying "Do you want to buy the car?" a salesman will ask, "Would you prefer red or blue?" The first question focuses attention on whether to buy the car; the prospect asserts control by saying "No." The second question lets the salesman control the purchase decision by focusing attention on the color of the car and letting the customer assert control there. It is easier for the customer to say "Red" or "Blue" or "Green" than "I don't want to buy."

People drive cars instead of riding buses because they want to take control of their travel. Manufacturers of high fidelity equipment put extra knobs on their products because customers want to feel in control of the sound—even though in practice they rarely use them.

The same principle applies to friendly software design. Obviously, the program must be in control if it is going to function correctly, but the more control it can let the user exercise, the better the user will feel. And the better he will like the program. Users tend to feel controlled in many situations—when they must look something up in an instruction manual, when they have to enter data in a particular format, and when they must complete one task before they can initiate another. We can't always avoid situations where the user feels controlled, but we should be sensitive to them, look for them, and try to minimize them when designing software.

Just as users like to control their environments, we designers like to control ours. Because of this inclination, we too frequently think of designing a program that asks the user for the information our program wants when it wants it. The better we are as software engineers, the better we are at getting our program to control its environment. When this is done at the expense of the user's control, our natural instincts cause us to design unfriendly software. Our fourth counterproductive instinct is that we want our programs to take control.

Controlling the user is fine from the program's point of view; it gets the information when the program needs it in the form required. But if from the user's point of view, he is answering the questions at the computer's convenience, the designer is controlling the user in the crudest way.

This kind of software design is the rule instead of the exception. Programs are first designed for the convenience of the designer. Only afterwards, if at all, is any thought given to the special problems of the user.

Many voice recognition systems provide an example of this. They require that the user "train" the system by reciting twenty or thirty words in a specified order beforehand. More interesting approaches are possible: A simple primer could show the user how the system works and ask the user to say the commands aloud as each new command is introduced. If this were done well, the user would learn about how the system works and be unaware that this process was necessary for the system to recognize spoken words.

VisiCalc's design as a spreadsheet program avoids this pitfall. It gives the user control. Users are given a blank sheet of paper and can put numbers, formulas, and text wherever they want. The user can move the cursor around freely. This gives him a feeling of control. Similarly, a user can try putting a new value in a cell because it can be easily changed.

An important type of control we can give our users is to make their actions provisional. For example, in VisiCalc or most word processors, a left arrow hit by mistake can be undone by a right arrow. Some of the more advanced systems, such as Xerox Star, have adopted Warren Teitelman's UNDO command, which undoes the effect of the previous command.

If our decisions are provisional instead of binding, we are willing to take a risk because the cost of a mistake is small. All user input is in some sense a risk. We must minimize the inadvertent damage a user is likely to do. If a system allows its users to browse, or to think of their actions as being provisional, they will be more comfortable using it.

Provisionalism is important for two reasons: It makes the user less defensive and it encourages people to browse while using the product. Browsing enables users to see more things, and helps to build up a model in the user's mind of what the program does.

13. SUPPORT THE PROBLEM-SOLVING PROCESS.

Where were you when the page was blank?

Truman Capote
in response to John Huston's criticism of his script

Many writers work best by first writing a rough draft without worrying about spelling and other details. Only after the draft is completed do they rewrite it with a critical eye. During the first draft, the right brain— the creative side— is dominant and the writing flows creatively. During the rewrite, the left brain— the analytic side— becomes dominant, as the writer corrects and improves the details. If during the first draft the writer has to spell each word correctly and correct each grammatical error before proceeding to another sentence, creativity would be arrested.

Brainstorming and other techniques for enhancing creativity are based on this idea. By relaxing our critical faculties, we can produce more creative solutions to our problems.

The VisiCalc model supports the creative process. The user need not specify in advance how wide the columns are or how many decimal places should be displayed. Rows and columns don't have to be given names or titles. The user does not have to start in any particular place, such as the upper-left hand corner. The user— like the writer producing a first draft— can get the job done with a minimum of petty annoyances, free to attack the work creatively. Later, the user can go back and specify column widths, numbers of decimal places, labels, and whatever.

Unfortunately, much computer software inhibits the creative process. The thrust of computer science and computer language design is toward languages that require excessive specification. A user must specify types and get the syntax right before he can see if his thoughts make sense, or, indeed, before his thought processes can be formed at all.

The aims of such work are desirable— robustness and maintainability are important to program development. Certainly, nothing is so destructive to user acceptance as unreliability.

However, languages that require detailed specifications inhibit trying new ideas. Being able to invoke the error-checking machinery that such languages provide is useful— like being able to use an umbrella when it rains. However, no one walks around with an open umbrella all the time.

In good weather, umbrellas fold compactly. The devices that ensure robustness and maintainability in our languages should do the same. It is no accident that languages that are the least restrictive and most interactive (and thus, least controlling), such as BASIC, FORTH, and LISP, have proved popular despite being outside the mainstream of computer science.

I expect that Smalltalk will prove to be an important language. Like BASIC, FORTH, and LISP, it is interactive and supports the problem-solving process. Furthermore, Smalltalk is a visual language. Useful metaphors such as windows and paper are its bases for communication.

This restrictive approach to language design permeates our thinking as software engineers, and given an application, our inclination is to design a language for it. We should try to design environments to help people find the solutions for their problems, instead of languages for people to present their solutions in.

14. AVOID FRUSTRATING THE USER.

For years in our office we have kept before us the concept that what we are working on is going to be ridden in, sat upon, looked at, talked into, activated, operated, or in some way used by people individually or en masse. If the point of contact between the product and the people becomes a point of friction, then the industrial designer has failed.

If, on the other hand, people are made safer, more comfortable, more eager to purchase, more efficient—or just plain happier—the designer has succeeded.

Henry Dreyfuss

No one has yet invented a scale for unhappiness or discomfort or uneasiness, and it is therefore not possible to set up performance standards for them. Yet these misfits are among the most critical which occur in design problems.

Christopher Alexander

Only a poor writer uses a long, obscure, or foreign word or phrase when a short, common, or vernacular one will do. It frustrates the reader, who will either look up the word in a dictionary (unlikely) or read on, slightly confused (more likely). Similarly, avoiding unnecessary complexity and the resulting user frustration is central to good design. A good design minimizes the frustrations experienced in using it.

One common source of frustration is the user's manual. Too frequently, our software designs expect the poor user to live with a thick manual. The user is frustrated at having to refer to the manual in the first place, frustrated because the manual can't be found, and finally, frustrated because the information can't be found in the manual. I view a manual as a software designer's list of failures.

Ideally, a software product should be obvious to use; where it isn't obvious, the designer should provide helpful information and eliminate the need for a manual. Someday we should be able to realize that ideal, and our software will require as much preparation as watching television does. Today, however, most programs are more like Verdi operas; they communicate in a foreign language and require reading notes in advance to have any idea of what is happening. Of course, if done with the genius of Verdi, our programs might attract a devoted following across cultures, but they will appeal to the masses only in a culture that understands the language.

Another major source of frustration is waiting. No one likes to wait in line and no one likes to wait for a computer. There are no magic times I can give you for how long a computer can keep a user waiting under different circumstances. The important question the designer must ask is, "When and how often do users perceive themselves as waiting?" The second question is, "How can that perception of waiting be reduced?"

When you're using WordStar, for example, and do something that requires that the whole screen be redisplayed, WordStar first displays the line where the cursor is located. While this time-saving feature might not be important to a new user, it is helpful to an experienced one who can continue working without waiting.

In his seminal book, *Notes on the Synthesis of Form*, the architect Christopher Alexander describes architectural design in a manner that is also true for computer software design. He says that we can't define good design, except as the absence of bad design or "misfits."

Alexander observes that good design is the lack of such misfits. We can never know all the possible misfits ahead of time; though our designs keep getting better, they will always be flawed. A completely frustration-free design is always impossible. Faced with conflicting objectives and sources of frustration, the designer has to decide what flaws to accept so that overall frustration will be kept to a minimum.

Alexander's concept is more general— he refers to a "misfit" between the form (design) and the environment. Thus, Alexander includes a host of other considerations the designer must keep in mind, including such engineering considerations as "Is there enough memory?" and "What is the allowable cost?" The designer should take the overall view of the design problem and get the best fit between the environment as a whole and the product, not just between the user and the product.

15. HELP THE USER COPE.

A good salesman knows that no matter how good a presentation is, the customer will still have questions and concerns. He knows he must help his prospects cope with these problems. This does not mean simply giving the customer additional information; it also means providing additional services, such as gift wrapping in retail stores or financing in automobile sales.

Salesmen are experts in helping the user cope. They are prepared for many of the potential problems a customer will have—they call them objections—and when the prospect raises an objection, the salesman is prepared to cope with the problem. As one example, if the prospect indicates he does not have enough money to purchase a car, the salesman shows him how he could get financing.

For our part, while designing the Craig translator, we faced this problem: What should we do if the user typed in a word that was not in the dictionary? The conventional solution (chosen by both of our competitors) was to display judgmental statements such as "NOT FOUND," and provide no way for the user to cope. We designed our translator to provide the user with information that described the problem and helped solve it.

First, the M-100 flashes the unrecognized word with question marks, indicating the word that it did not recognize and stating that the program did not recognize it. The user can then hit the search key, which finds all the closest matches to the unknown word.

The search routine subtracts one letter at a time from the right side of the word until it finds a match in the dictionary, then displays all the words in its dictionary that begin with the remaining letters.

For example, if the user entered SUGEST, the search routine begins to delete characters, getting SUGES, SUGE, and finally, SUG. At this point, the program alternately displays SUG--SUGAR and SUG--SUGGEST until the user types a space to accept the displayed selection.

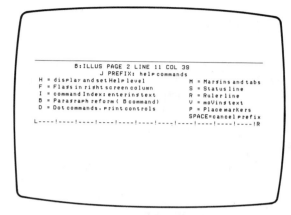

```
        B:ILLUS PAGE 2 LINE 11 COL 39
             J PREFIX: help commands
 H = display and set Help level        M = Margins and tabs
 F = Flags in right screen column      S = Status line
 I = command Index: entering text      R = Ruler line
 B = Paragraph reform ( B command)     V = moVing text
 D = Dot commands. print controls      P = Place markers
                                       SPACE=cancel prefix
 L----!----!----!----!----!----!----!----!----!----!----!R
```

Figure 18: The WordStar help screen.

Used by permission of WordStar International Inc.

Thus, misspellings and incorrect word endings become a minor annoyance instead of a major problem for the new user.

If the word is not in the dictionary in any form, the user is usually presented with enough information to recognize that fact. The user sees the information we provide as describing the problem, whereas the competitive translator's "NOT FOUND" is seen as frustrating and unhelpful.

The program itself can help the user cope. WordStar does a good job of this: it has a series of "help screens" that list and describe the available commands for the user and briefly describe their functions. These screens are on the top third of the CRT, leaving the rest of the display for the text. Although this allows less space for the text, the information is often useful. The user can always turn off the help screens if he wants to.

WordStar also has a HELP command that gives the user a list of topics— entering text, moving text, place markers— for which it provides helpful information. The user needs to refer to the manual only on occasion.

There is rarely an excuse for not providing coping information. Even on some of the simplest timesharing programs I wrote years ago, the commands "HELP" and "?" list the major commands with brief descriptions of their functions.

Figure 19: If the user types a word into the Craig translator that is not in its dictionary, the translator alternately flashes the word and question marks to the user. The user can type the search key and the translator will find the best matches. In this case, it finds SUGAR and SUGGEST.*

16. RESPOND TO THE USER'S ACTIONS.

Memory is a more fluid medium than perception because it is farther removed from the checks of reality.

Kurt Lewin
quoted by Arnheim

Any salesman will try to get feedback from a customer about the customer's likes and dislikes in order to gauge the effect of the sales presentation. Similarly, most actors feel more comfortable with a responsive audience and thus prefer stage to film. Audience response helps them judge their impact, so they can adjust their actions accordingly.

Everyone has a strong inclination to build a view of reality that may or may not prove to be valid. The effective communicator knows this and will actively stimulate feedback as a reality check. By making the user's actions immediately visible, our programs can influence the users to modify their perceptions of reality to agree with the computer's view of reality.

We can respond to our users' actions in several ways. By continually updating the cursor position on the screen, a program can make the effect of the cursor-moving command immediately visible. Any reasonably good word processor works to a large extent on the principle "what you

*Please flip through the next few pages to see the sequence of messages that the translator presents.

see is what you get"; it responds to inserts and deletes by displaying their effects. Spreadsheet programs respond to the changing of a variable by making its effect visible.

A good response shows the user how the computer interprets his intentions. If, for example, the user starts to delete a file by mistake, the response can make the effect of the action visible while there is still time to correct it.

When I find myself driving behind a truck and can't see the road ahead, I get uneasy. I would prefer to drive behind a car— my visibility is much better. Now think of your user operating your program; will it feel like driving behind a Mack truck or a sports car?

17. DON'T LET THE USER FOCUS ON MECHANICS.

We are not won by arguments that we can analyze, but by tone and temper, by the manner which is the man himself.
Samuel Butler

A good writer expends considerable effort to eliminate the reader's thought or effort by writing clearly and simply and providing the readers with any information they need.

On the other hand, the lazy writer leaves work for the reader. A writer who uses obscure words will have the reader reaching for a dictionary. If the writer's train of thought is hard to follow, the reader will probably stop reading.

Consider two ways by which we can move a cursor on a screen. In one interface, we have to type 10U to move the cursor up ten lines; in the other, we type U ten times— that is, UUUUUUUUUU. Superficially, the first interface is better because we type three characters instead of ten. But to use the first method— 10U— we must first count the number of lines we have to go up, possibly making a mistake, and then we must type three *different* keys.

With the second method, the operation is different. We type U's until we get close to where we want to be, slow down,

The Elements of Friendly Software Design

and finally stop typing U's. We don't have to count, or type more than one key, or divert our thinking from what we are doing. We have only to recognize when we get where we want to be. With the second method, the user is involved less in the *mechanics* of doing the task than in doing the task itself.

When we designed an intelligent telephone, we wanted to store forty frequently called phone numbers but had room for only twenty dial keys. The initial design had space for two telephone numbers by each of the twenty keys, and a bank-select key that could be used to select between the top or bottom of the two numbers. With this design, the user had to think as follows: Is my number in the top or bottom bank? Am I in that bank? If not, then I hit the bank-select key. Now I can hit the key next to the number I want to dial.

This thought process was substantially simplified by replacing the bank-select key with a bank-shift key. The user could dial any of the twenty numbers on top by hitting the key next to the number, or dial any of the twenty numbers on the bottom by hitting the bank-shift key and the appropriate number key. For the novice, these two interfaces are similar, because they both require thought. However, after using them for a time, commonly used key sequences become a part of the subconscious—the user needs only to think of his goal, not of his current mode. With the initial design, the user must consider both his goal and his current mode.

A typist has a similar thought process. Without thinking about where the keys are—that knowledge is stored in the subconscious—the typist is free to think about the words and sentences that are being written.

When this happens, the user acts instinctively; one feels the product is an extension of oneself—just as a tennis player feels that a tennis racket is an extension of himself and a driver feels that a car is an extension of himself.

18. HELP THE USER TO CRYSTALLIZE HIS THOUGHTS.

The average person has a writing vocabulary of 10,000 words, but a reading vocabulary of 50,000 words. Except for practiced writers, the Japanese or Chinese person who can read and speak his language fluently will be unable to write it without constantly referring to a dictionary of ideograms.

These are examples of a general principle: People are better at recognizing something than they are at recalling it.

Life insurance salesmen know this. They know that when they approach people about life insurance, people frequently say they don't need any. But the prospect often does in fact have an unrecognized need. The salesman brings out this need in the prospect.

The salesman asks questions such as "How many children do you have?" "Do you want them to go to college?" "What kind of college do you have in mind—a state college or Harvard?"

During this exchange, prospects go through a thought process during which they begin to recognize a need in their own minds for insurance. Since the prospect did not perceive his need for insurance initially, this process is called creating a need. In fact, the need was always there; the salesman merely got the prospect to recognize it.

Writers and filmmakers crystallize thoughts in the minds of their audiences. Sometimes they add little new information, but simply verbalize or organize existing information so that members of an audience see something they knew only piecemeal or subconsciously before. Frederick Brooks's *The Mythical Man-Month*, for example, does not tell

us much that many of us who have experienced several large software projects did not already know. But it crystallizes our experience and thoughts.

Many of our users have a fuzzy idea of what they want to do or what the program can do. Our products should present themselves to users in a way that helps them recognize what they want, instead of requiring them to spend time formulating their problems or recalling the various commands.

Menus can be an effective tool for the designer because presenting a user with options gives him an opportunity to recognize what he wants to do. Menus can even be used on single-line display devices. The intelligent telephone I designed has several menu-driven commands. The user who wants to forward calls to another phone depresses the call-forwarding key several times, and the options appear one by one: FORWARD ALL, FORWARD BUSY, FORWARD NO-ANS, and so on. The options keep cycling through so users can browse once or twice before committing themselves. The user just depresses the SELECT key when the desired option appears.

Think of a time when you had to go someplace you hadn't been for a time, and weren't sure you remembered how to get there. Certainly you could not have given someone else directions how to get there. I suspect that as you made your trip you recognized familiar places and were able to muddle through— finding the correct turns and, eventually, your destination. Similarly, a program that displays visual cues and other information will help users recognize their options and muddle through. It may not be perfect or logical, but it is a lot better than having your user refer to the manual every step of the way.

CHAPTER THREE

19. INVOLVE THE USER.

Resist the temptation to make everything bigger and more gorgeous when you need strong communication.
Frank Thomas and Ollie Johnston

A writer or filmmaker tries to get the audience involved in the story. This is frequently done by making a character sympathetic. In *E. T.*, Steven Spielberg achieved his effect by getting the audience to empathize with the title character by involving it in E.T.'s attempt to go home.

A salesman will involve his prospects. For example, in trying to close a sale, he might ask his customer to write a list of the advantages and disadvantages of a purchase decision. This gets the prospect physically involved. From the physical involvement, psychological involvement follows, and the chances of a sale improve.

The software designer starts out with an advantage; because the users must be physically involved with the product, it is easier to get them psychologically involved. Generally, the user's task will be something that already involves the user. The designer's job is to present that task to the user in an interesting and transparent way.

Several of the principles explained in this chapter can be used to help get the user involved in a task. But I have listed this as a separate principle because it poses meaningful questions for the designer: "Is my user involved?"; "What is preventing him from becoming more involved?"; "What else can I do to get my user involved?"

20. COMMUNICATE IN SPECIFICS, NOT GENERALITIES.

Prefer the specific to the general, the definite to the vague, the concrete to the abstract.
William Strunk and E.B. White

I have learned that the mind of a good merchant, and also of a good artist or good scientist...starts out with the most specific, the most concrete, and then reaches for the generalization.

Peter F. Drucker

George Orwell translated a passage from the King James Bible into "modern" English to show how communication deteriorates when we use generalities instead of specifics. First his translation:

> Objective consideration of contemporary pheno-
> mena compels the conclusion that success or failure
> in competitive activities exhibits no tendency to be
> commensurate with innate capacity, but that a con-
> siderable element of the unpredictable must in-
> evitably be taken into account.

Now the original:

> I returned, and saw under the sun, that the race
> is not to the swift, nor the battle to the strong,
> neither yet bread to the wise, nor yet riches to men
> of understanding, nor yet favor to men of skill; but
> time and chance happeneth to them all.

Even though the King James version of the Bible was written hundreds of years ago, it communicates more effectively. This extends to other communications crafts. The writer, business executive, or salesman tells a story to illustrate a point. The advertiser shows how a real person uses Tide to clean clothes, instead of describing the cleaning properties of Tide.

There is a reason for this. We think better in specifics than we do in generalities— especially when we are doing something new. This does not mean that thinking in generalities is impossible or undesirable; it means people find it easier to understand specific instances before they understand the general case.

VisiCalc does a good job of helping users think in specifics. As a simple example, the user who wants to add up a column of figures puts SUM(Al, A5) in the place where the sum should appear. The sum appears, and the user's spreadsheet looks like Figure 22 below.

From the user's perspective this is just adding a column of figures. But the program forces him to do it in a way that enables it to save the formula— SUM(A1,A5)— in cell A7. Now, if the user wants to change the third item from 33 to 44, the program has the information it needs to change the 237 to 248, which it then proceeds to do.

The user was thinking about adding five specific numbers, but in fact wrote a general-purpose program for adding any five numbers. Two other examples are shown in Figures 20 and 21.

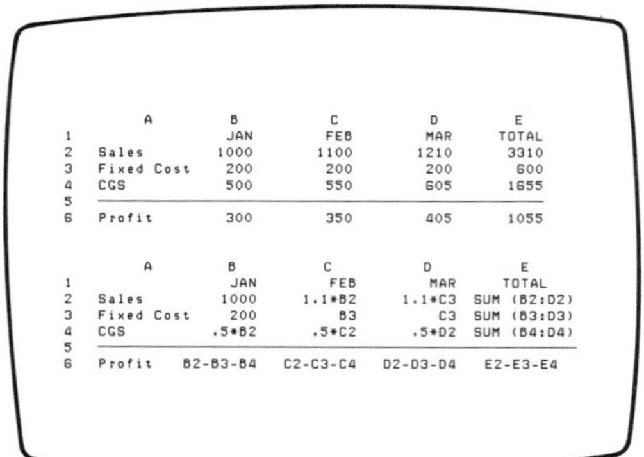

Figure 20: The top screen shows a simple spreadsheet calculation as it appears to the Visi-Calc user. The bottom one shows what is actually stored. Only two cells hold numbers. All other cells hold formulas and calculate the numbers they display.

Figure 21: This figure differs from the previous one only in that 1000 was changed to 2500. Of course, most of the numbers displayed are changed since they depend on the changed number in B2. Since the user looks at the top picture rather than the bottom one, he can think in specifics. For him to use the bottom one, he would have to think in generalities.

© Lotus Development Corporation. Used with permission.

	A	B	C	D	E
1		JAN	FEB	MAR	TOTAL
2	Sales	2500	2750	3025	8275
3	Fixed Cost	200	200	200	600
4	CGS	1250	1375	1512	4137
5					
6	Profit	1050	1175	1312	3537

	A	B	C	D	E
1		JAN	FEB	MAR	TOTAL
2	Sales	2500	1.1*B2	1.1*C3	SUM (B2:D2)
3	Fixed Cost	200	B3	C3	SUM (B3:D3)
4	CGS	.5*B2	.5*C2	.5*D2	SUM (B4:D4)
5					
6	Profit	B2-B3-B4	C2-C3-C4	D2-D3-D4	E2-E3-E4

Figure 22: Addition of numbers on a VisiCalc screen.

© Lotus Development Corporation. Used with permission.

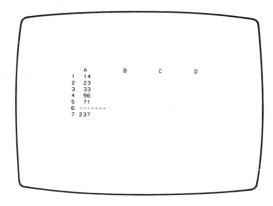

The process of programming consists of generalizing a problem, solving the general case, and finally plugging in specific data to solve the specific case. This forces programmers to think in generalities, and once we have made the transition from the specific to the general in a particular problem, we rarely go back to the specific to communicate with our users. We design our user interfaces to communicate in generalities instead of specifics without even realizing it. This is our fifth counterproductive instinct.

21. ORIENT THE USER IN THE WORLD.

Have you ever walked into the middle of a conversation to find out that everything was understandable except for one crucial fact, like the person or subject being discussed? You lack a world view and are frustrated. The naive communicator is likely to forget to provide a world view for the audience, but the experienced communicator always considers this problem. Frequently, the solution is something as simple as a title like "CASABLANCA 1941" at the beginning of a movie. Without something like this, the viewer (or reader) will feel disoriented.

The journalist knows the importance of completely orienting the reader, and will be sure that every story answers the five "W"s: Who, What, Where, When, and Why. And How.

WordStar's work screen shows the file being edited and its page number, thus orienting users in case they get lost. The Xerox Star (Figure 23) shows the current page in the file as a black rectangle in a vertical column. The rectangle's position in the column indicates the page's position in the document; its height indicates the length of the page compared to the whole column.

The user may at any time ask such questions as "Where am I?" "What am I doing?" "What do I do next?" The easier it is to answer such questions, the better your design will be.

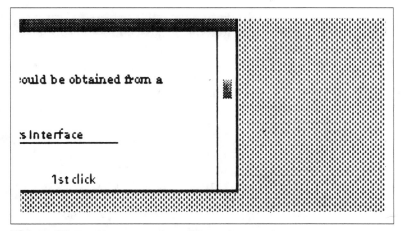

Figure 23 Used by permission of Xerox Corporation.

22. STRUCTURE
THE USER'S INTERFACE.

*The art of cinematography...is in every fragment of a film,
being an organic part of an organically conceived whole.*

Sergei Eisenstein

*Work from a suitable design.... Design informs even the
simplest structure, whether of brick and steel or of prose. You
raise a pup tent from one sort of vision, a cathedral from
another. This does not mean that you must sit with a blueprint
always in front of you, merely that you had best anticipate
what you are getting into. To compose a laundry list, a writer
can work directly from the pile of soiled garments, ticking them*

off one by one. But to write a biography the writer will need at least a rough scheme; he cannot plunge in blindly and start ticking off fact after fact about his man, lest he miss the forest for the trees and there be no end to his labors.

William Strunk and E.B. White

The single most important thing contributed by the screenwriter is the structure.

William Goldman

A fundamental challenge for engineers is to bring organization and structure to a design. A good structure gives the designer intellectual control over his design and helps him think about and communicate a design effectively. This is one reason that structured programming is useful.

We consider the internal organization and structure of a program, but when users are involved, it is even more critical to organize and structure the interface.

Writers are constantly aware of structure. Consider the simple sentence: "These are trying times for men's souls." Now consider: "These are the times that try men's souls." The content of both is the same. But a simple change in structure renders a dramatic difference in their respective impact. The writer considers the structure not just of the sentence, but of the paragraph, the chapter, and the volume.

Any communication, whether it is a sales pitch, a TV advertisement, or a film, has a definite structure that considers the effect in the mind of the audience.

The designer of friendly software designs an organization for the user and communicates it. Menus help describe the structure to the user, but the organization that is important is not what appears on the screen; it is that which is created in the user's mind. Just as good tailors do not let their seams show and good carpenters don't let their nails show, a good designer's organization does not intrude into the user's mind. Thus, for example, the good designer would not force the experienced user to go through a series of menus to get something done.

WordStar illustrates one way a program's organization can be communicated to users. A help screen displays

frequently used one-character commands. These commands are divided into six categories, an organization that helps users organize WordStar's capabilities in their own minds.

Probably the most important job that the designer must do— one that no one else can do— is to make the product an organic whole. The task of an architect is similar: When designing a house, he considers where the house faces, how much space the various rooms will have, how the rooms fit together, how the plumbing fits in, and, of course, what it will cost. The solution is structured and presented to the client.

Since people are better at recognizing problems than they are at generating original ideas, the client will have several suggestions: the living room should be larger, the location should be changed, a picture window should be added. But if the basic structure is sound, the architect can incorporate many changes without too much effort. Other changes may not be so easy to implement without destroying the fundamental structure: Making the living room larger might mean making the dining room smaller, which might easily prove unacceptable to the client.

The problem is more complex than I have painted it. There are always the risks of overlooking something that will prove to be a problem later. The architect must get as much client feedback as possible and use it to improve the design. But to avoid losing control of the design, the architect structures a solution so that it solves the client's problem while maintaining the organization he needs to deal with unexpected surprises.

Structure is just as important to software designers. Anyone can critique a user interface, but the designer, in considering any change, must ask, "How does it affect the

```
        B:ILLUS    PAGE 2 LINE 11 COL 39              INSERT ON
CURSOR: ∧A = left word      ∧S = left char  ∧D = right char   ∧F = right word
        ∧E = up line        ∧X = down line
SCROLL: ∧Z = up line        ∧W = down line  ∧C = up screen     ∧R = down screen
DELETE: DEL=char left       ∧G = char right ∧T = word right    ∧Y = entire line
OTHER:  ∧V = insert off/on  ∧I = tab        RETURN=end para  △U⁻= stop
        ∧N = insert a RETURN  △B = reform to end para  ∧L=find/replace again
HELP:   ∧J displays menu of information commands
PREFIX KEYS    ∧Q ∧J ∧K ∧O ∧P    display menus of additional commands
L----!----!----!----!----!----!----!----!---!----!----!----!----!----R
```

Figure 24: This is another WordStar screen that helps organize the user interface by categorizing various commands: *move cursor, scroll, delete, help,* and *other.*

Used by permission of WordStar International Inc.

rest of the design?" and "What does it do to the overall structure?" Good ideas that have minimal effect can be readily incorporated. Those that would sacrifice the basic structure must be carefully considered.

A quality that distinguishes the professional from the amateur designer is the ability to maintain control of structure while evolving the design. A good designer will do his initial design so that changes can easily be incorporated. If necessary, he will abandon one structure and replace it with another one, but will always maintain intellectual control of the design. Some amateurs will be unable to change their structures in response to new demands. Others will be responsive to such demands, but will lose control of their designs in the process.

The Elements of Friendly Software Design

Figure 25: "Shoe" by Jeff MacNelly.

Reprinted by permission: Tribune Media Services.

Our sixth counterproductive instinct is that we structure our designs as machines that must work, instead of as thoughts in the mind of the user. Our organization is aimed at solving the mechanical problems of the program's function and not the problem of communicating to the mind of the user.

23. MAKE YOUR PRODUCT RELIABLE.

Consider two applications: One takes one hour of your constant attention to do a job. The second takes two hours. Which would you prefer? The first one, of course— it takes only half the time. But suppose I give you some more information: The first application actually is four times as fast as the second one— but after it does the job in one half hour, it destroys all the work and you have to redo everything from scratch. Total time, one hour. Now, do you prefer the one-hour application or the two-hour one?

Most people don't answer this question. Most people cringe. The actual amount of time spent is less important than the psychological factors involved. A system should never let its users down. A half hour's work lost is frustrating—whether due to hardware failure, a software bug, or a mistake by the user. Our systems should prevent or at least mitigate such damage.

There are many techniques for making systems reliable: structured programming, proof of correctness, testing, quality assurance techniques, and methodologies for designing reliable hardware and software. But because they are primarily engineering techniques, they do not concern us here.

There are things that the designer can do to mitigate reliability problems. Some systems automatically keep backup copies of files—if the main file is lost, an old version is better than none—and the designer could have the word processor periodically save the latest version of the file being updated on disk.

24. SERVE BOTH THE NOVICE AND THE EXPERIENCED USER.

Language grows by introducing new words, but a language consisting only of new words and a new syntax would be indistinguishable from gibberish.

E. H. Gombrich

Good writing and good films frequently appeal to a broad audience. Shakespeare's plays attracted the masses of his day as well as the intellectuals of later ages. D. W. Griffith and Charlie Chaplin's films appeal to all classes of people.

The Elements of Friendly Software Design

The makers of video games design their games to start out easy and get progressively harder—always challenging the user.

Software designers sometimes design for the novice user and sometimes for the experienced user. But frequently we must design for both. The program should be easy enough for the novice to use, yet versatile enough for the expert. In this light, it is important to realize that every expert was once a novice. Most users' knowledge is dynamic. They learn and change, and their interactions with your program will form an important part of that change. Things that are useful to the novice often bore the experienced user, while those things that are second nature to the experienced user can baffle and confuse the novice.

One of our problems as designers is that we quickly become experienced users and this causes us to lose our empathy with novices.

In WordStar, several one-character commands can be followed by a second letter to form other commands. Inexperienced users find that after typing the first character of a command, WordStar pauses, waits for one second, and then displays a screen filled with choices for the second letter of the command. Experienced users can type the two-character command quickly and the screen will never be displayed. Not only do users have the advantage of getting multiple menus without the "seams" showing, but both the naive and experienced user are well served by this approach.

```
        B:SLIDES     PAGE 23 LINE 4 COL 41
                       PRINT CODES MENU
   B - Boldface        X - Strikeout          O - Non-break space
   D - Doublestrike    Y - Change ribbon color. C - Printer pause here
   V - Subscript       A - Alternate pitch    H - Overprint character
   T - Superscript     N - Standard pitch     RETURN - overprint line
```

Figure 26: WordStar can serve both the experienced and novice user. If the novice wants to type a special printing character, he types Ctrl-P, waits a second, and then selects a letter from this menu. He may also type a B for Boldface. The experienced user types the same thing, Ctrl-P then a B; but since he does not pause after the Ctrl-P, the above menu is never displayed.

Used by permission of WordStar International Inc.

25. DEVELOP AND MAINTAIN USER RAPPORT.

I must follow my people. Am I not their leader?
Benjamin Disraeli

Effective communication starts with getting close to the audience, and this means achieving rapport. Anyone whose profession is to persuade people knows this. The

salesman gets rapport and uses it to sell products; the advertiser uses it to get potential customers to perceive a product in a certain way.

John O'Toole, of the advertising agency Foote, Cone and Belding, suggests that the advertiser frame his message so the prospect who sees it says: "'Hey, they are speaking to me.' Talk to him in a way that gets him nodding in agreement before you try to sell him something."

Developing rapport with someone— whether in person or via the mass media— means meeting him at his level and emphasizing your similarities. Once you have achieved rapport, you are in a better position to lead a person in the direction you want him to go. A person will modify a position to agree with yours rather than lose rapport with you. Over a period of time, a series of such slight modifications in that person's behavior can evolve into a major change.

Winston Churchill was a master at using this principle. Once, when he attended a dinner party, his hostess told him that a distinguished guest had taken an expensive salt shaker from the table and put it in his pocket. She didn't know what to do. Churchill offered to take care of the problem.

How would you have handled it? How would you get back the salt shaker without antagonizing the distinguished guest? Think about it— if you want to design friendly software, this is the kind of problem you are going to have to solve.

Churchill put another salt shaker in his own pocket and approached the guest. First, he achieved rapport by establishing commonality with his audience. He took the salt shaker out of his pocket and said, "I think we've been seen." Second, he used the rapport he had created to lead his audience in the direction he wanted: "We'd better put them back."

Our designs should communicate with the user at his level.

When he designs a word proccssor for secretaries who have not used one, the designer can achieve rapport by making it operate as much like a typewriter as possible. If rapport can be achieved, then the designer can introduce the user to other word processing capabilities. A word processor should after all be more than a typewriter. A major value of a program's achieving rapport is that the rapport can be used to advance the user's knowledge.

An applications system for tire retailers provides an intriguing example of the importance of rapport. Triad Systems, after enjoying spectacular success in developing and marketing an applications system to handle accounting and inventory control for the automotive parts marketplace, developed a similar system for tire retailers. Triad's tire system substantially increased its users' profitability by its sophisticated back-office accounting systems, but its sales force lost market share in one regional market to a less sophisticated system.

Why was this unsophisticated system so successful? When a prospect walks into the store, the tire salesman's thinking runs something like this: "What model car does this customer have? What are the most expensive tires I have in stock for that car? The next most expensive? The least expensive? What else can I sell this customer? Whatever happens I can't let him leave here without tires!"

The successful program asked the salesman for the car model, and it found all the tires that fit the car and listed them on the screen— starting with the most expensive and going to the least expensive. The tire retailer was most interested in selling tires, and the program helped him sell tires in the same way he normally did. Not only did the program complement the owner's thought process when he was there, it replicated the process for a new clerk when the owner wasn't there. It achieved rapport.

This small company in one regional market had done such a good job of achieving rapport that Triad Systems withdrew its product from the market and redesigned both the hardware and the software to provide this capability. They feel that by making their program achieve the same kind of rapport with its users, they will be able to get their customers to use their sophisticated back-office accounting systems.

26. CONSIDER THE FIRST IMPRESSION.

In my stories I try to figure myself as a prospective buyer of a magazine standing in front of a hotel newsstand. Would my story title make me pick up the magazine to look at it? Would the first hasty glance through the story make me buy the magazine, and would a reading of the yarn make me a regular subscriber?

Erle Stanley Gardner

The designer's main concern is to make the user happy with the product. But the designer also needs to consider the problem of getting the customer to purchase the product.

In this sense, a software designer is similar to the industrial designer who specifies beige and other light colors for vacuum cleaners so that they won't appear to be heavy. The consumer's first impression of a product is important to generating sales. Similarly, a writer will spend proportionately more time on the opening paragraph of an article than on the body of it because it is essential to get the reader's attention and interest at the beginning.

If you are designing a personal computer product that is sold in a computer store, you must realize that the clerk probably doesn't know how to use your program. If it is sold in a department store, the clerk won't even know how to run a computer. The product must be able to demonstrate itself and sell itself. The language translator I designed could display words and their translations continuously. This attracted attention and generated interest from potential customers at the point of sale.

27. BUILD A MODEL IN THE USER'S MIND.

The supreme question must be, what impression will the introduction of this detail produce upon the mind of the spectator?
Jasper Maskelyne

What a painter inquires into is not the nature of the physical world, but the nature of our reactions to it.
E. H. Gombrich

One thing should be obvious by now. Designing friendly software is not an engineering job. Or, if it is an engineering job, what is constructed is an illusion in the user's mind.

The filmmaker deals in illusion. This is obviously true where special effects are concerned: a one-foot-high burning model can look like a towering skyscraper on fire. The camera operator can tilt the camera to photograph the cockpit of a fighter plane, so that the plane looks like it is descending at an angle. In these cases, the viewers will usually be unaware that they're not seeing the real thing. The filmmaker's only concern is the image that remains in the viewer's mind.

The Elements of Friendly Software Design

Figure 27: In the "learn" mode, the translator displays successive words with their translations. This is important at the point of sale. By giving the potential purchaser a feeling for what the translator does, it makes a good first impression.

Alfred Hitchcock gave a simple example that illustrates that what is in the mind of the audience is what is important. Consider a five-minute film sequence of a man and a woman talking in a room. The conversation is ordinary, the sequence dull. Now, just before that sequence, insert a brief scene where the audience is told, unknown to the man and woman, that a bomb will explode in the room in five minutes. The whole sequence becomes interesting, involving, and suspenseful to the audience. But the five-minute sequence is unchanged. The only thing that is different during those five minutes is what is in the mind of the audience.

Magic is primarily a form of communication; it is concerned with constructing a false picture in the audience's mind. It may come as a surprise to the layman, but the least important part of magic is the engineering of tricks. The essence of magic is communicating an illusion; the professional magician is primarily a communicator.

First, the magician must be an effective showman who entertains his audience. To this end, he builds up the suspense of an illusion, tells jokes, and otherwise develops entertaining patter— the equivalent of a salesman's pitch.

Second, the magician must be an expert at misdirection, the psychology of deception. The magician determines what effect he wants to make believable to his audience. The effect must be impossible, if it is to be magic. The magician then designs a performance, the purpose of which is to communicate the illusion of that effect to the audience.

While sleight of hand and special magic equipment play a part in magic performances, misdirection plays the major part. A magician who has an envelope that contains a marked $20 bill he wants to remove will probably use misdirection. He might ask for a volunteer from the audience and then select an attractive woman. Everyone's attention will focus on the woman while the magician replaces the $20 bill from the envelope with a piece of paper the size of a $20 bill.

To more effectively communicate the illusion of the bill in the envelope, the magician might ask the woman to feel the envelope and tell the audience what is inside. She

will almost certainly say a $20 bill; after all, it feels like a $20 bill, and it was there a second ago. Because the audience's image of what is happening leads it to believe there is a $20 bill in the envelope, the magician can produce some wondrous effects. The magician's skills are not so much the skills of an engineer; they are those of a communicator.

We have a similar opportunity to create the effects we desire when we design friendly software. The reality of what our programs actually do is of no importance to the user; only the mental model of what they do is important. Our task as designers is not so much to design and create software that carries out a function as it is to design and implement a believable and communicable illusion, or model, for our users.

A spreadsheet program, for example, does more than just use the metaphor of the spreadsheet— it communicates an image of the spreadsheet to its users. For example, when a user moves the cursor off the screen to the right, the program shifts the whole screen a column to the right, bringing the cursor back onto the screen. This movement helps convey the illusion of a window into a large spreadsheet.

28. MAKE YOUR DESIGN SIMPLE...

Sometimes one has to say difficult things, but one ought to say them as simply as one knows how.

G. H. Hardy

Vigorous writing is concise. A sentence should contain no un-necessary words, a paragraph no unnecessary sentences, for the same reason that a drawing should have no unnecessary lines and a machine no unnecessary parts....

William Strunk and E. B. White

Perfection, then, is finally achieved, not when there is nothing left to add, but when there is nothing left to take away.

Antoine de St. Exupéry

To write simply is as difficult as to be good.

W. Somerset Maugham

Good design, like good writing, is simple and economical. Simple design makes the product easier to maintain and use. No magic formula will enable us to create simple designs; they are the result of creativity, false starts, and hard work. But when we can achieve most of our design objectives while making something simple, our results are likely to be good.

If something is complex, it can fail in many ways: Its design, obscured by its complexity, can be unsound; it can be difficult to use; and it can be difficult to learn and understand.

Both the internal design and the user interface can have simplicity, but the interaction between the user and the program is what concerns us here, and frequently we have to sacrifice the simplicity of internal design to make the user interface simple. In a word processor, for example, we might want commands that move the cursor left or right one word. Defining what a word is will be complex algorithmically if it is to appear simple and natural to the user. We must consider diacritical marks, apostrophes, dashes, and backspaces.

Similarly, the definition of alphabetic ordering in the phone book, which was designed to be simple and natural for phone users, turns out to be complex algorithmically when implemented in a sorting program. The designer should, of course, localize these complexities in a single function instead of infecting the whole design.

Simplicity in the user interface can cause design complexity in other ways, but the good designer looks at the tradeoffs involved and is often willing to pay the price of implementation complexity to achieve user interface simplicity.

The kind of simplicity that is most useful occurs when the designer is able to look at a problem from a perspective that exposes its inherent simplicity.

VisiCalc is elegantly simple. There is an array of cells into which the user can put text, numbers, or formulas. This simple concept is extremely powerful. Like most good design, VisiCalc is obvious in retrospect. It makes us ask: "Why didn't I think of that?"

Simplicity does not come easily— it is the result of work. However, I must warn the designer that people are generally unwilling to pay the cost of simplicity. They would prefer to pay for quantity, which is more easily measured than value. We pay doctors to make us well when we are sick; it would make more sense to pay them when we are well, and not pay them when we are sick. People seem willing to pay

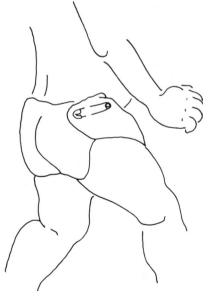

Figure 28: Design should be simple...

software designers in proportion to the garbage they leave in their designs, instead of the garbage they take out.

This brings us to our seventh counterproductive instinct: Our natural desire is for simplicity of the program and its design instead of simplicity in the mind of the user.

29. BUT NOT TOO SIMPLE.

[continued from above] This requires not that the writer make all his sentences short, or that he avoid all detail and treat his subjects only in outline, but that every word tell.
William Strunk and E. B. White

Five lines where three are enough is always stupidity.... But to eliminate expressive words in speaking or writing— words that intensify or vivify meaning— is not simplicity. Nor is similar elimination in architecture simplicity. It may be, and usually is, stupidity.
Frank Lloyd Wright

Every good artist, every good workman, has a passion for economy; if you can do a thing in one stroke, don't use two; if a certain mood or atmosphere is essential to the illusion you are after and it requires a hundred strokes, use them.
Dudley Nichols

Make things as simple as possible— but no simpler.
Albert Einstein

There are two kinds of false simplicity. First, there is the error that Strunk and White, Frank Lloyd Wright, and Dudley Nichols point out: While the essence of a design should be simple, the details need not necessarily be.

When the user issues a command, feedback that clarifies what that command accomplishes is useful and valuable detail, not added complexity. A good piece of craftsmanship is rarely as simple as it appears; it is the craftsman's skill that makes it appear simple.

Einstein points out the second kind of false simplicity. Sometimes people think they are being simple when they are

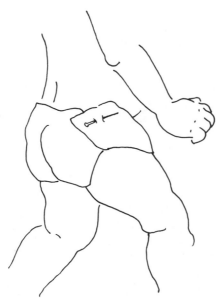

Figure 29:   ...but not too simple.

only being simplistic. A word in a word processor can be defined as a series of alphabetic characters, but since this definition ignores the problems of apostrophes, dashes, and other diacritical marks that can be in a word, it ignores the essence of the problem.

30. YOU NEED VISION.

The most important thing is to have the vision. The next is to grasp and hold it.... You must see and feel what you are thinking about.

Sergei Eisenstein

Imagination is more important than knowledge.

Albert Einstein

A pedant would have us believe that good writing is following the rules of grammar. That is the easy part. The first problem is to have something to say; the second problem is to be able to say it, even if ungrammatically. The last and easiest part is to get someone to copyedit it.

The design of a good user interface does not come from knowing an extensive amount of literature on user interfaces, or worse yet, an extensive knowledge of software algorithms. It comes from having a vision of what the product should be. The knowledge must then serve that vision. When Beethoven composed his music, he put aside such workaday considerations as whether the musicians could play all the notes or not. He had a vision and he was communicating it to his audience. He knew that if the vision was any good, the musicians would be able to figure out how to play the notes eventually. The designer's vision should direct his search for knowledge; knowledge should not inhibit his vision. This brings us to our final counterproductive instinct: As designers, we let our knowledge inhibit our vision.

After Francis Ford Coppola had made a few grade-B movies, he began to direct his first major picture, *Finian's Rainbow.* He hired a young assistant to help him on the set and quickly found him useful. As he said: "I was very grateful to have someone of my own generation around to discuss what I was trying to do as opposed to what I was able to do." A good communicator starts with a vision; he then thinks of the images he wants to create in the audience's mind. Then he considers the effects that will produce those images, and finally he considers the technology that will produce these effects. Most programmers and engineers start with the technology. Francis Ford Coppola's young assistant, by the way, was George Lucas.

The ultimate question for the writer is "Does my vision work?" The filmmaker asks the same question. And so should the software designer.

Figure 30: Opera. Since opera is usually in a foreign language, it is generally incomprehensible to most people. Many computer programs communicate in "computerese" and are similarly incomprehensible to those who are not cognoscente.

Designing for Innovation Acceptance

There is nothing more difficult to carry out, nor more doubtful of success, nor more dangerous to handle, than to initiate a new order of things. For the reformer has enemies in all those who profit by the old order, and only lukewarm defenders in those who would profit by the new order, this lukewarmness arising partly from fear of their adversaries, who have the laws in their favor; and partly from the incredulity of mankind, who do not truly believe in anything new until they have had actual experience of it.

Niccolò Machiavelli

C omputers will probably prove to be the most innovative thing to affect the average person since the automobile. People's acceptance of computers will, however, be slowed by their natural resistance to change. As designers, it is to our advantage to understand what we can do to make our products overcome people's resistance to change.

Everett Rogers discovered that people's perception of five factors associated with an innovation determines how fast they will accept it. One factor—you could write a book!—is ease of use. Here are the other four.

Relative advantage

The most important factor that determines whether someone will accept an innovation readily is the advantage it has over the existing way of doing things.

One reason VisiCalc penetrated the market so quickly is that it is much better than either pencil-and-paper or large computer approaches to doing financial analyses. A good user interface can emphasize a product's advantage over existing ways of doing things. For example, VisiCalc's automatic recalculation whenever a cell entry is changed makes this advantage immediately visible to the user.

The automobile demonstrates what we will pay for an innovation that has an important advantage: It is faster, more comfortable, less bother, and cleaner than horses, and it gives its users mobility and control of their travel. We find its advantages so great that we have asphalted a good part of the United States, accept 50,000 traffic deaths per year, and pay a substantial portion of our incomes to keep our motor vehicles running.

Hand-held language translators had no real advantage over simple phrase books. However, the Craig language translator I designed was the easiest to use and the most functional of the translators. It was interesting and it got substantial media attention. It outsold the competition by a factor of at least five to one. But it offered no real advantage over a phrasebook, and the word of mouth was that hand-held translators were not useful and the market collapsed. It was a successful gadget, a high-technology pet rock.

Compatibility with user's environment

Since basic human nature resists change, our designs, no matter how innovative they are, should minimize the changes the users perceive they need to make in how they do things. A typist who has never used a word processor would more readily adopt a product she perceived as a typewriter with extra features than one she perceived as a word processor. Even though she might see a higher status in using a word processor, she would be inclined to resist it just because it was different.

People resist change in social status even more than they resist technological change. Only a few years ago, business executives would not use personal computers because they saw them as fit for use by clerks and programmers. They did not see themselves as clerks. Even less would they want others to see them as clerks. VisiCalc changed this. Businessmen find it a useful tool they can use in discussions with associates. As the personal computer changes from a low-status item to a high-status item, it becomes easier to get executives to use computers for many things.

Scientific calculators show the importance of designing a product to be compatible with the way people do things. Hewlett-Packard, the first company to make scientific calculators, created a product that had such an advantage over the existing method— the slide rule— that it took less than ten years for slide rule production to drop below buggy whip production in the United States. But even though standard notation ($2 \times 3 + 4 =$) is compatible with the way most users think, Hewlett-Packard designed its calculators to use Reverse Polish Notation or RPN (2 ENTER $3 \times 4 +$).

Following Hewlett-Packard's success, other manufacturers entered the market, but they designed their products to use standard notation. Hewlett-Packard is known as the Cadillac of calculators and it has a loyal base of happy customers who love RPN now that they have learned how to use it. Nevertheless, new customers are unfamiliar with RPN and this poses a marketing problem for Hewlett-Packard. The purchaser's decision is no longer between the slide rule and the calculator, but between different scientific calculators, and the incompatibility of RPN notation with his normal way of thinking becomes a major factor.

Trialability

One reason personal computers in general, and VisiCalc in particular, have proven so successful is that their cost is small enough to enable anyone to try them easily. Furthermore, the VisiCalc and WordStar user can learn to do simple things quickly without having to know all the system's capabilities.

The designer who can make a product that is compatible with the user and easily tryable is achieving rapport, an element of good design discussed in the last chapter.

Observability

The more visible an innovation is, the more quickly it will be accepted. This is one value of advertising: It increases the visibility of a product. People are more likely to try something they can see than to ferret out something that is not there for them to see. And the more they see it, the more willing they are to try it.

The designer can make a product observable in several ways. First, he can make the product so that it is interesting at the point of sale. Second, he can design it so that it is naturally used where people see it. Finally, it can make several of its features visible to the user and thus stimulate their use. And now....

And now let me say that five factors that do *not* affect the rate at which people adopt something are ease of use, relative advantage, compatibility, observability, and trialability.

What? I said the factors that affect the rate of adoption are not ease of use, but the user's perception of ease of use; not relative advantage, but the user's perception of relative advantage; not compatibility, but the user's perception of compatibility; not trialability, but the user's perception of trialability; not observability, but observability by potential users.

Figure 31: Sculpture. Picasso could look at a toy Volkswagen and see the head of a baboon; more important, he can get us to see the same toy Volkswagen as the head of a baboon. Effective communication means getting people to see what you want them to see.

PICASSO, Pablo. *Baboon and Young.* 1951. Bronze (cast 1955), after found objects, 21 × 13¼ × 20¾. Collection, The Museum of Modern Art, New York. Mrs. Simon Guggenheim Fund.

CHAPTER FIVE

Seeing and Friendly Software Design

Seeing consists in the grasping of structural features rather than the indiscriminate recording of detail.

Rudolf Arnheim

The designer of a program thinks at various levels at various times. There is the high level of global program structure and data formats, and there is the more detailed level—the number of characters a field should have, or the sequence of control characters necessary to display something on a screen.

The same is true of "friendly" software design. At the highest level—the user's—software must be easy to use. At a low level, one can consider details of user convenience, such as precise wording of messages. It is between these extremes that the most crucial, difficult, and judgmental thinking occurs.

The thirty principles I presented earlier help the designer think at these middle levels, but it is still necessary to put these useful principles into perspective at a higher level. The most relevant statement about our work as designers is the one that Griffith gave: We have to get our audience to see. But before we can do that, we have to learn more about perception and seeing.

PERCEPTION AND PRECONCEPTION

I very rarely think in words at all. A thought comes, and I may try to express it in words afterwards.

Albert Einstein

We all realize that the ability to read is something we must learn; we are not born with it. Similarly, the ability to appreciate music requires learning. But it probably comes as a surprise to most of us that seeing is something we learn. We are not born with the capability. Some people can't read maps. Primitive tribes who are not familiar with photographs cannot "read" them. People have to learn how to "read" movies. In *Visual Thinking*, Arnheim tells about a Russian who, banished after the revolution, moved into the countryside hundreds of miles from the nearest city. Highly educated, he continued to read the current newspapers and magazines and listened to the radio. Yet, fifteen years later, when he went to Kiev to see his first film (a Douglas Fairbanks thriller), he could not understand what was going on in the film. To someone who has never seen a film, a pan shot of houses looks like the houses are moving; a closeup shot is not seen as related to the previous long shot. We find this hard to appreciate because we have experienced films all our lives and learned to "read" them at a young age.

Few of us are aware of how much our preconceptions influence what we see. We see what we expect to see. Consider the picture below.

Figure 32

What is it a picture of? Is it a rabbit or a duck? As you look back at it you will find that you can see it as either a rabbit or a duck; it is an ambiguous figure. You will also notice that if it looks like a rabbit, it does not look like a duck; and if it looks like a duck, it does not look like a rabbit. You cannot see it as both a duck and a rabbit at the same time. Once we have formed a preconception of what it is, we interpret input data as confirming our view of things. Our preconceptions control much of what we see.

This is the reason that few people think they know how to draw. In fact, most of us do have the ability to draw reasonably well, but our preconceptions inhibit us from accurately seeing what we are trying to draw. You can demonstrate this with a simple experiment that has to do with how the brain "sees."

The brain has two sides— the left, logical brain and the right, creative brain. The left brain handles language, mathematical and symbol manipulation, and organization. It imposes logical order on things. The right brain handles images— both visual and mental— and is the creative part.

When you or I (as differentiated from an artist) draw a chair, we would let our left brain dominate the process. The left brain would use its information about what chairs look like. We "see" the brown of the chair as being uniform and do not distinguish the various shades caused by reflected light. What we really see, whenever we look at anything, is the simplest thing in our experience that is not strongly contradicted by our senses.

We "see" the four legs as having equal length, although the closer legs are longer on the visual image. We would see the back of the chair as symmetrical, when— because the chair is being viewed at an angle— it is not symmetrical in the visual image. We let the left brain take control from the right brain and use the information stored in it about chairs, instead of using the image that actually falls on the retina.

Some extremely sophisticated mental processing is going on; our brain has seen many chairs and has compiled a "chair" recognizer that recognizes chairlike things. The advantage of this is that we quickly recognize chairs and call on our mental model of them. We cut through the details to see a "chair." Once we see that chair, our perception of it becomes as strongly influenced by what our experience has told us about chairs and chair legs and chair backs as it does by the specific chair we are looking at. We don't see *the chair,* we see *a chair.*

Because our experience of what chairs are like gets in our way when we try to draw the chair, the result is generally poor

If we could let the right brain work unassisted, it would see the chair without using any left-brain knowledge of a "chair," and we would draw the chair reasonably well. We can, in fact, "anesthetize" the left brain by preventing it from seeing recognizable images.

For example, if we draw something upside down, the left brain doesn't recognize it and lets the right brain take over. When I give this exercise in my seminars on friendly software design, about half the people say the picture they drew is much better than they would have expected. You should try it. It is described, along with other techniques to teach drawing, in Betty Edwards's *Drawing on the Right Side of the Brain.* It demonstrates that the (non-artist's) problem is not one of drawing but one of seeing.

Our inability to draw is symptomatic of a more general phenomenon: Our view of the world is strongly biased by our previous experiences, our expectations, the language we use, and the theories we have. What we really see, whenever we look at anything, is the simplest thing in our experience that is not strongly contradicted by our senses. We see what we expect to see. Our left brain generally imposes its view on what we see, and this makes it difficult for us to see anything new or different unless it is blatantly obvious.

In his classic essay "Politics and the English Language," George Orwell, the clearest and most perceptive twentieth-century English essayist, points out how easy it is to let our preconceptions do our thinking for us:

> What is above all needed is to let the meaning choose the word, and not the other way about. In

prose, the worst thing one can do with words is to surrender to them. When you think of a concrete object, you think wordlessly, and then, if you want to describe the thing you have been visualizing, you probably hunt about till you find the exact words that seem to fit it. When you think of something abstract you are more inclined to use words from the start, and unless you make a conscious effort to prevent it, the existing dialect will come rushing in and do the job for you, at the expense of blurring or even changing your meaning. Probably it is better to put off using words as long as possible and get one's meaning as clear as one can through pictures or sensations. Afterwards one can choose— not simply *accept*— the phrases that will best cover the meaning and then switch round and decide what impression one's words are likely to make on another person.

In his book *Notes on the Synthesis of Form,* Christopher Alexander points out how these preconceptions have influenced architecture.

The Roman bias toward functionalism and engineering did not reach its peak until after Vitruvius had formulated the functionalist doctrine. The Parthenon could only have been created during a time of preoccupation with aesthetic problems, after the earlier Greek invention of the concept "beauty." England's nineteenth-century low-cost slums were conceived only after monetary values had explicitly been given great importance through the concept of "economics," invented not long before.

In this fashion the self-conscious [logical leftbrained] individual's grasp of problems is constantly misled. His concepts and categories, besides being arbitrary and unsuitable, are self-perpetuating. Under the influence of concepts, he not only does things from a biased point of view, but sees them biasedly as well. The concepts control his perception...until in the end he sees nothing but deviations from his conceptual dogmas, and loses not only the urge but even the mental opportunity to frame his problems more appropriately.

George Orwell or Christopher Alexander could just as well have been talking about computer science. After a new and useful paradigm proves successful, a set of techniques associated with it is developed, and it is difficult for its practitioners to reconsider the validity of the paradigm in a changed environment.

Computer languages illustrate this. It started with the paradigm of the FORTRAN batch compiler compiled by John Backus, a magnificent advancement in its time. Batch processing was the earliest way that computers were used. Because the computer could only run one job at a time and was expensive, you had to wait several hours or even days after you submitted your program before it would be run and the output returned to you. The result was to get as much done as possible on any given run, and a compiler like FORTRAN would take a program of several thousand lines of what is source code (a language intelligible to both the computer and to people), compile it into machine language (a language intelligible by computers but not by people), and then run the resulting program.

When interactive environments (time-sharing and, more recently, personal computers) became common, this cumbersome method was no longer necessary. A user had his own computer and didn't have to wait for others to finish before he could run his program. One could write an interpreter— a language that would "compile" one line of code, run it, then compile another and run it, and so on. The advantage of this method was that a user who made an error in the first line was saved from waiting several minutes for the whole program to compile. The user could fix the error quickly and continue without having to start again at the beginning.

The biases of the batch processing compiler have held sway, however. Language developers had developed several FORTRAN, COBOL, and other compilers for batch environments and developed a whole technology to do it. When interactive computers became common they immediately built the same type of compilers they had built for batch environments, without questioning the basic assumptions.

Mainstream language developers have come to value the attributes of structure, maintainability, and elegance of syntax. These attributes are certainly desirable, but as languages become more refined, it becomes harder to start from scratch. Languages such as Pascal, C, and Ada are mainstream languages developed well after time-sharing and minicomputers had shown the value of interaction, but interaction is only superficially part of their design.

Languages like BASIC, LISP, and FORTH have rejected the batch-compiler paradigm. They attract loyal groups of users. Some of these languages are hard to read and maintain, and even somewhat inefficient, but these problems are not fundamental to interactive languages.

Interactive languages are largely ignored by the mainstream computer science community, which judges them with the biases of the batch-compiler paradigm and finds them lacking in important attributes. The following that interactive languages have attracted should focus designers on analyzing what makes these languages successful, and what assumptions they are making in determining what is important in a language.

Alan Kay is a happy exception to most language designers. At Xerox's Palo Alto Research Center, he developed an environment that was interactive and visual but still used many of the techniques developed in computer science. The resulting language, Smalltalk, is fundamentally an interactive language, but it has many of the capabilities of advanced languages. While his purpose is to develop the software for the notebook-sized computer of the future (he called it Dynabook), Smalltalk has strongly influenced the design of the Xerox Star, Apple's Lisa, and a whole host of other products.

We can't always be aware of our preconceptions in perceiving things, but if we recognize that we have hidden assumptions, biases, and preconceptions, we will be in a better position to identify them, put them aside, and look at things in a fresh light. If we don't recognize them, we will be like the tailor who visited the Pope. A friend of his asked, "What was he like?" The tailor replied, "Forty-two short."

SEEING THE PROBLEM

Every child is an artist. The problem is how to remain an artist after he grows up.

Pablo Picasso

Discarding the baggage of the conventional way of looking at things is important in science. However, most scientists spend their lives working within a proven paradigm— unquestioningly accepting a conventional way of seeing. Newton's laws are an example of such a paradigm. However, major scientific discoveries came from seeing things differently. Einstein looked at the same data that everyone else did, but he was able to see something different. What he had to say on how he invented relativity theory is instructive:

> A normal adult never stops to think about problems of space-time. These are things which he has thought of as a child. But my intellectual development was retarded, as a result of which I began to wonder about space and time only when I had already grown up. Naturally I could go deeper into the problem than a child with normal abilities.

Dan Bricklin and Robert Frankston, the authors of Visi-Calc, saw the problem of designing computer programs for financial planning not as people saw it in the past (as data structures or specific applications), but as an array of cells into which the user could put numbers, simple equations, and text. Obvious as this concept may be in retrospect, at the time it was a major intuitive leap in seeing the problem in a simple way.

OBSERVING PEOPLE

All of my experience tells me that the advertising person who studies people as they really are [will be] the most successful.... The best creative people I know have always been amateur social psychologists.

John O'Toole

Most writers are avid readers. Most filmmakers are avid moviegoers. The effective communicator constantly observes how others communicate and how people react.

Henry Dreyfuss, a founder of industrial design, made a practice of walking through department stores looking at what was for sale and observing people's reactions and behavior.

If we are going to design software for people, we have to observe how people, including ourselves, use products and what they use them for. We should also observe how other designers have solved their user interface problems.

We have to ask questions: How do users interact with a new product or a familiar product? What expectations do they have? What frustrates them? What do they find natural? What is unnatural? What do they tend to remember and what do they forget? What do they like about a product and what do they dislike? Which features do they use frequently? Which do they use rarely? Why?

We must, of course, qualify what we observe. Observations about people who can type aren't applicable to those who can't, and observations about doctors are not necessarily applicable to lawyers. But if we are observant and ask questions when we see someone using a computer program or when we use one ourselves, we will become sensitive to how users see things. These observations should provide the raw data we need to improve our design products.

MAKING THE USER SEE

My task which I am trying to achieve is, by the power of the written word, to make you hear, to make you feel— it is, before all, to make you see.

Joseph Conrad

The task I'm trying to achieve is above all to make you see.

D. W. Griffith

The whole object and difficulty of the art (indeed of all the fine arts) is to unite imagination with nature.

John Constable

The likeness which art creates exists in our imagination only.

E. H. Gombrich

Image-making, artistic or otherwise, does not simply derive from the optical projection of the object represented, but is an equivalent, rendered with the properties of a particular medium, of what is observed in the object.

E. H. Gombrich

Art is the lie that makes us realize the truth.

Pablo Picasso

The final aspect of seeing is getting our audience to see. The designer must communicate to the user what the program does and how it does it. If the designer does this well, the program will seem simple, obvious, and natural to the user.

Consider the chair I described earlier. You or I would take a photograph of it by pointing the camera at it and snapping a picture. We would get a mediocre picture. However, a professional photographer would want that chair to communicate something— maybe that it is old, or sturdy, or worn. To accomplish this, he will consider how the lighting, composition, and point of view could help him achieve his effects better. He will consider a myriad of details and will communicate what he sees by manipulating these details to get the effects he wants. He determines what is in the picture and, as Picasso says, he lies. He does this to force the audience to focus on what he wants it to see.

Figure 33: A good artist can put just a few lines on paper and stimulate an image in your mind. Notice how little detail is provided in this picture from the *Mustard Seed Garden Manual of Painting*. Images are not on paper, they are in our minds.

From the *Mustard Seed Garden Manual of Painting*, 1679–1701.

The same is true with any communication. The communicator structures the photograph, sales pitch, or other user interface to get his audience to see what he wants it to see. The map of the London subway system shown in Figure 34 is more useful than an accurate map would be. All

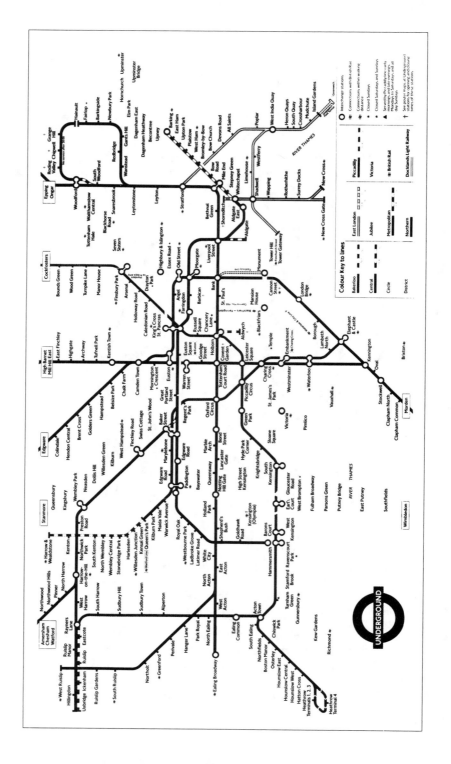

unnecessary detail is removed and what remains is a clear statement of what it is important to communicate. In the painting in Figure 33, only the barest suggestions of lines convey an image to the observer.

The effective communicator strives for psychological accuracy, not technical accuracy.

A spreadsheet program presents itself to users as a window into a giant spreadsheet. This is what the designers envisioned. But to see something is one thing; to make someone else see it is something else entirely.

The details of the user interface can be designed to reinforce the model being communicated. As we noted earlier, moving the cursor off the screen shifts the window one row or column—putting new cells on the screen. The user sees the window into a giant spreadsheet move—like a camera moving in a film. It appears natural and reinforces the visual illusion we are trying to build in the user's mind. If the whole screen has to be redrawn to accomplish this illusion, that is only a technical detail, as long as it can be done in a way that does not confuse the user.

Figure 34: A subway rider needs to figure out how to get from one station to another and know how long the trip will be. By suppressing irrelevant details and changing other details to simplify the image, this map presents its information clearly.

Figure 35: Music. The great, yet simple melodies of Beethoven's symphonies are the result of his constantly refining his music until it could no longer be improved. Sometimes, as in the *First Symphony* shown here, he actually tore through the paper.

Prototype, Revise, and Rewrite

Plan to throw one away.

Fred Brooks

Rewrite and revise. [The writer can use] scissors on his manuscript, cutting it to pieces and fitting the pieces together in a better order.... Do not be afraid to seize whatever you have written and cut it to ribbons; it can always be restored to its original condition in the morning, if that course seems best. Remember it is no sign of weakness or defeat that your manuscript ends up in need of major surgery. This is a common occurrence in all writing, and among the best writers.

William Strunk and E.B. White

The two most important tools an architect has are the eraser in the drawing room and the sledge hammer on the construction site.

Frank Lloyd Wright

What is written without effort, is read without pleasure.

Thomas Babington, Lord Macaulay

An artist never really finishes his work, he merely abandons it.

Paul Valéry

Any writer or filmmaker goes through several drafts of something before feeling that it will have the intended impact on his audience. That is rarely true with software. One reason most software is "unfriendly" is that we don't test it in actual use. Often, we test the program only to remove bugs. Too frequently, we copyedit and publish our first drafts.

Software managers sometimes blame poor planning or design when a program is difficult to use. The implication seems to be that next time the planning and design will be better and the program will be easier to use. This is partially true—we all learn from experience.

However, planning and design alone are not enough to make programs friendly. The real problem is that even the best of us do a poor job of visualizing the end product in actual use.

The textbook way to develop a computer program is a three-step process: design, code, debug. When you finish one part, you begin the next. With this method, the basic design is determined early and changes are minor. It works well for software projects where there are proven product specifications, such as compilers for existing languages.

There are two kinds of planning, however. One has been called the "Cook's tour." It is a carefully scheduled tour; everyone knows exactly where they are going and how they are going to get there. This plan keeps everything on track and serves to insulate people from the unexpected. In an attempt to preserve the plan, people's bias is to refuse to recognize things that don't conform. There is another type of planning, the "Lewis and Clark" method. Here, everyone is going on an adventure and no one is sure exactly where they are going or exactly what they are going to find. The purpose of a Lewis and Clark plan is to handle the daily necessities during the trip. It is this second type of planning that is most useful in developing friendly software. It facilitates the expected adventure and change.

A writer makes an initial draft and then begins to revise and rewrite. Hemingway, for example, rewrote the ending of *A Farewell to Arms* thirty-nine times. He had trouble "getting the words right." James Michener has protested that he is "not a great writer" but he is "one of the world's great rewriters."

Filmmaking involves constant revision. Scriptwriters spend months rewriting before a film script is acceptable. Even after the script is ready, Neil Simon will bring the actors together to read it. "Why," he says, "should I wait until the very first day of rehearsal to find out I'm going to be in trouble?"

With *The Goodbye Girl*, Simon brought the actors together for readings three times before he was satisfied that the script was finished. He said that if he had started shooting with the original script, he could not have saved the film. He did "a month's rewriting before shooting began."

Shooting begins, rewriting continues. It continues on the set when problems are discovered; writers will spend all night rewriting a scene so it can be reshot the next day. After shooting ends, editing begins. This can take six (or more) months.

Robert Towne, the "script doctor" who fixed the problems in the scripts of several fine films— most notably *The Godfather*— explained the reason for so much revision:

> You are always miscalculating in a movie, partially because of the disparity between what you see on the set and what you see on the screen. No matter how skilled you are in anticipating what the image is going to look like finally, you can still be fooled. So you have to rewrite, and be rewritten— not because the original is necessarily badly *written*, but because ultimately if it doesn't *work* for a film it is bad.

In other arts, revision is the rule. Beethoven's draft manuscripts survive today, and from them we know that those great, simple, wonderful melodies were the result of many revisions. Picasso typically painted one or two pictures a day. Yet, his most powerful painting— *Guernica*— was the result of six weeks of constant revision.

If you accept the premises that designing friendly software is a communications craft and that we can learn from the experiences of other communications craftsmen, you must accept the necessity of constantly revising your programs to get them to be easy to use. We cannot expect success the first or second time. If our program is at all innovative, we can't expect it to be right even on the third or fourth time.

Figure 36: This is Picasso's first drawing of *Guernica* on the actual canvas.

Copyright 1991 ARS, N.Y./SPADEM.

Figure 37: Picasso has completely redrawn the statue of the soldier. He has taken the baby away from the woman on the right and given her the leg that used to belong to the falling woman on the extreme right.

Copyright 1991 ARS, N.Y./SPADEM.

Once we recognize that prototyping and revision are crucial to friendly software design, we can plan for it.

I like to sketch out a working prototype and then, in response to various people's reactions, continuously upgrade

Figure 38: The completed painting. Picasso has raised the head of the horse to replace the arm of the statue of the fallen soldier, and to make that work he has moved the bull so its body would be to the left of its head rather than to its right. Picasso constantly revised his paintings to get them to "work."

it into a finished product. I find it tremendously valuable to get something working quickly. It forces my perspective to coincide with the user's and focuses my attention on his problems. These problems generate creative ideas and my designs become more user-oriented. Frequently, I story-board a program I am developing. (Chapter 10 gives an example of this.)

It is important to test a program while it's still easy to change its basic structure; if one waits, any basic structural changes become difficult, if not impossible. If the user interface starts working late in a project, the rest of the system has usually achieved its final structure and any but detail changes are hard to make. The ego, time, and effort spent bringing something to fruition can easily blind its developers to its shortcomings.

Every good artist gets emotionally involved in his work, but he must be able to step back and view it objectively. Sometimes he must even abandon it and start from scratch.

A good artist must, in William Faulkner's phrase, "be willing to kill his babies."

A prototype can also be used to sell a product concept to management or to potential users. It provides a common data base for those involved in a project. Too frequently a product proposal is like the proverbial elephant viewed by six blind men—each senses things differently. A good prototype, like a movie storyboard, can reduce misunderstandings and focus attention on the real problems, misunderstandings, and opportunities.

The production code for the Craig translator was written in machine code for a single-chip computer that had little ROM and less RAM. First, however, we prototyped the translator using a high-level language on a completely different CPU—an 8085. While several times larger than the production machine, the prototype was portable and thus we could more easily simulate the ultimate user's interaction.

The prototype, since it had extra space, freed us from petty problems and allowed us to concentrate on the crucial ones. We could write a "rough draft" of the program and make major revisions easily. We had the first working version in about five weeks. Although we spent almost five months revising the user interface, we were able to begin production coding ten weeks after starting the project. Here are some of the benefits we got from prototyping the translator:

It stimulated ideas and we developed several major improvements to the original concept. Many of these affected the fundamental design, but since they showed up in the rough-draft stage, the changes were not costly. We came up with the search feature for misspelled words. This search feature became a major constraint on the data structure design; if we had designed the data structure before we did our user testing, we never would have been able to design in this feature.

We were able to postpone several design decisions until late in the project. We replaced the rudimentary data structure, which worked fine for prototyping purposes, with the production data structure later in the project. Even the details of this decision were postponed until two weeks before we made final ROM masks. If we had made some of these design decisions earlier, we would not have been able to exploit some of the unexpected ideas that made the translator better.

We extensively revised and refined the user interface. You would be surprised at the amount a user interface can change if you approach it as a rough draft to be revised several times, instead of as something that has to be shipped when it works.

All this work paid off. Even if it was a high-technology pet rock, the Craig translator proved to be the easiest to use and the best selling translator in the marketplace.

Rob Barnaby developed an early version of WordStar and used it to write both his programs and instruction manual. As a result of this, he was able to identify quickly those areas where the user interface had to be revised and capability added. The second thing he attributes his Word-Star success to is his having renovated a house; he found it forced him to focus on identifying and doing the five percent of the tasks that had the greatest impact.

Most projects of any size are structured to give visibility to what is important to the project manager: progress versus schedule, and money spent versus money budgeted. This makes it easy to monitor progress, allocate resources, and estimate costs. But it is also necessary to structure projects to give visibility to those things that are important to the user.

The next time your program begins to work, think of how you might make it better. Ask yourself this: If Ernest Hemingway, James Michener, Neil Simon, Frank Lloyd Wright, and Pablo Picasso could not get it right the first time, what makes you think you will?

"Well, back to the old drawing board."

Figure 39: Cartoon. By the standards of a Rembrandt, a Peter Arno cartoon is simple and rough, yet communicates effectively. What *The New Yorker*'s Harold Ross looked for was not precision in drawing, but good staging and effective communication.

Drawing by Peter Arno; © 1940, 1968 The New Yorker Magazine, Inc.

Advice to the Beginning Designer

Anything that is written to please the author is worthless.
Blaise Pascal

There is nothing to writing. All you do is sit down at a typewriter and open a vein.
Red Smith

If you want to learn how to make your software more friendly, I suggest you start by writing for nontechnical audiences. First, the thought processes you use when you write will carry over to designing friendly software. They are both communications processes. Second, the ability to write (always a useful skill) will enable you to write user's manuals. They are part of user interfaces and the responsibility of the designer. It will also be easier to find writers who can provide a good critique of your writing than to find software designers who can provide a good critique of your user interfaces.

Let me tell you how I learned to write. I learned to write (or should I say didn't learn to write) in school. In grammar school, I advanced from not learning penmanship to not learning spelling and punctuation. In high school and college, I didn't learn composition from a succession of English teachers. In my humanities courses at the Massachusetts Institute of Technology, where writing was not graded harshly, I got straight D's.

In retrospect, I can identify two reasons I didn't learn how to write. I had little that I wanted to communicate, and I had a string of English teachers who were concerned with form instead of substance and who, as a result, taught me neither.

Although learning to write was not my top priority in school, I did try to learn. I remember getting involved in one paper. The teacher found it interesting, read it to the class, and then because of errors in spelling and grammar, gave me a C.

My teachers failed to teach me either how to spell or how to write. I say *they* failed because teaching is a communications craft. The teacher, like the writer or software designer, must accept the responsibility for success or failure.

How, then, did I learn to write? I had to write a series of design papers describing a communications system design. I had something to say and I had to communicate persuasively to get my design accepted. Fortunately, Butler Lampson, for whom I was working, proved to be a helpful and sympathetic editor.

Good communication is not about following rules and form. In fact, the form is the easiest part—you can always correct it later, just as you can change the precise wording of user messages late in a project. I'm not saying that such details are not important; they are extremely important and you must attend to them before your product is finished. But these details are subordinate to the overall communications design, and you should not let them distract you from focusing on the structure and substance of your design.

You must learn to think like a writer: in terms of images, clarity, and impact. I find it fascinating to see how members of different professions think. Lawyers, businessmen, accountants, engineers, programmers, and writers all think differently. As a designer of user interfaces, it is crucially important that you observe how your audiences think, so you can design your user interfaces with their thought processes in mind.

You must realize that you are communicating *with* someone. This is probably the reason many of us are poor writers. We forget how much of our knowledge is subconscious and we assume much of that knowledge when we reread our writing (if we reread at all). We think of putting our information down on paper the same way a computer generates a core dump—a mass of meaningless numbers that make perfect sense to the computer and almost no sense to anyone else. The information may be there if you know how to find it, but it is not structured in a form that communicates effectively.

To evaluate what you have written, *you must put yourself in your reader's place.* You must wipe your mind clear of everything you know that your typical reader is not likely to know. Try to read your writing as your reader would. Does it make sense? Could it be clearer? Could it be more persuasive?

You can't wipe your mind completely clear. Your reader must start out by knowing how to read English, for example. Similarly, if your typical reader is a competent programmer, it might be appropriate to assume he can understand a PASCAL program. The point is to be consciously aware of what you are assuming your reader must know to understand what you have written. Consider a simple message that so many programs give: "Boot Disk." What does that assume of the user?

As an exercise for the technically oriented reader, write a paragraph explaining what "Boot Disk" means for the nontechnical readers of this book. Show it to your grandmother. If she understands it, you got the right answer.

Learn to listen. As a programmer, you are used to getting feedback from computers about bugs in your programs. You readily accept this feedback and modify your communication to the computer as a result.

Whether I write English or friendly software, I look for a critical audience. I expect my work to have bugs and its design to be flawed. Only by getting user's reactions to it will I discover my design flaws and bugs and improve my craftsmanship.

When someone in my audience says, "I don't understand this," "How about being more specific?" or "I couldn't get interested in it," I react the same way I do when I get a syntax error from a compiler: I say, "I have a problem." I probably won't accept the suggested solution, but I will accept the validity of the reaction and recognize that I have a problem to solve.

Know that you will have to do much revising. This process is important—not just to improve the particular work, but also to improve your craftsmanship so that your future projects will be better.

Recognize that effective communication and clarity of thought are identical. This doesn't mean that your initial thinking can't be fuzzy; it can be fuzzy, if you recognize it as such. Striving to find out what to say frequently means striving to find out what you are thinking, and this often requires that you go through a fuzzy stage if you are to reexamine your preconceptions. If your work seems unclear, it might be because your thinking is unclear. When this happens, it is often best to rethink what you are saying.

Read, observe, and practice. Read what other communicators say about how to communicate. Observe effective communication—in the books you read, in the advertisements you see, or just in listening to people talk. And, of course, use other people's programs to see what they do well and badly. Be aware of when they are effective, when they are not, and why.

Figure 40: Painting. Most of Rembrandt's paintings, such as *Portrait of Jan Six* (1654) were of Dutch community leaders done on commission. He was like the portrait photographer, commercial artist, or industrial designer of today who brings his art to tasks he is hired to do, rather than the artist who pursues art for its own sake.

Oil paints were invented about 1100 and first used by painters about 1400. Earlier paints dried quickly and could not be painted over. Oil paints allowed the painter—for the first time—to rework his painting until he achieved his desired effect. Without this ability, Rembrandt would never have been able to capture the expressive face of Jan Six for us.

The Craft of Friendly Software Design

An honest job of design should flow from the inside out, not from the outside in.

Henry Dreyfuss

A screenwriter should have knowledge of direction, of cutting, of all the separate functions, before his imagination and talent can be geared effectively and skillfully to his chosen line of work.

Dudley Nichols

In *The Mythical Man-Month*, Fred Brooks points out the importance of conceptual integrity. Conceptual integrity is consistency of purpose in design. Yet Fred Brooks discusses conceptual integrity in products that either have well-defined specifications (such as a FORTRAN compiler) or are systems whose designers are typical of the users (such as operating systems). Conceptual integrity is a broad concept that should encompass a technical solution in the context of a market, its users, and the users' problems.

Marketers generally know users and their problems, but don't understand software design; software engineers know software design but generally don't understand users and their problems. People who understand both are hard to find.

As a result, management splits product design into marketing and software engineering. The negotiated specifications that result are frequently acceptable solutions. No one person fully understands both the user's problems and the technological possibilities, and hence there is no one person who can develop a truly innovative solution.

Developing a product, particularly an innovative one, can be like solving Rubik's cube—everything is interconnected. Making one person responsible for red, yellow, and blue and another responsible for white, orange, and green can generate more problems than it solves.

In *Technology and Change,* Donald Schon shows that entrepreneurial firms innovate because a single individual—the entrepreneur—understands both the market and the technology, and can make good design tradeoffs between marketing and technical objectives while still maintaining conceptual integrity. Because an established firm is divided into marketing and engineering, there is no one who understands the details of both, and can make tradeoff decisions. The resulting design, a product of compromise, will lack consistency of purpose and thus, conceptual integrity.

Conceptual integrity is crucial in communications, where one or two individuals usually provide the vision and most of the critical work. Books are generally written by one author. Even films, which by nature are a collaborative group effort, are the result of the vision and work of a few individuals. In any creative group effort everyone contributes, but someone must be the boss. A movie director's success, like a symphony conductor's, will largely be determined by how much he can get everyone to contribute; but one person is responsible for the integrity of the whole; one person is the boss; one person makes the final decisions, and everyone accepts them.

The designer must know both the subject he is presenting and he must know the limits and opportunities of software technology. He also must immerse himself in his user's world. Only then can he see neglected possibilities, unworkable requirements, and the myriad details from which he can form a solution that has conceptual integrity.

My experience suggests that most software designers are both poor writers and poor designers of friendly software. I don't think this is a coincidence: Both are forms of communication. The average software designer has the logical skills of a software engineer but not the visual thinking skills of a communicator. You will never really be successful until you have both.

Henry Dreyfuss, the industrial designer, believed in knowing the technology. Early in his career (in the infancy of industrial design) he was one of ten artists who were offered $1,000 by the telephone company for ideas on the form of future telephones.

He declined the commission because he strongly believed that designs of external form alone were irrelevant. He insisted on working with Bell engineers to learn the technology so that he could design "from the inside out."

The telephone company didn't accept his terms; it felt this would limit artistic scope. But when the designs other artists submitted proved unsuitable, the telephone company hired Dreyfuss to work the way he wanted. Dreyfuss had a long association with the telephone company. His many designs included most versions of the familiar desk telephone.

Friendly software design must also flow from the possibilities that software technology can offer us.

Someone who doesn't know the technology can't design software because he doesn't know the techniques of the craft. A writer who wants to become a filmmaker has to learn the techniques of the craft that Dudley Nichols refers to in this chapter's opening quotation. Similarly, people who are not experienced software designers don't know what the technology makes possible; what it makes easy and what it makes hard; what is fundamental and what is detail. They don't understand the technical risks or problems.

VisiCalc was designed by software developers with strong technical experience. Bob Frankston had ten years of software development experience, including several years with the M.I.T. Artificial Intelligence Laboratory. His partner, Dan Bricklin, headed up a word processing project at Digital Equipment. Similarly, Rob Barnaby, who developed WordStar, had eighteen years' experience, several of them with Bolt, Beranak and Newman, a company that has been a leader in computer science research since it developed the first working time-sharing system.

From my own experience with the Craig language translator, the most useful thing we did to help the user cope was to develop the search function I mentioned earlier. I came up with this idea because I could visualize both the technical possibilities and the user advantages of such a function.

I am not saying that someone need be an expert software designer with many years of experience. Indeed, the success of some software amateurs shows the fallacy of that. What I am saying is that one cannot attain proficiency in any communications medium without having expertise in the medium— software technology, here. The successful software amateurs I know learned the software medium and ceased to be amateurs.

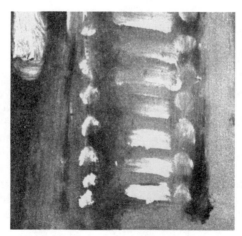

Figure 40A: In his earlier years, Rembrandt painted his subjects precisely; he copied everything he saw in great detail. As he became more experienced, his main concern was with the effect his paintings had on their observers, and he left out much of the detail. In his early days, he painted gold buttons and gold braid in meticulous detail. In this painting, done late in his career, he achieved his effect with a minimum of strokes.

Because programmers are notoriously bad communicators, we need people who can both communicate and program to design friendly software. Thus, we are faced with a dilemma: Who has the needed communications skills and the software skills to design friendly software? Some programmers will acquire the communications skills and make the transition; others will have to come from outside the field.

Figure 41: Architecture. Frank Lloyd Wright preached organic architecture. A building should be designed to fit naturally into its environment while serving the needs of its occupants. "Falling Water" could have been built in no other place. Software, too, must be organic. It should be designed to fit naturally into the environment in which it will be used.

The Moment of Truth

Mr. Griffith urged us to mingle with audiences in movie theaters to observe their reactions. "It doesn't matter how you feel when you're playing," he said. "I'm not interested in that. I'm interested in what you make an audience feel. You may be crying or having hysterics, but if you're not making the audience feel that way, you're not any use to my story. Go to a movie house and watch the audience. If they're held by what you're doing, you've succeeded as an actress."

I have often sat in the balcony, staring at faces to measure the effect of a scene. More than once I've put my face directly in front of a spectator's face; instead of being distracted, I found, he would move his head aside in order not to miss a second of what was happening on the screen. Then I would know that I had achieved what I was striving for.

Lillian Gish

The last woe, and sometimes the last straw,...is that the product over which one has labored so long appears to be obsolete upon (or before) completion.... This always seems worse than it really is.... The real tiger is never a match for a paper one, unless actual use is wanted. Then the virtues of reality have a satisfaction all their own.

Fred Brooks

And I promise you disappointment in every film, for it is far removed from the perfection of imagination, as is everything that is realized.

Dudley Nichols

It is nothing to bring a picture in on schedule or under budget. The hard part is making a good picture—I don't care what your schedule or budget is!

Blake Edwards

F or both the artist and the engineer, the ultimate question is "Does it work?" But the connotations of the word *work* are different for the engineer and the artist. For the engineer, the test of whether something works is objective; for the artist, it is subjective. For the engineer, something works if he has successfully overcome the problems posed by physical reality. For the artist, something works if he has gained entrée to his audience's mind and had the effect he intended.

For many crafts, and friendly software is one such craft, both the objective engineering tests and the subjective artistic ones must be applied. And in the end, for those of us who work hard and view our work realistically as engineers, and critically with an artist's eye, if things are never as great as we imagined them, they will never be as bad as they might have been. If things work well, we have to count ourselves lucky; if they work badly, which will too frequently be the case, the shock of the experience will force many of us to learn those lessons that can only be learned by doing and failing.

Figure 42: Advertising. The Doyle, Dane Bernbach ad campaign helped crystallize the needs of a significant portion of car buyers. Its advertisements communicated the position of the Volkswagen as an inexpensive, reliable alternative to the big, "made in Detroit" car.

Works in Progress

GLENDOWER. *I can call spirits from the vasty deep.*
HOTSPUR. *Why, so can I, or so can any man;*
But will they come when you do call for them?
William Shakespeare
Henry IV, Part I, **act iii, sc. i**

Today we use calculators the size of credit cards to do everything ten-pound mechanical calculators did twenty years ago. In 1986[*], computers the size of wallets will have the power of the room-sized superbrains of the early 1960s. If such a computer is to be any more useful than a rock to the average person, someone will have to write software that will communicate its capability effectively. This will not be easy; such computers will have small keys and a small display. Nevertheless, I will try to show how we are approaching the design of two such products at my company, QuickView Systems.

The products described here are an electronic funds transfer device, which we call Viewcheck, and an electronic index file for names, addresses, and phone numbers, which we call Viewdex. Eventually, both products could fit into your shirt pocket. As this is being written, we are still in an early stage of the software design; both products are likely to have evolved considerably by the time you read this. Viewdex will probably even be available in the local stores. In this sense, I'm taking at least a page from Thomas Edison's book: His approach to inventing something was first to announce

---

[*] This is what we believed in 1982.

that he had invented it, then to invent it. Committing himself in public put pressure on him to make his invention work. If such a system worked for him, it might work for me. If you are going to do anything innovative, sometimes you just have to jump off a cliff and hope you land upright....
Geronimo   o   o
                       o
                           o
                              o
                                o
                                  o
                                    o
                                      o
                                        !

VIEWCHECK: AN ELECTRONIC FUNDS TRANSFER DEVICE

People have been talking about electronic funds transfer (EFT) for some time. The idea is when you make a bank transaction, electronic signals would instantly debit your account. Banks would like to adopt such a system because it would reduce, and maybe eventually eliminate, the need for checks. Checks mean handling, moving, and storing paper; large volumes of data entry; and time delays in effecting transactions. With electronic funds transfer, these problems would go away. One problem in making this work is to get people to stop using checks. Some banks are trying to do this by having people pay their bills by phone; others are trying to get them to use home computers.

My intention here is not to analyze the technical or market complexities of electronic funds transfer, or to make a detailed design of such a product. It is to present a basic version of what the product would be, especially as perceived by the consumer. If the basic concept makes sense, then more detailed analyses of other aspects become appropriate. However, I would not present the something here if I did not feel that I could make it work as a practical and useful product.

First, we don't want to call the product an automatic funds transfer device, or even a home computer. We want to start with something more familiar. To the average consumer I would say:

"Would you like an intelligent checkbook that keeps track of all your checks and balances your account automatically? Would you like it to be a personal bookkeeper that keeps track of your tax records for you? Would you like this intelligent checkbook to be your personal representative to your bank's computer?"

We have changed from meeting the bank's needs (EFT) to meeting the consumer's needs— automatic checkbook balancing, saving of tax information, and other things. I think this comes closer to meeting real user needs than an EFT device, and, to the consumer, it sounds more friendly, interesting, and useful. Of course we have to design a product that can deliver on what was promised in the previous paragraph. If the user finds it difficult or time-consuming to use, he won't want it.

What we really want to build is an illusion machine. The machine will present one illusion to the consumer and another to the banker. The consumer will think he is writing checks; the banker will think he is effecting electronic funds transfers. The consumer is familiar with checkbooks and writing checks in terms of our user interface, and that is where we will start. This will help us gain rapport with our user. The illusion it presents to bankers is that of an EFT device, which helps us gain rapport with the bankers.

Let's see how you as a consumer would see the intelligent checkbook. You would purchase a hand-held computer the size of a checkbook. The picture of the Sharp 1500 below shows you that such products are within today's technological capability. To write a check, you would type in the name of the payee and the amount and then pass a blank check through the printer. The intelligent checkbook would print out the check (and the stub if you wanted one) and automatically fill in the date and check number. Once signed, this would be a valid check.

The intelligent checkbook eliminates manual book-keeping. Since the only way to write a check is to enter the information into the computer first, a record is made of the check and the amount is deducted from your account. You can't forget to list any checks you write. The intelligent checkbook keeps track of your balance; computers don't make errors in subtraction.

Of course, once every month or so, you should plug your intelligent checkbook into a telephone; it will call your bank for you and receive a list of the checks and other

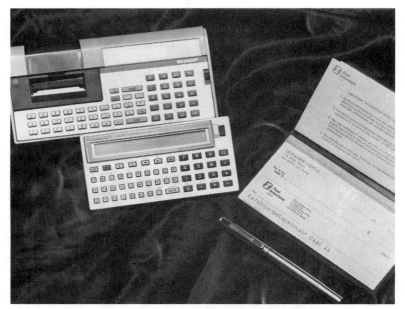

Figure 43: The technology to make an intelligent checkbook is available today. The normal checkbook on the right is larger than the Sharp 1251 hand-held computer (in the middle). It contains enough RAM memory (4000 bytes) to keep track of 50 to 100 checks. The larger hand-held computer in the background is an earlier Sharp product which has a built-in printer.

disbursements it paid, as well as any deposits made on your account. Your intelligent checkbook, like any good book-keeper, will reconcile these transactions with the ones it stored when you wrote the checks, and will tell you about any differences between its copies of your records and the bank's. You could either accept these differences (typically bank charges and deposits you forgot to record) or reject them (bank mistakes).

You could do this at your convenience on any day of the month, not just at the bank's convenience at the end of the month as you do now. The intelligent checkbook would be your computer keeping track of your money for you. It would be your designated representative to your bank's computer. If you wanted, your intelligent checkbook could display your outstanding (uncashed) checks and tell your exact balance, with and without outstanding checks.

To help you even more, your intelligent checkbook would have a list of expense categories such as entertainment, travel, and medical. You could, if you wanted, add other categories. Whenever you wrote a check, you would be presented with a menu of categories. Since you would have to make some selection, even if it was *unknown,* you could not forget to record some expense type. (By making choosing a category as easy as selecting *unknown,* we give you con-trol— while making it easy for you to select the appropriate expense category.) We entice you to give the intelligent checkbook this information when it is fresh in your mind, and we do it in an unobtrusive way. The information gathered in this way should make writing tax returns less difficult and let you generate expenditure reports. The hard part of the problem is solved; all the relevant information is in the computer. The easy part is generating the reports.

Now the banker is probably saying, "How do we get rid of the checks?"

The user could just plug the intelligent checkbook into a cash register or other device at a retail establishment (into a telephone if he wanted to pay a bill he got in the mail). The amount of the bill and the payee would be entered directly into the checkbook, and when the checkbook wrote the check, it would send an electronic transaction to the retailer's cash register or over the telephone. The check that was printed would not be a real one; the fine print would say it was a record of an EFT transaction. But since all the records would be the same, the consumer wouldn't care. This approach will work with both checks and EFT transactions, depending on what is available at the retail establishment, and thus is ideal if one wants to wean the customer from checks to EFT transactions. It can even generate credit card vouchers if the user wants to select them. (A credit card account could be treated as a series of checks and a monthly loan to cover them, or it could be treated as a separate checking account.) The electronic signal or the checklike piece of paper generated could represent any of several different types of transactions, but these all could be converted to simple checking account transactions.

The intelligent checkbook could also be plugged into an automatic teller machine when you need cash. Or you could make a phone call to direct your bank to "write a check" for the phone, electric, and other bills. You could print the "check" or not, as you desired. Pretty soon you will be doing electronic funds transfers without even realizing it; you will still think of writing checks.

You might think it more work to write a check with an intelligent checkbook than to write a normal check. But this is not true, for in writing a normal check and recording it in your checkbook, you write about eighty-four characters of information, plus your signature. But with an intelligent checkbook, you don't enter the payee twice, but once; you don't enter the amount three times, but once; and you don't enter the date at all— it is generated automatically.

Typically, you will enter twenty-one characters when you write your first check to someone. But when you write a second or third check to the same payee (by far the most common case), your intelligent checkbook will guess who you are writing it to. For example, if you type *PA* and if the only company whose name begins with *PA* to whom you have written a check in the last year is Pacific Telephone, your intelligent checkbook will find "Pacific Telephone" and ask you to confirm it. This is another ten characters you won't have to enter twice— you will only have to enter eleven characters, on the average, compared with eighty-four with a normal checkbook. That is an eight-to-one improvement.

See how easy it will be to spend money?

I have not gone into the details of the user interface, or how the intelligent checkbook might work with home banking or credit cards. These details can be fleshed out later. My objective has been to present what I want you, as a consumer, to perceive about the product. In any design, this is a critical first step. If most of you, as typical consumers, want an intelligent checkbook, then the basic idea is probably sound. But if you and other consumers don't want one, it is pointless to work on the design details. The basic concept would have to be changed first.

VIEWDEX®: AN ELECTRONIC ROLODEX FILE

The second product is a simple index file system, similar to a name-and-address book or Rolodex™ file. It would replace address books that get cluttered with crossed-out names, addresses, and telephone numbers. Not only do such address books get messy, but names get misplaced: "Mason" might accidentally get filed under *N,* and even if it was filed under *M,* it would just as likely be at the end of the *M* 's as at the beginning. Such address books don't let us find someone whose name we have forgotten who lives in Chicago or Nebraska, or who works for General Electric. I am sure we could all use an electronic address book that fits in our shirt pocket and has the advantages of a normal address book or Rolodex file without the aforementioned problems.

Although we expect to see pocket-sized products in the next few years, the first products would be notebook-sized and limited to about a hundred "index cards" with names, addresses, and phone numbers. We are currently designing our first such product. It is called Viewdex and will run on the Epson HX-20, a notebook computer that has four lines of twenty characters.

The small screen of the HX-20 creates several problems in designing a useful program with a good user interface. But this constraint also forces us to focus on the essence of communication with our users.

In describing how this product might work, I will refer in passing to style elements and show pictures of what the

Figure 44: A challenge for software design is the Epson Model HX-20, which only has four lines of 20 characters in its display. However, even within these constraints it is possible to build an interesting and easy-to-use software product.

typical screens would be like. You should look at this as an early storyboard of the program. In its simplest form, the user interface contains a screen of characters that gains *rapport* (Element 25) by presenting a *metaphor* (Element 7) of the familiar index card.

```
Heckl, Pl C 965-0327
Presidnt QkVw Systms
146 Main St Suit 404
Los Altos Clfr 94022
```

You will notice that several of the fields have been compressed to fit on the display: "Heckel, Paul C" has been compressed to "Heckl, Pl C." Still, you get a *visual image* (Element 4) of the information on the card. The database is preloaded with a few simple cards so that the *first impression* (Element 26) is that of a filled-out, familiar index card.

If you want to look at the next card, you type a down arrow.

```
Hllmn, Mrty 555-0986
Lawyer Hllmn & Hllmn
1234 Cresenda Circle
Mountn Vw Clfr 94022
```

Similarly, typing an up arrow moves the screen back to the previous card.

```
Heckl. Pl C 965-0327
Presidnt QkVw Systms
146 Main St Suit 404
Los Altos Clfr 94022
```

If you want to look at more information in a field, you hit the Q key to call the QuickView command.

```
<NAME=Heckel Paul C>
Presidnt QkVw Systms
146 Main St Suit 404
Los Altos Clfr 94022
```

This shows both the name of the field (NAME) and the information in it. The normal, unQuickViewed screen simply has the *specific* (Element 20) data for a card on it and not the more general field names. Even if the name is longer than the screen's width, it can still be displayed. If, for example, my name has been put in as "Heckel, Paul Charles," the Rolodex card would look like this:

```
Hckl, Pl Ch 965-0327
Presidnt QkVw Systms
146 Main St Suit 404
Los Altos Clfr 94022
```

The QuickView command would start the display of the same information, and on finding out that the name did not fit, it would rotate it in characters from the right while deleting vowels from the left. Over time, it would look like this:

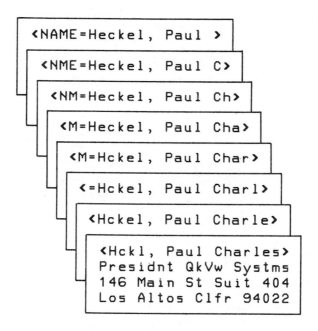

A name that is longer than the total width of the screen has been displayed. When you see this effect, you find it *interesting* (Element 3), and the name, QuickViewed on top of the selected (underlined) field, appears where your eyes are *focused* (Element 8). You are not *frustrated* (Element 14) by having your fields restricted to a specific length as in most full-screen database systems. If you miss something and want to see it again, you can; you already have your hand on the QuickView key, so you hit that key a couple of times to get the message redisplayed from scratch.

Most of the time, you can get most or all of the information you need just by looking at the card with the compressed fields. However, if you need to QuickView a field, you can move the cursor with the left and right arrows. Hitting a right arrow and then the QuickView key would produce, respectively:

```
Heckl, Pl C 965-0327
Presidnt QkVw Systms
146 Main St Suit 404
Los Altos Clfr 94022
```

```
<PHONE=415/965-0327>
Presidnt QkVw Systms
146 Main St Suit 404
Los Altos Clfr 94022
```

Another right arrow and another QuickView would produce:

```
Heckl, Pl C 965-0327
Presidnt QkVw Systms
146 Main St Suit 404
Los Altos Clfr 94022
```

```
Heckl, Pl C 965-0327
<TITLE=President>
146 Main St Suit 404
Los Altos Clfr 94022
```

Hitting any key stops the current field's being Quick-Viewed. Using the left and right arrows to select fields is a natural action whose effect is immediately *acknowledged* (Element 16). The left and right arrows provide a *provisional* browsing action that prevents you from becoming *defensive* (Element 11); if you hit one too many right arrows, a left arrow will correct the situation. This, in combination with the QuickView function, gives you a strong feeling of *control* (Element 12).

You can also search for something. To search for a particular person, you select the name field and depress the search key, resulting in a QuickViewed search message:

```
<SEARCH NAME=  ...>
Presidnt QkVw Systms
146 Main St Suit 404
Los Altos Clfr 94022
```

If you were looking for someone named Smith, you might type *Sm.*

```
<SEARCH NAME= Sm...>
Presidnt QkVw Systms
146 Main St Suit 404
Los Altos Clfr 94022
```

This *leverages* (Element 5) your knowledge that three dots (...) mean something has been left out, and the program communicates to you that it will look for a name beginning with *Sm.* However, you can hit the search key again and see a different search option:

```
<SRCH NME= Sm EXACT>
Presidnt QkVw Systms
146 Main St Suit 404
Los Altos Clfr 94022
```

Since you are probably not looking for a Mr. Sm, you would hit the search key again to see the next option:

```
<SRCH NME=  ...Sm...>
Presidnt QkVw Systms
146 Main St Suit 404
Los Altos. Clfr 94022
```

This would match *Sm* anywhere in the name. If you hit the search key once more, the program cycles back to the first search possibility:

```
<SRCH NAME= Sm...>
Presidnt QkVw Systms
146 Main St Suit 404
Los Altos Clfr 94022
```

Not only does this communicate your options to you *visually* (Element 4), but stepping through the options with the search key helps you *crystallize* your thoughts (Element 18) about what you are searching for and how you tell the program to do that search. Now, you can confirm your action with a carriage return. After you hit the carriage return, the program stops on the first match.

```
Smith, John 395-0278
Sales Manager      TXQ
1829 Jones Avenue
Brentview Clfr 99099
```

The application behaves somewhat differently at this point. For example, hitting a right arrow will display two underlined fields:

```
Smith, John 395-0278
Sales Manager      TXQ
1829 Jones Avenue
Brentwood Clfr 99099
```

The up and down arrows will only stop the search at cards that match the search criteria. One cursor is locked onto the field being searched. This helps keep you *oriented* (Element 21) in your world, as does the message displayed if you QuickView the field being searched, which will display the message "NAME-*Smith, John*, SEARCHING FOR *Sm*..." Since this message is so long, it will rotate in from the left in the normal fashion.

You can edit a field by selecting it and depressing the change key, which displays:

```
<Heckel, Paul C>
<CHANGE NAME TO: >
146 Main St Suit 404
Los Altos Clfr 94022
```

Left and right arrows now move the cursor. Del deletes the current character and Ins inserts a space. If you move the cursor all the way to the left, and then fill in the middle name—

```
<ckel, Paul Charles>
<CHANGE NAME TO: >
146 Main St Suit 404
Los Altos Clfr 94022
```

the *He* in Heckel is still there. You can see this by moving the cursor back to the beginning:

```
<Heckel, Paul Charl>
<CHANGE NAME TO:  >
146 Main St Suit 404
Los Altos Clfr 94022
```

You can then accept the change by typing a carriage return.

```
<Heckel, Paul Charl>
   <NEW NAME IS:  >
146 Main St Suit 404
Los Altos Clfr 94022
```

This *acknowledges* (Element 16) what you just did and *focuses* (Element 8) your attention on it. If you did the right thing, any concerns you have are immediately dispelled. If you made a mistake, you know how to correct it. Also, this helps build an *illusion* (Element 27) in your mind of how the product works. After one second, or when you type another key, the message is cleared.

This is not the complete functional capability or the complete user interface: We will have additional capabilities.

To make this interface work, we will have to impress several things upon your mind. First, only one key, the carriage return, changes data. Every change is *provisional* (Element 11) until that key is hit. This is reinforced by a brief, confirming message every time this key is hit, which will help build the *illusion* in your mind (Element 27) that the carriage return changes data.

Second, there is a clear key that you can always depress. This stops whatever you are doing and clears the card. Clear, when depressed, flashes CLEAR CARD. Clear

Figure 45: QuickView, an arctic blue fox, is our company's mascot.

restores you to a comfortable place, reestablishing *rapport* (Element 25) with the program and *reorienting* (Element 21) you in the world.

Third, function keys cycle in what they do, giving various options before going back to the first one. Pushing the search key several times selects different search options, and pushing the QuickView key several times might select different types of QuickView display. Left and right arrows wrap around, moving between the first and last fields of the card. Up and down arrows wrap around, moving between the first and last cards of the card deck. Giving each of these keys at least two options reinforces exploring to see what is possible.

Fourth, minor actions are easily correctable. Until you hit a carriage return, no matter how confused you get, you can always hit Clear to get out of it. Simpler recoveries are also possible. Hitting an up arrow can correct an extra down arrow. The option cycling of function keys repeats itself after

152

Figure 46: The Sharp Model 5000 is an example of a portable computer that will fit in your briefcase and can be used by salesmen and businessmen to keep track of name and address files and other personal information. This is typical of the high-end portable computers that QuickView software will run on.

three or four options at the most, so you won't get frustrated if you pass what you want.

Fifth, we want the user to see our software as quick, agile, and clever. That is the reason we have a fox for a mascot. It is an arctic blue fox that was born in June 1983. We like to think that we selected a fox because it is *small*— like the displays our software runs on; *clever*— like our software technology; *curious*— our software encourages browsing; and *quick*— you can get the information you want with a few simple keystrokes.

The real story is a little different, however. A good friend of mine purchased a baby arctic blue fox. (She had raised several animals in the past, including a red fox, so she knew how to get state approval and understood the problems of raising a wild animal.) Several of her friends came by to look at this cute, scared little animal, and my friend was wondering what to name it. That's when, without thinking, I opened my mouth. I said, "If you call it Quick-View, I'll pay for it." So she said, "Here, QuickView! Here, QuickView!" QuickView, the blue fox— corporate mascot and my godpuppy— is growing up fast. She has tripled her weight in less than two months, has grown a bushy tail, runs around the house, and lets people pet her.

We think the QuickView technology presented here holds promise for a variety of applications. The intelligent checkbook could use it. It could be used for reminder lists, day calendars, data and sales order entry, and time and expense accounting. We expect to develop such products for the HX-20, Radio Shack Model 100, NEC 8200, and other computers.

Eventually, such applications will keep track of your names, addresses, and phone numbers; your reminder lists; and your daily calendar. It will be a while before such a product can fit in your pocket. However, today computers such as the Sharp Model 5000, which fits in a briefcase, can make these applications cost effective for salesmen and traveling businessmen. Of course, a salesman has somewhat different needs from a consumer. He needs a prospect and sales follow-up, and possibly a sales order entry application. Whether it is the size of an 8½" × 11" pad of paper or fits in your shirt pocket, the small-screen portable computer will enter an explosive growth phase over the next few years. Whether you are a salesman, a businessman, or a housewife, it will only be useful to you if it has useful, friendly, and communicative software. It might take a few years for the right hardware to support these systems to become available, but when it's available, QuickView will have the software for it.

Figure 47: Film comedy. Before Charlie Chaplin, film comedies featured cardboard characters and primitive plots that were subordinate to the gags. Chaplin revolutionized film comedy by creating believable characters and plots, to which the gags were subordinate. His Little Tramp became a three-dimensional character who could be transported into a variety of different movies— including *The Kid, City Lights, The Goldrush,* and *Modern Times*— and even into IBM advertisements for its personal computers.

Roses And Cabbages: Familiarizing and Transporting User Interface Metaphors

Written with Chuck Clanton

An idealist is one who, on noticing that a rose smells better than cabbage, concludes that it will also make a better soup.

H. L. Mencken

Point of view is worth 50 I. Q. points.

Alan Kay

Form follows function.

Louis Sullivan

The Pulitzer prize-winning Civil War historian James Mc-Pherson considered the question: If Abraham Lincoln had been president of the Confederacy and Jefferson Davis the president of the U.S., would the South have won? In an essay on the subject, he gives examples of Lincoln using metaphors for communication and inspiration, in contrast to Jefferson Davis who "seemed to think in abstractions and to speak in platitudes." His conclusion is indicated by the title of that essay: "How Lincoln Won the War with Metaphors." Metaphor, it would seem, is a powerful tool.

Another example of the power of metaphor can be found in this book, which uses the metaphor of communication for software user interface design. This metaphor enables readers of this book to see things in a new way and to make new connections with what they already know. A metaphor is useful not just in the information it communicates, but in the structure it provides and the connections it invokes, enabling the audience to use its existing knowledge.

As you may recall, Element 7 of Chapter 3 is "Communicate with metaphors." We classify computer metaphors as familiar metaphors that make a program easy to learn; and as transporting metaphors that provide a framework into which the user can transport a variety of problems and thus think about and achieve power over them. We feel that both types of metaphors have an important role in user interface design.

Software's power is usually considered an engineering rather than a user interface design issue; user interface design is usually relegated to problems of ease of use and ease of learning. The problems of power and interface are closely related and the task of design is to create unified solutions that solve both problems as if they were one, to make a solution that is "of-the-thing-not-on-it" in the terms of Louis Sullivan. Louis Sullivan was an architect in Chicago at the end of the last century when steel girders, electric lights, and elevators were creating new possibilities in architecture.

While his contemporaries went to past architecture to copy forms going back to the time of the Greeks, Sullivan looked outside of architecture to understand how to use the new technologies. He went to nature and observed that, in either a spider or a flower, "form follows function." In these words, Louis Sullivan distilled the essence of the solution to the problem of design and defined the direction of much of twentieth-century architecture. Rather than disguise the height of his buildings, he designed them to emphasize and glory in their tallness. In his Chicago Amphitheater, he designed the electric lighting into the structure, rather than on it. Earlier, auditorium lights had hanging chandeliers added on to the basic structure as an afterthought, like a new feature added to a program. Sullivan's protégé, Frank Lloyd Wright, modified his mentor's dictum, "Form follows function," to "Form and function are one." The same point is made in the quotation in Chapter 5 from the English painter John Constable: "The whole object and difficulty of the art (indeed of all the fine arts) is to *unite imagination with nature.*" Our job as designers is similarly to unite the form the user experiences with the function of the product.

People learn to use computer software that gives its users real power over their problems even if it is difficult to learn. People tend not to use applications that address limited problems and give their users little power even when they're easy to learn and use. This is consistent with our worldly experience. We all acquire skills that are difficult to learn but powerful. Everyone learns to walk, read, and drive a car, and also learns the skills of a professional. These skills are used repeatedly, and once learned, they are taken for granted and the effort expended in learning them is forgotten. So, too, computer spreadsheets and word processors are powerful tools that people take for granted once they learn to use them; yet learning to use one's first spreadsheet or word processor takes considerable time and effort.

The history of the Apple Macintosh also illustrates how power is more important to computer software success than ease of use or ease of learning. When it was introduced, the Macintosh was promoted for its user interface of the future, a perception that has proven to be true, though in the beginning the Macintosh came close to failing. The Macintosh attracted a substantial base of enthusiasts in the first year, but its sales were drying up by the second year. Only when PageMaker was introduced, providing power that conventional PCs did not and opening up a new marketplace, did the Macintosh succeed. Ease of use and flashy interfaces may kindle computer use, but power fuels it. Now that the value of desktop publishing is established, font-based text and graphics have become standard and have created expectations for what other applications should provide.

One way to empower computer users is by increasing the number of applications that they can use. The classic methods of doing this are by improving learnability and promulgating user interface standards. According to the classic method, user interfaces can be made easier to learn and use by designing them carefully. However, even in an ideal world, different applications have different purposes, so optimizing each application independent of the others leads to differences that users must remember. As the user moves from one application to another, he must learn a different model of how each application works. The different experiences and tastes of designers further increase differences between applications.

The Xerox Star pioneered the use of a standardized user interface across multiple applications to address this problem. It provided consistency of artifacts such as menus and windows. It also provided consistent commands across its standard applications that helped make conceptual models of individual applications similar. While Apple retreated from the consistency of commands between applications with the Macintosh, it extended this consistency of artifacts to multiple software vendors by providing user interface guidelines. Such guidelines are useful, as much of what a user learns in using one application is transferable to another. As someone uses more and more applications that follow the guidelines, the cost of learning each new application approaches the cost of learning the different conceptual model for that application. User interface standards are probably the major reason Macintosh owners use substantially more applications on average than MS-DOS users. However, the different conceptual models underlying different applications still inhibit the learning of new applications.

CREATING RICHER CONCEPTUAL MODELS

Every application presents a conceptual model—a set of concepts such as equations, cells, words, characters, files, or other objects, and a set of rules or commands for manipulating them. A program's conceptual model is where the user interface and the software's power meet; it is where form and function meet. The design of the conceptual model is an important, but often overlooked, part of user interface design. The spreadsheet is the best example of a rich conceptual model. Users transport many different applications into the spreadsheet's conceptual model, few of which were envisioned by its authors. When introduced, VisiCalc took time to be accepted: the conceptual model of a spreadsheet was new and different to computer users; its power was not apparent at first; and its interface took time to learn. Learning one's first spreadsheet or even one's first word processor takes time and effort. The real value of a powerful conceptual model becomes clear only when a user has learned it and acquired skills in using it. People will learn something uniquely valuable to them even where the interface is difficult. Why else would anyone learn to play the violin?

As time passes, spreadsheets and word processors are becoming easier to learn and use because of incremental user interface improvements. But a major reason they are easier to learn and use is that their underlying conceptual models are more widely known; in most offices, several people understand these conceptual models and can help newer users. The problem new concepts face in gaining acceptance is that they are likely to be seen as different, even counterintuitive. Furthermore, new ideas come into the world rough-hewn, and it takes time to shape their ends into a more polished form.

To understand how conceptual models work in practice, observe how people actually use productivity tools. Once they master one, they will use it for many tasks rather than learn a more appropriate tool or even use one they already know but don't use much. A spreadsheet user, for example, will use a spreadsheet to write a letter rather than learn to use a word processor. Writers will keep a text file of names and addresses rather than learn a database. A dBASE user will use dBASE for budgeting rather than learn a spreadsheet. These uses are awkward compared to using the appropriate tool; however, this is how people behave. In

CHAPTER ELEVEN

The Society of Mind, Marvin Minsky presents two principles about how the mind works that address this issue:

The Investment Principle— our oldest ideas have unfair advantages over those that come later. The earlier we learn a skill, the more methods we can acquire for using it. Each new idea must then compete against the larger mass of skills the old ideas have accumulated.

Hence, we are reluctant to learn a word processor if we know how to use a spreadsheet.

Papert's Principle— some of the most crucial steps in mental growth are based not simply on acquiring new skills, but on acquiring new administrative ways to use what one already knows.

As a result, once we know how to use a spreadsheet, we will use it for more and more tasks and might write letters with it.

Fertile conceptual models are ultimately more valuable to users than a polished interface. They shape thinking processes in a way that makes it possible to use them for a broader variety of applications. But that which makes them so valuable— people's inclination to use what they know on whatever new problems they face— is also what makes it difficult for them to gain acceptance.

Frank Lloyd Wright described how when he worked for Louis Sullivan, the latter kept saying that architecture should be "of-the-thing-not-on-it." A good conceptual model is one whose applications are of it, not on it. In other words, the application and the conceptual model become one in the users mind; form and function become one.

FAMILIARIZING AND TRANSPORTING METAPHORS

Metaphor: The myth that there is a clear distinction between representations that are "realistic" and those that are merely suggestive.... Metaphor is no mere special device of literary expression but permeates virtually every aspect of human thought.

Marvin Minsky

The software metaphor, like the literary metaphor, is a device for enriching communication between author and audience. The desktop metaphor invented at Xerox PARC and popularized on the Macintosh is such a *familiarizing* metaphor: it draws on the user's prior experience to make the file system application easier to learn and understand. It is the "rose" in user interface design.

A computer whose operating system is organized by a desktop metaphor is easier to learn than one based on MS-DOS; but it does not make possible things that MS-DOS does not do. It assists with developing an intuition for the computer environment. But even so, computer files are not the same as paper files, and in more complex operations the metaphor can be misleading. The desktop metaphor has no "magic" properties like the spreadsheet's cell equations, automatic recalculation, or the ability to let users transport a variety of applications into its domain. Despite its familiarity, the desktop metaphor is no stronger than MS-DOS.

Benjamin Whorf observed that language influences human thought by shaping how we think. Another linguist, George Lakoff, observed that metaphor in language shapes our thought process. The conceptual models and metaphors that underlie the programs we use also influence our thinking.

The archetypal example of a transporting metaphor is the spreadsheet metaphor. We use the term *transporting* because users can transport many different applications and problems into its domain. While the value of a familiarizing metaphor is in its ability to facilitate learning, the value of a transporting metaphor is in how rich it is— how broad a range of problems can be transported into its domain and how powerful a mastery it provides once learned. If the familiarizing metaphor is the "rose" mentioned in the quotation that begins this chapter, a transporting metaphor is a "cabbage." By analogy, a toy truck is a familiar toy; but an Erector Set is a transporting toy.

Thomas Kuhn pointed out that dramatic advances in science occur when we have paradigm shifts— new ways of looking at things. Similarly, new transporting metaphors dramatically advance computer usage. Incremental improvements in user interface design, like incremental or "normal" scientific advancement, are important for their cumulative effect. New conceptual models have two similarities to the paradigm shifts of science.

First, they unify or generalize, making much existing knowledge special cases. In discovering the laws of mechanics, Newton unified the problems of a falling apple and the moon revolving around the earth by treating them as special cases of the same conceptual model, subject to the same laws. Both problems could be transported into the equations of Newton's model, as can much else. VisiCalc unified the problems of budgeting and cash flow projections on computers by letting them both be transported into computer spreadsheets.

Second, new conceptual models provide a new point of view. As you may recall, the duck-rabbit figure back in Chapter 5 can be perceived as either a rabbit or a duck, but not both simultaneously. So, too, a paradigm shift usually prompts one to see a rabbit where once one saw a duck. It takes time to perceive something from a different point of view, and more time to restructure one's mental world to fit the new perception. However, once that perception takes over, the world is never seen in the same way again. Once the value of the spreadsheet was recognized, it permeated many people's thinking deeply.

MENTAL MODELS

A few years ago, a new traffic island with a traffic light was installed in an intersection near my office. In the following month, cars twice drove into the intersection, turned left and crashed into the traffic light. These drivers made the turns based on the mental model of that intersection that they had built up from their daily commutes. The model that worked well in the past no longer reflected reality and led to disaster. Drivers quickly adjusted their mental models to include the traffic island and there were no more accidents after a month. This is a simple example of how we build and use mental models of the world even to the extent of dismissing contradictory information.

How we behave is based largely on our mental models. We have models about automobiles, how to steer them, how to make them go faster or slower, how we fuel and fix them, how they are used in streets and parking lots, how we should stop at stop signs and stop or go according to traffic lights, and the domains in which cars are useful (going to work or the supermarket) and not useful (going to England). As drivers, we have developed an extensive set of skills and connections with the real world to use with these mental models.

Our mental model of the automobile has connections to many areas, such as how cars are manufactured, financed, and insured, and even areas such as drilling for oil, refining it, and distributing it to gas stations. We can think of our mental models as the tip of the iceberg of larger models of reality. They are the visible one-tenth of the total that is supported by the remaining nine-tenths. The value our models have comes from the connections they make with the real world. That is why drilling for oil is, in a sense, part of the larger conceptual model of driving a car.

People have always built models to explain the world and so make it more predictable. Some, like the model of the flat earth are naive from today's perspective. Subjects as diverse as theology and physics are concerned with developing conceptual models that explain aspects of the world. The great breakthrough in medicine was not to treat symptoms, but to diagnose the underlying disease, thus determining the appropriate model, and then both treat the disease based on its model and develop a more accurate model based on experience with the disease. Similarly, legal jurisprudence is a conceptual model developed to resolve disputes in a predictable way. And anyone who knows accounting understands that double-entry bookkeeping is a conceptual model into which a wide variety of problems can be transported.

In the same way that we once developed models of the flat earth, users of computer programs invariably build mental models of how programs work. Anyone who has spent time supporting users knows that they offer explanations for "bugs" based on these models that are strange to someone who knows how the program actually works. Our nature as people is to construct mental models of the world. The models an average person constructs are likely to be primitive, whether it is a model of gravitation, of the behavior of other people, or of how a computer program works.

METAPHORS AS CONCEPTUAL MODELS

Cross-realm correspondences can enable us to translate entire families of problems into other realms, in which we can apply to them some already well-developed skills. However, such correspondences are hard to find since most reformations merely transform [from] one realm into a disorderly accumulation in the other realm.

Marvin Minsky

"The time has come," the walrus said,
"To talk of many things:
Of shoes— and ships— and sealing wax—
Of cabbages— and kings...."

Lewis Carroll

As people operate using mental models in the real world, so too they operate with mental models in using computers. We believe that the most critical aspect of user interface design is the designing of conceptual models that can be understood by users and communicated to users, and that provide a useful framework in which users can think.

In designing and evaluating conceptual models, we must consider the whole iceberg, not just its tip; we must consider not just what the software does, but what connections to the real world it evokes. Many conceptual models are artificial in that they have few connections to their potential users' real-world knowledge, or those connections they do have are not part of an organic whole. To a user, an artificial conceptual model seems arbitrary, but a metaphor, especially a familiar one, seems natural. From the user's perspective, metaphor evokes existing mental models, provides connections to the real world, and provides a natural organizing mechanism. From the designer's perspective, metaphor provides a useful map for exploring and evaluating design alternatives.

Conceptual metaphors typically are part literal and part magical, although they need be neither. Computer metaphors are literal in that they literally copy the parts of the metaphor from the real world to the computer. Potent conceptual metaphors invariably contain magic— something whose real-world analogy, if any, is not organized or connected to the rest of the metaphor in the same way it is in the real world. The automatic recalculation of equations in the spreadsheet is an archetypal example of such magic. It is hard to give a good definition of magic. However, if, when someone understands something about a computer metaphor, he says "Aha!", it is probably potent magic; if he says

"Okay," it is probably not. The more Aha!s, the better the conceptual model.

Let's look in a little more detail at how the metaphoric component of a conceptual model makes the job easier for both the designer and the user.

Metaphors provide familiarity.

Users can think in a familiar territory. Objects and rules are not arbitrary things to be memorized, but have real-world connections that aid thinking.

Metaphors provide an objective map of reality.

By selecting a real-world analogy, both the user and the designer can work from a common map. Even if most users' copy of that map is incomplete and of poor quality, the original exists, not subjectively in the designer's mind, but objectively in the real world.

Metaphors communicate.

By invoking a common mental model in two people, a metaphor provides a framework for human communication. This makes communication easier, both between the user and his program and between different users in discussing how a program is used. Once a user is fluent in a metaphor, he is seduced into framing applications within that metaphor when he begins to think about them, and as a result he thinks about the applications in partnership with the computer from the start.

Metaphors simplify.

Like Newton's model of gravitation, a good metaphor provides a simple conceptual model— a few equations— into which complex problems can be transported. The spreadsheet metaphor and the card and rack metaphor (to be described) are simple models into which many applications can be transported.

Metaphors unify.

Good metaphors provide a unifying framework for looking at classes of problems. Again, the spreadsheet and card and rack metaphors provide a unified way to look at large families of applications.

Metaphors assist invention.

Metaphor has always been important to invention and this benefits both the designer and the user of software. The metaphor of the gas distribution system helped Edison invent the electric light bulb. A light bulb, like a gas light, is useful only in the context of a distribution system. Edison designed a distribution system of generating plants, power lines, light bulbs, and billing based on the metaphor of gas distribution, before detailing the design of the individual components. For such a system to be economically feasible, electric light bulbs had to work at 100 volts, and Edison looked to invent a light bulb that would work at 100 volts, rather than one that would work at a more convenient 5 volts. In using metaphor, the designer can profit by understanding as much as possible about the real-world original; this will suggest ways to extend the metaphor where connections to the real world are automatically provided. Effective metaphors evoke possibilities in users' minds that had not occurred to the designer.

Metaphors constrain.

Henri Poincaré defined invention as "avoiding the constructing of useless combinations, and as constructing the useful combinations which are in infinite minority. To invent is to discern, to choose." A good metaphor also does this. We work within the constraints of a spreadsheet in the same way that we work within the constraints of the 110-volt electrical system. The effective designer tries to reduce the constraints, not by working against the metaphor and readily adding features that do not naturally fit within it, but by working with the metaphor and pushing its boundaries to enlarge the domain in which it is useful. The constraints of a good metaphor define natural standards, as opposed to artificial standards such as the Macintosh guidelines.

Metaphors support change.

Louis Sullivan said, "The problems of architecture are growth and organization." Alfred North Whitehead observed, "The art of progress is to preserve order amid change and to preserve change amid order." Similarly, the art of designing a good transporing metaphor is to preserve a simple, natural conceptual model amid the changing uses to which it will be put, and to preserve the ability to change the applications amid the constraints of that model. With a spreadsheet, for example, the rows and columns provide the orderly framework, and the ability to change equations and add and delete rows and columns provides the ability to support change.

The following table illustrates the basic differences between familiar and transporting metaphors.

	Familiar (Rose)	Transporting (Cabbage)
Example	Desktop	Spreadsheet
Number of Tasks	One	Many
Helps	Learning	Thinking
Types of Problems Addressed	Static	Dynamic
Primary Use	Application	Productivity Tool
Learnability	Easy	Medium

THE RACK METAPHOR

As the first edition of this book was going to press, we were designing Zoomracks, a transporting metaphor based on the metaphor of cards in a rack, like a time-card rack. Zoomracks was introduced in 1985, Apple's HyperCard in 1987. Since HyperCard is better known than Zoomracks— it is bundled with every Macintosh— and since we are publishing HyperRacks, a HyperCard add-on that brings Zoomracks capability to HyperCard, we will use HyperCard as the point of reference here when possible in describing the card and rack metaphor. In its essence, the card and rack metaphor consists of three basic objects, described below.

Cards

Visually, the cards are like index cards except in that they are separated into fields. In database terminology, one can think of a card as a record. Figure 48 shows an example of a card in a HyperCard stack. While Zoomracks supports

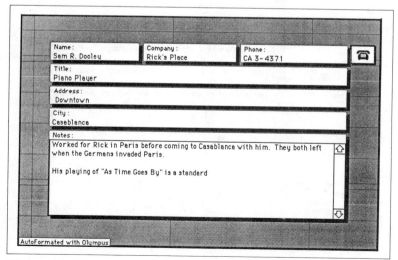

Figure 48: Name and address format in a HyperCard stack.

only fields on cards, HyperCard supports graphics and buttons as well.

Fields

The fields are all of indeterminate length. The actual field limit is an artifact of the implementation, but is the same for all fields; Zoomracks fields are 250 lines of 80 characters each, HyperCard fields are 30,000 characters. At first glance, the fields on a card seem to be literal, like the blanks on a form. However, through the magic of scrolling, the user can view or edit all of any field. Through the magic of zoom, the user can expand a field to show a larger window (this is done with a single command in Zoomracks or with a simple, one-line program in HyperCard). Figure 49 shows a field zoomed to reveal additional information. The fact that all fields can be arbitrarily long frees the user from the constraints of a field's normal display area.

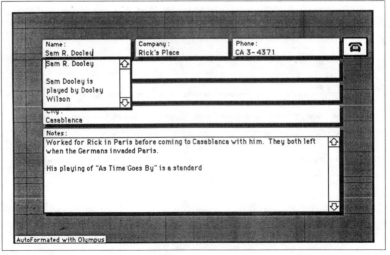

Figure 49: The selected field, DEARNAME, has been zoomed to show more information.

Racks

Cards are organized into racks, whose real-world analogue is time-card racks or similar systems. If a card is similar to a record, a rack is similar to a file. The rack metaphor gives the user navigation and overview capability in a natural way. The first line of each card is visible so the user can view many cards in a rack at once. HyperCard only displays one card from a stack at a time. However, Hyper-Racks displays a window of the first lines of several cards from a stack as if they were stored in a rack on top of the current card, as is shown in Figure 50. Both HyperRacks and Zoomracks can display multiple racks side by side as well as only a single rack. The first line of the cards forms a list of the essential fields, uniting the concepts of lists and cards in a natural way. This rack view a) maintains the integrity of the metaphor by letting users view information from many cards, and b) encourages the user to format essential information on the first line where it can be seen.

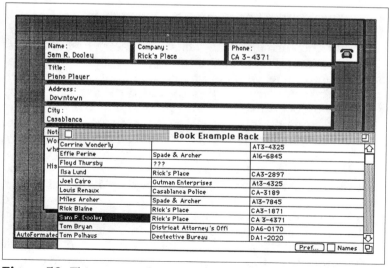

Figure 50: This screen shows HyperRacks' rack window on top of a HyperCard card. Notice that the selected field and card, Sam R. Dooley, is highlighted in the rack window.

CHAPTER ELEVEN

This is an example of how a good conceptual model constrains a user's thinking and becomes part of how he thinks about his problem. Racks also provide a natural method of visual navigation. A simple command lets the user zoom in to view only a card. The user can reformat the card and, by changing the arrangement of the fields on the first line, change what is seen in the rack window.

Information in the racks can be viewed in many ways while maintaining the integrity of the metaphor. In addition to the display of one card or the first lines of several cards in Rack mode, or the current field zoomed, there are other viewing modes. The user can display one rack or several, and can display the field names before the field text or display just the field text. A Search Lock mode, shown in Figure 51, constrains the display to only those cards that meet the last search criteria. All display modes are independent of each other and can be combined for a rich variety of views.

In both Zoomracks and HyperRacks, the commands operate on the conceptual model directly, and are the same in all viewing modes. The basic implementation consists of a database, a viewboard, and a command processor. The viewboard specifies which racks are to be displayed, the current field and card on these racks, and their viewing modes. User commands such as Edit change the data in the database if appropriate. User commands do not update the screen directly, but set viewboard data and dirty flags to specify what should be redisplayed and how. Later, when there are no input commands to process, the screen is updated to reflect what the viewboard says should be displayed. As a result, a command such as "go to next card" only has to update the pointer to the current card in the viewboard and does not have to deal with the multiple display modes. Later, a redisplay module updates the screen to the state specified by the viewboard. A useful side effect of this implementation is that if the user enters several commands in such rapid succession that the redisplay module is not called until they are all processed, then the redisplay will update the display to reflect the final result from all the commands, and not display any intervening display images.

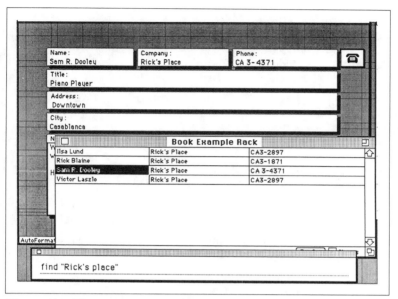

Figure 51: This screen shows Find Lock mode. Here, only the cards for people in Rick's Place are displayed. In Find Lock mode, the navigation commands such as Next Card only navigate to cards matching the search criteria— those visually displayed in Rack mode.

The conceptual model was designed to emphasize the similarity of operations on cards, racks, and fields, as Figure 52 shows. This array forms the basis of a HyperRacks command palette shown in Figure 53, which can be used instead of menus.

Since all fields are scrolling text fields of the same length, the basic conceptual model is simpler than in a standard database with its typed fields. Of course, a field's text might have meaning as a number or a date and there are operations that can interpret fields as such. But the user can always treat any field as text of indeterminate length, copying one field to another field or adding text (possibly annotating a date), without needing to know about a field's type. The user (or a program) can take advantage of a field having a date if he desires. In a conventional typed database,

Command	Rack	Card	Field	Inverse Command
Zoom	Zoom Rack	Zoom Card	Zoom Field	Zoom
Next	Next Rack	Next Card	Next Field	Previous
Previous	Previous Rack	Previous Card	Previous Field	Next
First	First Rack	First Card	First Field	Back to
Last	Last Rack	Last Card	Last Field	Back to
Back to	Back to Rack	Back to Card		Back to
Create	Create Rack	Create Card		Cut
Cut	Cut Rack	Cut Card	Cut Field	Paste
Copy	Copy Rack	Copy Card	Copy Field	
Paste	Paste Rack	Paste Card	Paste Field	Cut

Figure 52: Zoomracks' command matrix. Most of the Zoomracks commands fit into a matrix that emphasizes the similarity of operations on cards, racks, and fields, allowing the user to make connections between commands. The Inverse Command column specifies the command that will undo the command in that row. Thus, Zoom commands toggle and are their own inverses; Next and Previous are inverses of each other. We created the Back to command to be the inverse of commands that go elsewhere.

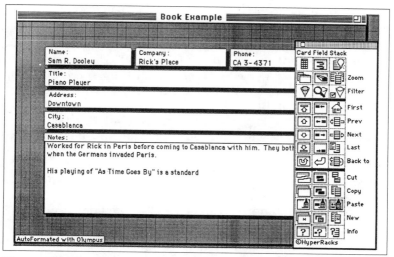

Figure 53: HyperRacks Palette for HyperCard. This palette implements the card and rack command matrix for HyperCard.

type data informs the database structure at a more fundamental level and proves to be pervasive in its use and a source of a lot of constraints on and error messages for the user.

A problem in the design of most computer software is to free the user from the constraints imposed by the size of the display screen, what Frank Lloyd Wright called the "tyranny of the box." Normally, one puts fields and other objects within the box (display screen) as if they were wooden blocks of various sizes and accepts the constraints of both the box and the blocks. While the blocks can be added and moved around, their total area can never exceed that of the box. Windowing accepts the limitations of the blocks but rejects the limitations of the box; the box becomes a window frame and there can be as many blocks as desired; to see them, the user pans left, right, up, and down. The card and rack metaphor does the reverse; it accepts the limitations of the box, but rejects the limitations of the wooden blocks. It treats the blocks as if they were made of compressible foam. No matter how full the box, one can always find room to move a block to another line or add another block, since all the foam blocks automatically compress to make room. This compression can be in the x and y directions, which is what Zoomracks does, or it can be in the z direction as in HyperCard, where the foam blocks can partially cover each other so they will fit within the constraints of the box.

This technology provides magic that is basic to the program. There is always room to add a new field or move one to another line so that all the fields can be shown without explicitly changing the size of other fields. This is important in creating or modifying existing applications, as the user is freed from the concern of whether enough information will fit. If more room is needed the field can always be zoomed for the purpose.

The window ("box") can be expanded or shrunk, and the fields will be expanded or shrunk proportionately. Figure 54 shows how HyperRacks uses this magic to display a rack resized to be narrower: All three fields are shrunk proportionately. Thus, detail of each field is sacrificed to keep the big picture, whereas with conventional windowing the big picture is sacrificed to keep the detail, on the theory that it is better to show all of one field than parts of all three.

This magic subtly pervades the program. If n racks are displayed, each rack and each field can be compressed to $1/n$ of its single-rack width. Both products have a Zoom Name command that toggles between displaying fields without their names and with more text from the field, and displaying fields with their names but with less text from the field. Fields automatically resize to fit.

Since this technology is display-size independent, the applications can be used on computers with any size display screen. This can be particularly valuable on computers with small display areas that fit into shirt pockets, as is described in the previous chapter. The user can use the same application and user interface on a small-display area computer as on his desktop. One value of this technology is that in

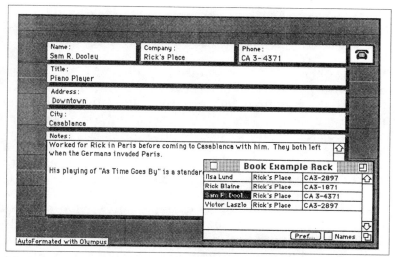

Figure 54: Here, a rack has been narrowed using the Smart Zoom. The fields have their proportional widths maintained as each field is shortened.

eliminating constraints on field sizes, it eliminates both the need for the user to make certain decisions and a source of mismatch errors.

The rack metaphor itself provides a form of compression. By putting the most useful fields together on one line, the designer of the application, whether a professional or an end user, is forced to determine which fields on the card are most essential. The rack forms a natural standard; the user doesn't have to consult User Guidelines to find out where to put the essential fields; it becomes obvious to him in using the rack metaphor. Even more important, even without consciously deciding what fields are essential, the designer will find some more useful than others when making overviews and navigating, and thus will naturally put those fields on the rack line and will likely make other subtle changes in his application to fit within that constraint.

CHAPTER ELEVEN

SPECIAL USES
OF THE RACK METAPHOR

Rather than let the immediate needs of specific applications warp the conceptual model, we integrated the applications at the metaphorical level, enriching the conceptual metaphor in the process. The rack metaphor's richness comes from the fact that three simple objects— racks, cards, and fields— can be used, like an Erector Set, to construct a variety of applications with little or no programming. With the (temporary) exception of menus, everything that is shipped as part of Zoomracks is a special case of the basic metaphor. The details of the examples that follow are less important than the fact that they show how such a variety of applications can be made to fit naturally within the framework of the rack metaphor. Many require some simple magic in order to work, usually a few additional commands.

Macros

While HyperCard keeps its programs as scripts in buttons on stacks, Zoomracks macros are stored one per card in a macro rack that is arbitrarily assigned rack slot 1. Users can view, edit, copy, rename, move, or delete macros just as they can any other card in a rack. One field is the macro name, a second the macro text, and a third a comment. Keeping to the basic idea of the transporting metaphor, the macro rack is like all other racks, except for having a few simple magic functions:

- A Record Macro command lets the user define a macro and give it a (single character) name, and then creates a new card in the rack and stores the macro there.

- A Playback Macro magic command accepts the macro name and then finds and executes the macro.

By typing a number sign (#) and a number between the macro command and the macro name, the user can specify a number of times to execute the macro. After each execution of the macro, the current card is advanced to the next card in the rack. If Find Lock mode is on, the macro will be executed for only the "find-locked" cards (to which navigation and display would be restricted). The result is to provide visual looping and conditional capabilities that don't use language constructs like **repeat** and **if**. While less general than the looping and conditional capabilities found in programming languages, the visual capabilities are easier to use and understand than programming language constructs and thus are more useful to the average user.

We arbitrarily assume that racks whose names begin with "MAC" are macro racks and should be magically loaded into macro slot 1. When a macro rack is loaded, if there is a macro called "$" in that rack, it is magically executed on loading.

Word processing

Each field is a scrolling window on which a word processor operates. Neither HyperCard nor Zoomracks has a full-featured editor, but both can be and are used as simple word processors, and both could be upgraded to be full-featured text editors or to call the user's favorite word processor to edit the current field.

The card and rack metaphor is a natural way of keeping and organizing documents with, say, a Subject field on the first line and the Document field normally displayed on the second to last lines of the card. In Rack mode, all the subjects can be viewed and the user can zoom in on any card and view its Document field. Other fields, such as Project, Contact, Date, Follow up Date, etc., can be added to the first line when and if desired. Since word processing is a special case of the rack metaphor, someone who uses it for word processing and who already knows the metaphor gets extra power at no extra cognitive cost.

File system

In Zoomracks, a file system rack that has one card for each rack (file) on the disk is arbitrarily assigned to rack 0. As implemented, the file system rack has two fields: a Rack Name field and a Number of Bytes field. Other fields like a Comment field and Date Last Used field could be added. The file system rack has a simple magic capability: executing a Load command loads the rack named in the current card.

The current implementation is incomplete in that the File System rack is created from the MS-DOS file system from scratch whenever the user starts up Zoomracks, so any fields or information the user adds is lost between sessions.

Help

Zoomracks comes with two help racks. One provides general help information; a second has one card of help information for each Zoomracks command. There are two magic help commands:

- One Help command goes to the Help rack that has general help on 20 subject cards.

- A second Help command, pressed after selecting a particular command on the menu, takes the user to a card in a second Help rack that describes that command.

A user can add or modify text, or search or even reformat Help racks just as he could any other rack.

Output forms

Zoomracks has an output form for each rack. The output form is associated with a rack and is the the same size as a normal field. It is interpreted as a template for printing a card or rack. The user can edit the output form (changing the print template) like any other field, and can cut, copy, and paste between the output form and any field. As a result, he can save different output forms as fields in cards in the same or other racks. Output forms have certain simple magic properties.

The Create Output Form command creates a default output form that prints cards as they appear on screen. This allows a user to start with and modify an existing output form, instead of having to create one from scratch. In addition, Print, Display, Output to ASCII File, and Output to Field all use the rack's output form as a template to output either a single card, or all the (possibly find-locked) cards in a rack. These commands interpret formatting information that specifies page length, headers, footers, placement of fields, size of fields, and length of fields. This capability supports form letters and invoices.

While users like the flexibility of our output forms, we feel a more visual solution is preferred and we think the gene metaphor described later in this chapter provides an alternative and possibly better solution to this (and other) problems.

Demo rack

Zoomracks comes with a rack that demonstrates Zoomracks' capabilities. The user goes through a rack of cards one at a time. In the process, he is asked to execute various macros that demonstrate Zoomracks' capability. To support this, we added a few special commands that can be edited into macros, one of which waits for the user to press a key before continuing.

Online tutorial

Zoomracks comes with a tutorial rack that demonstrates how each of the various commands works. It is similar in operation to the demo rack.

In addition to the above racks, Zoomracks was shipped with several sample racks including a name and address rack, a checkbook balancing rack, an invoicing rack, and a forms rack that includes several mail-merge letters.

USER FEEDBACK ON ZOOMRACKS

In August 1987, the same month HyperCard was introduced, we conducted an in-depth survey of 91 Zoomracks users. We were surprised at the diversity of personal applications they had developed using Zoomracks, despite the "obvious" deficiencies of many mainstays of programming, such as conditional expressions, looping, and the ability of macros to call other macros. Despite limited word processing and calculating capabilities, the conceptual model of cards and racks proved to be powerful and rich and was well liked by users.

The 91 users ranged from complete computer novices to highly skilled users. They used Zoomracks for a total of 125 different Zoomracks applications at home, business, and school at an average of 5.2 applications per user. At the same time, another survey reported that the average IBM PC is used for two applications, and the average Macintosh for six.

Several people have computerized entire small businesses with Zoomracks. Jerry Finzi, a commercial photographer who had never used a computer, developed and marketed to over twenty customers a photography studio management system that included applications for business development, project tracking, job estimation, job tracking, invoicing, correspondence, form letters, inventory, pricing, scheduling, shipping, ordering, bookkeeping, photographic slide management, and directories of photographic property houses. All of these applications are special cases of the rack metaphor. The unifying rack metaphor was a big help in enabling his customers to understand and use the system. Zoomracks satisfied enough different application needs—usually ten or more—to form the basis of marketable application packages in several areas: academic research, ad space sales, church management, horticulture (professional and home gardening), genealogy (professional and consumer), genetic engineering hypertext database, innkeeping management, home management, job searching, psychologist office management, law office, small business accounting, computer service support, teaching, telemarketing, and writing. We ported three external products to Zoomracks: 100 legal contracts, 125 business letters, and a desk organizer.

The fact that such a diversity of applications fits within the unifying framework of the rack metaphor attests to its power as a transporting metaphor. It should be particularly valuable to software vendors of vertical market products, especially since it makes it easier to add new applications to an existing product.

Using a transporting metaphor for a variety of applications emphasizes the similarity of applications and de-emphasizes their differences. This contrasts with the standard development technique of designing different conceptual models for different applications. In communicating with people, one could treat doctors, lawyers, students, programmers, and clerks as all different and requiring different methods of communication; or, one could treat them all as special cases of human beings for each of whom different facets predominate and who have different additional properties. This second method, which emphasizes similarity, is likely to be better because the information gained in dealing with one type of person is more likely to be usable when dealing with another type. So, too, transporting metaphors provide the same common conceptual model across a wide realm of applications.

ZOOMRACKS AND HYPERCARD

In the summer of 1987, Apple Computer introduced HyperCard, with a conceptual model similar to Zoomracks' and with different but complementary strengths and weaknesses. HyperCard supports building applications with an object-oriented programming language, HyperTalk, as opposed to Zoomracks' macro language. While Zoomracks has a rich variety of viewing modes, HyperCard can only display one card at a time. (HyperCard 2.0 now displays cards from multiple stacks, but no more than one card in a stack.)

CHAPTER ELEVEN

HyperCard has facilities for interaction and presentation—graphics, animation, and type styles. Zoomracks provides application-specific programmability with macros that are arbitrarily stored in rack 1; HyperCard provides its programmability as HyperTalk scripts in buttons on the stack image. Clicking the mouse on the button executes the program.

Zoomracks' macro capability includes programming capability in that the user can edit in additional commands, including simple looping and conditional commands. This approach gives the user the capability to start with very simple macros and grow into using a sophisticated programming language. HyperCard's aesthetic strengths make it more attractive and easier for the person who uses canned applications. Zoomracks is limited to a character interface; its presentation is less attractive and its canned applications are less polished. A beginner developing personal applications can do more in Zoomracks without macros than in HyperCard without HyperTalk.

Since HyperCard does not have the unifying rack metaphor, lists are implemented with scrolling fields in a less general way and a variety of methods is used for navigation. The result is not only a lot of application-specific work on the part of each user, but also a proliferation of navigation methods.

Because of the complexity of HyperTalk and the multiple graphic layers, HyperCard is primarily used by application developers and computer enthusiasts. Zoomracks, on the other hand, is used by end users who create their own applications. Zoomracks is RAM based and does not support graphics, so it is faster than the disk-based HyperCard. Much more than HyperCard, it was designed to support the ready evolution of simple, quickly created initial racks into sophisticated applications as a user's needs grow. HyperCard does not support change as well. Simple changes often require the skills of a graphic artist, a programmer, or both. The difference between Zoomracks and HyperCard audiences highlights the different aims and philosophies of their respective designers. While the two metaphors strongly overlap, each pushes at different boundaries. Since their strengths are complementary, future products in the genre will likely combine both the unifying transporting metaphor and ease of change of Zoomracks with the strong visual presentation and interactive grace of HyperCard.

THE FUTURE
OF THE RACK METAPHOR

Designing a transporting metaphor requires both opening the metaphor up to support many applications, and structuring individual applications to fit within the metaphor's framework. To push the boundaries of any metaphor to support a variety of applications, the designer must push on the following four fronts.

Adding new applications

This is the most obvious method and is what the user does, but it is also something the metaphor designer must do because it illuminates the metaphor's limitations and stimulates new directions for evolution.

Extending the metaphor

This is the most important and critical way to push the metaphor because it directly extends the boundaries of the conceptual model. However, it must be done carefully; the designer should strive for simplicity, naturalness, and potent magic in the conceptual model, rather than just new functionality.

Adding new functional capability

This might be viewed as adding features. In Hyper-Card, this consists of the variety of HyperTalk commands, as well as the ability to incorporate external XCMDs and

XFCNs into HyperTalk programs. While it is important to support new capability, it is also important to make it subsidiary to the basic conceptual model.

In Zoomracks, we deliberately added as little capability that did not fit within the metaphor as possible, since we wanted to extend the metaphor and solve problems in the domain of the metaphor rather than in the domain of language. We knew we could add features later, resisting, for example, adding hierarchy or a dial-out capability to make phone calls. Alfred Hitchcock made the movie *Rope* as one continuous 90-minute sequence, denying himself the cut—the most basic technique of moviemaking. This let him explore the limits of the medium. If *Rope* suffered as a result of a minimalist approach, Hitchcock's future movies were better for his increased powers. Similarly, we felt if the early version of Zoomracks suffered from a minimalist approach, future versions would gain. If we were reluctant to add something new to the conceptual model, once we did do so, we pushed its boundaries to the limit.

Using illusion

At times, we might need to present something as being within the conceptual metaphor when in fact it is not. One example of this is accessing an existing online database as if it were based on the card and rack metaphor; here, the data is on another computer in an unknown data format. Another example is building a spell checker based on the rack metaphor where extremely efficient implementations are required for space and speed. In neither of these cases would it be possible to store the data in a standard rack, but one could present them to the user as if they were.

Ultimately, just as with the spreadsheet metaphor, some things will fit within the card and rack metaphor well, some not so well, and others not at all. Only time will tell how far the boundaries of the metaphor can be pushed, how large a family of applications it will support, and how valuable it will be. Below, we suggest some easy directions for the rack metaphor that have broad applicability.

Communications and electronic mail

Racks could physically reside on computers in the next room, the next continent, or both, instead of just the memory of the host computer. Scrolling through racks, using new racks, and copying cards, fields, and racks from one place to another could invoke appropriate back-end buffering and communications.

We think several communications applications fit naturally within the rack metaphor. For example, electronic mail could be cards in racks. One field of each card would contain the message, others might hold information such as TO, FROM, DATE, STATUS, etc. Rack mode would provide a list of messages. The user could select messages with Find Lock and could organize them into input, output, archive, and other racks as he wished. New capability to send and receive messages would be added.

Fax messages could be treated similarly to electronic mail. Since fax messages are graphic rather than textual, one field of the rack might contain the text form of the message and the second field the compressed image form; new functional capability would convert from one to the other.

Further, online databases on mainframe computers could be presented to users as cards in racks. Users would copy information between such databases and their own personal databases with the standard copy and paste card commands.

Finally, electronic bulletin boards could be presented to users as cards in racks, similar to online databases.

Relational databases

A rack of cards looks like a table and the rack metaphor operations can be extended to include relational database operations such as join and project. These operations could create new racks or pseudo-racks— racks that are presented as normal racks but are in fact assembled from the data in the other racks.

Spreadsheets

Formulas could be attached to fields or lines of fields to provide calculated fields, or spreadsheet functionality. Such calculations could be within a single card. Rack mode suggests that summary information from a card be placed on the first line, where it could be summarized with similar data from other cards in Rack mode.

Hierarchy

Hierarchy, or outlining, was left out of the rack metaphor because it added unnecessary complexity. Hierarchy, which was rarely requested by users, was the feature software professionals most frequently suggested on seeing Zoomracks. Interestingly, the invention of the relational database model was done by eliminating hierarchy from existing database models. While we expect to add hierarchy in the future, it will be an advanced part of the metaphor that will not be needed in most applications.

Spell checking

A rack could contain a list of words for a spell checker. Other fields could contain the word's source (Webster's dictionary or the user), date added, class of word (legal, technical, medical, corporate buzzword), and typical misspelling or comments about the word. The advantage of such a view of a spelling dictionary would be that the user could review recently added words, correcting or deleting them as necessary. He could also categorize words.

Menus

Menus are the only major Zoomracks construct that is not currently implemented within the rack metaphor. Menus would be racks with fields for the menu name, menu action, and comment. To extend the capability of menus to Hyper-Card buttons, one might add fields for the icon number, location, and button flag. Thus, a menu rack could specify both the location and function of a button, and a switch could determine whether the command is part of a menu or a button.

System shell

Using the rack metaphor as a file system goes part way towards eliminating the desktop metaphor or other file system and just using the rack metaphor. One could extend the metaphor by letting fields contain graphics, sound, and binary and other forms of data, as well as textual data.

Hypermedia

While Zoomracks, like HyperCard, was conceived and developed as an organizational tool to support a wide variety of applications, Apple's marketing of HyperCard as hyper-media and their calling it *Hyper*Card has emphasized the use of the metaphor as a hypermedia platform, and in the process has influenced the expectations of what hypermedia is.

Hypermedia should be considered within the overall framework of how information is used: its creation, its presen-tation, and its integration into the end user's work. Existing hypermedia products primarily address issues of presenting information, but do not address the issues of how users can integrate that information into their personal use. The rack metaphor provides an overall framework for the presenter to organize information prior to the presentation stage, and for recipients to integrate information into their personal "database" after the presentation stage. Cards or fields, for example, can easily be copied from a presentation rack to a personal use rack containing other information. Hyper-media requires links and pictures to be effective, but those problems must be solved within the framework of the total system.

In using any of the above or other applications, the user explores a different aspect of the unifying rack meta-phor. Each application emphasizes different portions of the overall conceptual model, so whenever someone uses a different application, he deepens his understanding of the conceptual model as a whole and acquires skills useful with other applications.

PAPER-BASED TRANSPORTING METAPHORS

The software that accounts for most personal comput-ing is modeled on paper metaphors. Paper has met the test of time as a tool for solving problems. It works for a wide class of problems, and because people are already skilled in using paper to solve problems, there are many metaphorical connections that users can make. The advancement of per-sonal computing occurred largely with metaphors that *rep-*resent paper in ways that are more powerful than the original. What follows not only shows how paper is used as computing metaphors, but gives credit to some pioneers.

Windowing systems

The concept of windows as a means of looking at part of a large sheet of paper was developed by Doug Engelbart at his NLS laboratory at Stanford Research Institute in the late 1960s. His system used two tiled windows on the screen. Alan Kay's group at Xerox PARC extended this concept to overlap-ping windows in the 1970s. Windows provide the magic ability to manage several pieces of paper. However, in the early stages of development, windows (like menus) are artifacts of an application and in themselves are weak as a transporting metaphor. Programmers may have constructed applications with windows; users did not.

Word processing

The most widely used transporting metaphor is the scrolling paper metaphor for word processing. This metaphor allows the user to feel as if he were writing on paper and deleting, inserting, and moving text as if from a marked-up prior version. Anywhere someone might use words on paper, they can use a word processor.

In contrast to the scrolling metaphor, the literal metaphor of sheets or pages of paper is familiar and superficially attractive, and formed the basis of early commercial word processors. However, the less literal, scrolling paper metaphor has become dominant. This is an example of how the cabbage of utility is more important than the rose of familiarity, and how potent magic is more important than strict literalism in making an effective metaphor: The magic of automatic pagination frees users from the constraints of sheets of paper for the tasks of writing and editing.

Spreadsheets

The earliest computer spreadsheet of which I am aware is a worksheet computer that allowed the user to record and play back macros of keystroke operations. This was patented by Robert Rahenkamp and William R. Stewart, Jr. at IBM. More of a rose than present-day spreadsheets, it mimicked the capabilities of paper spreadsheets, complete with their limitations: Adding a row or column might render a macro obsolete. The magic of putting equations into cells and natural order recalculation seems to have been first developed by Pardo and Landau to run on timesharing computers in the early 1970s and patented by them. Dan Bricklin and Robert Frankston reinvented Rahenkamp's worksheet and Pardo and Landau's cell formulas, and added windowing to make the first commercially successful spreadsheet: VisiCalc. Interestingly, Frankston says that horizontal or vertical recalculation, rather than optimum ordering recalculation covered by the Pardo and Landau patent, was a "breakthrough" in developing VisiCalc in that it freed scarce memory space for a larger spreadsheet in the early Apple computers. This is not surprising— compromise with the ideal is common in early manifestations of new ideas.

The spreadsheet is the classic transporting metaphor because of its power, its simplicity, and the richness of the applications it can support. The spreadsheet metaphor evokes connections to the paper spreadsheets, the paper-spreadsheet problem-solving skills of millions of people, and the thousands of problems that have been solved with manual spreadsheet methods. The computer, by adding the magic of formulas in cells, automatic recalculation, and windowing, makes present-day spreadsheets potent transporting metaphors.

Desktop publishing

Aldus PageMaker, together with the laser printer and Adobe's PostScript, popularized font-based typography on personal computers and mixed text, pictures, and page layout, thus creating the desktop publishing market. The desktop publishing metaphor makes connections to the cutting and pasting experience in text and graphic layout, typesetting of different fonts and font sizes, and the design skills of layout artists. It adds magic by providing the ability to automatically resize fonts and text and picture areas.

Table metaphor

Codd created the relational database model by simplifying the network and hierarchical database models into the metaphor of tables. He invented magical operations like selection, projection, and join to give the relational database the power to create new tables, and in the process, a wide range of applications.

When we look at how the above conceptual models work in practice, we can draw several conclusions. First, once a user understands and is skilled in using a conceptual model, he uses it for many tasks; indeed, it becomes part of his thinking process, determining what tasks he will attack and how he will attack them.

Second, each of a small number of these powerful conceptual models is responsible for a respectable amount of personal computer use. Together, these conceptual models are responsible for the vast majority of personal computer use.

Third, not all users need be familiar with the model on which the metaphor is based. While users who are not familiar with the underlying metaphor do not get the advantage of it immediately, later when they begin to see its metaphorical connections with the real world, they will deepen their understanding of the conceptual model.

Fourth, the more general model grows at the expense of the less general. Spreadsheets grew at the expense of specific financial applications; the personal computer and word processor grew at the expense of dedicated word processors.

Fifth, many of the metaphors described have taken on a life of their own, as we build up a large body of experienced users and push the boundaries of the conceptual models. They are beginning to leave their origins behind; the computer spreadsheet has pretty much replaced the paper spreadsheet, just as the horseless carriage has replaced the horse-drawn carriage.

Sixth, the metaphors described here transport problem solving out of the language domain into the visual domain. What would have been programs become equations in cells in spreadsheets. This is not to say that programmability is eliminated, but that it takes a subordinate role to the basic metaphor. Communication between user and computer is better when users are reacting to what they see and to a conceptual model they understand rather than having to think in the domain of language or programming.

THE GENE METAPHOR

The *gene* metaphor is a transporting metaphor used to encode and manipulate user interface formats. While it is useful in many environments, we describe it here in the context of HyperCard because the reader has acquired some knowledge of HyperCard by now and because HyperRacks provides the only implementation of the gene metaphor.

Some additional details of HyperCard are necessary to understand the gene metaphor. Each HyperCard stack has background objects (fields and buttons) that appear on all of the cards in the stack. Buttons contain HyperTalk scripts (which are executed by clicking on the button with the mouse) and provide the application's functionality. Background objects have properties such as height, width, text style, visibility, etc. Most object properties can be changed with HyperCard commands, and all can be changed with Hyper-Talk language constructs. The values of the properties of the background objects specify the visual format of the stack: where the objects are located, how big they are, the style and font of the text they display, etc. A HyperCard application is a stack of cards with background buttons whose scripts implement the application and whose fields contain data.

The gene metaphor addresses the problem of managing one or more visual display formats for a stack. One might want to have several visual display formats for the same stack, each having different fields (for data) and different buttons (for functions). For example, an application might consist of one visual format with a few buttons and fields for novices, and a second format with more buttons and fields for advanced users. It would be useful to switch between these two formats on the same stack. Different formats could also be used to implement different, but related, applications: A name and address stack might have a standard format (as shown in Figure 48), a format for printing labels (Figure 55), and a format for doing a mail merge (Figure 56). Each would have different buttons with different scripts. Switching between formats changes not only the format of the data displayed, but also the functionality of the application itself because the different buttons can be made visible. Normally, creating and modifying such formats takes substantial (HyperTalk) programming skills. The gene metaphor makes creating and managing multiple formats easy for programmers and nonprogrammers alike.

The gene metaphor is implemented as a HyperTalk script that encodes a complete specification of a format, just as DNA encodes a complete specification of an organism. Executing the script expresses its format and reverts the background to the format specified, independent of the background objects' current properties, just as expressing a DNA gene creates proteins and, ultimately, an organism. The gene script is stored in a HyperCard button and is invoked either by selecting and clicking on the gene button with the mouse or by selecting the gene button's name from a menu of gene

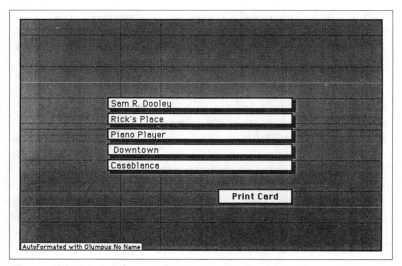

Figure 55: A label format for the stack shown in Figure 48.

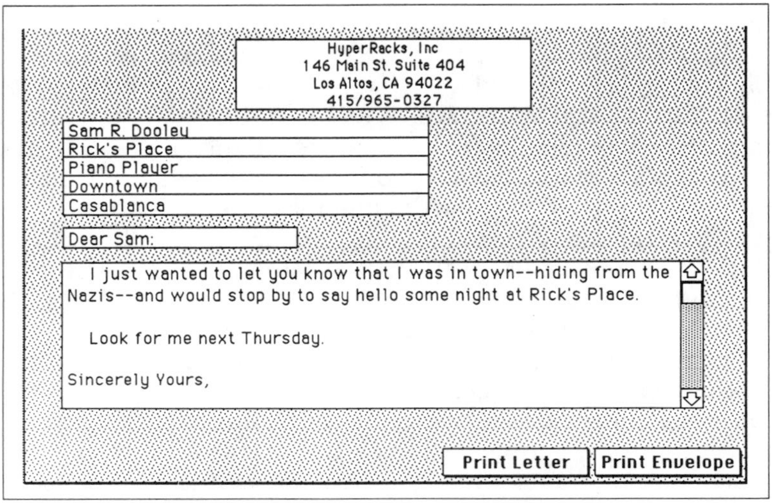

Figure 56: A correspondence or mail-merge format for the stack shown in Figure 48.

buttons (formats). Because the gene format is a normal HyperCard button, its script can be copied (cloning in genetic terminology), edited (genetic engineering of mutations), injected into the genetic information of another stack (conjugation), and combined with another stack's genetic information to produce a descendant format combining the properties of both "parents" (sexual reproduction).

The magic Keep Background Format command starts the process by creating a gene button to encode the current stack format. (Its analogy does not exist in nature, and genetic engineers cannot yet reverse engineer DNA from an organism.) The user has two ways to manipulate a format: in the visual domain, using HyperCard's standard formatting commands, and in the programming language domain by editing the HyperTalk gene script.

Gene scripts contain straight-line code and so are easy for novice programmers to understand. Only changes to object properties are compiled, making the script more compact and making it easier to effect global property changes and to edit out undesired property differences. Users with limited programming skills can edit a field width from "123" to "100," or delete the line "set height to 13" when the previous height of 12 should remain unchanged. Figure 57 shows the part of the gene script that encodes the format for the fields shown in Figure 48. A similar script handler called "on RevertButtons" for the button objects is not shown. Keep Background Format creates similar gene scripts for the formats shown in Figures 55 and 56.

The "genestart" at the beginning of a gene button script hides all objects so that objects not referenced in the gene script will be invisible. The script statements then specify (set) the current properties to be the properties of the

```
on Revert_Fields
  GeneStart "bkgnd Fld"
  . . .
  set textsize      of RNA to 10
  set width         of RNA to 125
  set height        of RNA to 13
  set left          of RNA to 43
  set_DeltaLeft_of_RNA_to 0
  set top           of RNA to 53
  set_DeltaTop_of_RNA_to 0

  nextObj Show, "bkgnd Fld id 5", "Name" --1 "43,53,168,66"

  set width         of RNA to 132
  set_DeltaTop_of_RNA_to     0
  set_DeltaLeft_of_RNA_to    135
  nextObj Show, "bkgnd Fld id 9", "Company" --2 "175,53,307,66"

  set width         of RNA to 151
  set_DeltaLeft_of_RNA_to    148
  nextObj Show, "bkgnd Fld id 6", "Phone" --3 "314,53,465,66"

  set width         of RNA to 422
  set_DeltaTop_of_RNA_to     33
  set Left of RNA to 43
  set_DeltaLeft_of_RNA_to    0
  nextObj Show, "bkgnd Fld id 8", "Title" --4 "43,86,465,99"

  nextObj Show, "bkgnd Fld id 10", "Address" --5 "43,119,465,132"

  nextObj Show, "bkgnd Fld id 11", "City" --6 "43,152,465,165"

  set style         of RNA to scrolling
  set height        of RNA to 113
  set_DeltaTop_of_RNA_to     83
  nextObj Show, "bkgnd Fld id 14", "Notes" --7 "43,185,465,298"

  GeneDone Hide --Unspecified Objects Hide,Show or AsIs
end Revert_Fields
```

Figure 57: Encoding of fields in name and address format for the stack shown in Figure 48.

first object in the format, and the "NextObj" command as-signs those current properties to the object specified by its argument. The properties of the rest of the objects are then defined by first specifying changes to the current properties and then assigning the current properties to an object with other "NextObj" commands, and repeating this for all objects. The only properties not specified in the gene script are the *script* property and the *name* property. The script property is not specified so as to draw a bright line between the user interface (encoded in the gene button script) and the application itself (encoded in the non-gene button scripts). The name property is not specified so as to ensure that objects will have the same name in all formats, even if a different format is selected after an object name is changed.

USING GENE FORMATS

A user can create a format by using HyperCard to arrange the format he wants, keeping the format with the Keep Background Format command. He can arrange other formats and keep them under different names. As many formats as desired can be created and saved in this way. Any format can then be restored (reverted to) by executing the associated gene button.

The multiple formats provided by the gene metaphor can be used in several ways, described below.

Task-specific formats

Stacks of cards can contain information useful for different purposes. For example, a name and address stack might be used for telemarketing, printing labels, writing correspondence, sending electronic mail, or sending faxes. Genes provide a means for specifying different formats for each of these purposes; switching formats becomes switching from one application (or subapplication) to another. By encoding applications into different formats, genes address the issues of complexity, organization, and customization involved in creating and maintaining applications by both the end user and the professional developer. If cards, racks, and fields each provide a dimension (two in the case of fields), then the ability of genes to specify applications provides a fifth dimension to the card and rack metaphor. This one aspect of the gene metaphor offers interesting potential.

User interface prototyping and testing

The gene script distinguishes an application's functionality (the button and field scripts) from its interface (the gene script). Alternate interfaces can be readily developed, saved in genes, easily reverted to, and tested or demonstrated. This is particularly useful if one wants to test prototype user interfaces in actual practice with real application data. After switching the format, the user can continue using the new format from where he left off.

Matching the user's level

Different formats could be used for different classes of users: novices who want just the bare minimum functionality, expert users who might want a great deal of functionality, and casual users who might want an intermediate level of functionality. Not only does this support the different needs of different levels of users, but it lets a user change levels by switching to a new gene format.

User customization and version control

If a user wants to modify an application by adding a few buttons of his own to add functionality, he can. The different formats for different versions can be saved as genes and reverted to later if desired. Different gene formats would invoke different versions of the copied button.

Splicing new applications into existing programs and data

Gene buttons can be copied from one stack to another to port a format or application. For example, a format that prints a name and address label could be ported to any stack that has names and addresses. To install a ported gene, the user must specify what should be done for each object referenced in the ported gene, and the ported gene's script must be modified to reflect the new object identifiers. For example, if a PRINT LABEL gene were ported to a stack, during installation some fields would likely be recognized by name (e.g., NAME, TITLE, ZIP); others might be selected by the user (e.g., COMPANY *vs* FIRM); and others (a PRINT LABEL button) would likely be copied from the origin stack.

Once installed, the PRINT LABEL gene could be used as a separate format and could be integrated into another existing format. When a new gene script is created, all the objects appear in the script and the user can make visible those he wants in the new format and then execute the gene script to invoke the new format.

Application update and installation

It is often difficult to install the application upgrades and it is particularly difficult if the user has modified the applications and has to deal with installing the modification into the new installation. This metaphor helps address these issues. Installing a new version becomes installing a new gene. If things don't work as expected, the user is less concerned about making an error, as he can switch between the original format and the new one. If the user has added new buttons with new functions to customize his application, then these buttons can be made visible and used within the updated application. The user can restore any of the formats of interest, whether old or new, customized or not.

While we think the gene metaphor holds promise, like any new idea, it will take time before we see how valuable it may prove to be in practice.

Transporting metaphors empower users. Unfortunately, such metaphors are few and take time for users to learn. Once mastered, however, they give users skills to solve a wide variety of problems. Only recently have we started to understand how important metaphor is to the thought process in both natural language and software. Both the roses of familiar metaphors and cabbages of transporting metaphors are valuable to user interface design, but we have concentrated too much on roses and not enough on cabbages. Ultimately, the power of metaphors to transport a wide variety of problems into a common framework is more important to the advance of computing than the classic human factors involved with ease of use.

Figure 58: Animation. Walt Disney and his animators made animation into an art form and in the process rediscovered the principles of communication.

CHAPTER TWELVE

Animation, Imagination, and Friendly Software Design

The universe is looking less and less like a great machine and more and more like a great thought.

Ortega y Gasset

When the outstanding violinist Isaac Stern was asked the difference between the great and the truly great, he replied, "The ability to communicate." It is the key ingredient in every art form and certainly the great strength of Walt Disney's genius.
Frank Thomas and Ollie Johnston

As I was finishing the manuscript for the first edition of this book, I read *Disney Animation: The Illusion of Life* by Frank Thomas and Ollie Johnston. The authors, Disney animators from 1935 until they retired in 1978, wrote the book to record how the great Disney films were made. In describing the thought processes that go into creating an animated film, they recreate the atmosphere in which those great films— *Snow White, Fantasia, Bambi,* and others— were created.

For anyone seriously interested in designing friendly software, that book is must reading. It describes a journey of discovery that is quite similar to the journey the developer of friendly software must make; it is a great source of

stimulation for what might and might not work; and it reinforces the points I made earlier.

In its essence, *Disney Animation* tells the story of the
invention of an art form, and the rediscovery of the principles of communication and theater. Its authors, who are
artists rather than writers, show by the interest and excitement they arouse in the reader that they have mastered the
principles of communication and that these principles are
indeed universal.

First and foremost, every scene and every sequence of a
Disney film had to be interesting. A dull sequence was revised
or eliminated; it was never left in because it was needed for
continuity. If we put in one-tenth the effort that Disney did
just to make his films interesting, our software would improve tenfold. (In an effort to avoid the awkward construct,
"Walt Disney and his artists," I use the word *Disney* throughout this chapter. When referring to Walt Disney specifically,
I will use his first name.)

Disney storymen and animators constantly look for "a
piece of business" that will bring a character to life and make
it interesting. A character never simply walks from one place
to another: too dull. He might be angry and show it in the
way he walks; he might drag something along; he might
scratch his head. But every character would do some piece
of business that was in character, advanced the story, and
was interesting.

The concept of "a piece of business" was a new one to
me. However, with the QuickView technology, I think we get
that effect when a long message that does not fit is displayed. You may remember that the vowels are deleted one
by one so new characters can be brought in from the right.
This is unusual and gives the product a certain personality
that people find interesting.

The early animators discovered that two related keys
to making a character interesting are exaggeration and
caricature. Reality must be the starting point: It is necessary
to identify the essence of an animal or a person, and this was
researched in great detail. But once the essence of a character was identified, it was caricatured and its movements

were exaggerated. This made the character more interesting than the real one on which it was based. This principle, the authors point out, is true of all art. Michelangelo's David is not proportioned like a real human being, nor is Disney's Bambi proportioned like a real deer. Bambi may be deceptively similar to the deer we know, but it is designed so that the animator can exaggerate its actions and thus make it interesting. (The difficult characters to animate are the human ones, such as Snow White. The animator's dilemma is that an accurately human character is difficult to make interesting, while the audience won't identify with a character that is a caricature).

This, too, was a useful insight. It suggests that the software designer's objective should not be to model *accurately* something the user is familiar with. VisiCalc provides an exaggerated spreadsheet, 254 rows of 64 columns. The largest normal spreadsheet is probably 50 rows of 15 columns. Similarly, automatic calculation is an exaggeration of something that is done on a real spreadsheet. In both of these VisiCalc examples, we see that the spreadsheet is used as a starting point, and that that aspect of it is exaggerated. It is this combination of familiarity and showmanship that makes the product interesting.

From the earliest stages of a film, the story was presented visually through story sketches. "Walt usually left out the dialogue until a sequence had been developed to the point where he could see just how little was really needed," say Thomas and Johnston. "If the idea could be communicated with an expression, an action, or a sound effect, or with music, he would not use dialogue. The storyman had to think in visual terms first, and when he did write dialogue, it had to tell something about the character and not be exposition." Hitchcock is quoted with approval: "When we tell a story in cinema, we should resort to dialogue only when it is impossible to do otherwise."

Software is also a visual medium; we should resort to English only when it is impossible to do otherwise. In designing friendly software, start out with a blank screen to fill, just like a filmmaker does. I think of filling it the same way— with pictures. Commands come later and then only to support the pictures. Words are used only as a last resort.

Disney used several techniques to focus the audience's attention where he wanted it. Two seem particularly appropriate to friendly software design: staging and anticipation.

First, staging is carefully considered. How should a particular scene be shown? Should it be indoors or out? What characters should be in it? How should they be arranged? What is in the background? Who should be in the scene? How should they be arranged? Should it be a frontal shot, a side shot, a down shot, or a moving shot; should it be a long shot or a closeup? The major consideration in any part of a film is always what is the most effective way to communicate the desired information to an audience.

Our software is staged too. How do we structure information on the screen? I think it would be useful to think of our software as consisting of a series of scenes which need to be staged appropriately. Much of our software staging is ill considered; more is unconsidered.

Disney rediscovered an old theatrical principle— anticipation. An actor telegraphs what he is about to do before actually doing it. Before a character would jump, for example, he would first bend his knees in preparation. This prepares the audience for what will happen so it is not taken by surprise. A related technique, called slow in and slow out, is used when going from one pose (or extreme) to another. The character moves slowly at first, then speeds up, then slows down before settling down on the next pose. Generally, there are fewer drawings for the middle three quarters of the action. Almost all of the drawings are at both extremes. This prepares the audience both for the movement and for the new pose.

Anytime the software designer wants to move the user's focus of attention from one place to another, a "slow out" could get the user to anticipate the general direction of the new focus. A "slow in" draws the user's eyes to the new focus of attention. As an experienced user, I sometimes use a Find command in WordStar and can't find the cursor on the screen afterward. An inexperienced user would have more trouble. The slow in-slow out technique might reduce that problem.

Whenever there is more than one thing on the screen, the audience is likely to get confused. Disney and his animators were always concerned about identifying the essence of what should be communicated in a scene and determining the minimum needed to say it. Every scene must be communicated clearly. Backgrounds, for example, are designed so they don't distract the audience from the action. Secondary actions in a scene always reinforce the primary action. Thus, for example, if the main action shows a character picking a flower, other characters in the scene look at or point in the direction of the flower, and this focuses the audience's attention on the flower. The action is always staged so that it is easy to see and not obscured by some other aspect of the scene.

A major problem with many computer screens is that they show too much. This indicates laziness on the designer's part. Instead of finding what is important to the user, and showing only that, he shows everything and expects his user to find what he needs. The user is often overwhelmed; what he needs is often not clear to him. This can be particularly serious for the new user, but it can be a problem for the experienced user as well. This does not mean that it is easy to make our software simple, clear, and easy to understand.

Audience rapport was important to Disney and his animators. "We involve the audience in our films.... We start with something they know and like. This can be either an idea or a character, as long as it is familiar and appealing. It can be a situation everyone has experienced.... But there must be something that is known and understood if the film is to achieve audience involvement." Or later, "*you are playing off images in the viewer's subconscious* [author's emphasis] and if people grew up thinking a certain way that is where you must start. To have a mean and cruel kitten terrorizing a family of nervous flighty bears is an uphill fight for everybody." An uphill fight, but not impossible. Steven Spielberg solved that problem when he made an alien a sympathetic figure in *E.T.*

But only a master of his craft, who understood the forces he was up against, could hope to succeed.

The italicized portion of the previous quotation emphasizes how the raw material for any communications craft is what is in the audience's mind.

Building a model in the user's mind is thought transference. Dave Hand, a Disney animation director, put it this way:

> Our entire medium is transference of thought. The thought is created first in the mind of the storyman...then transferred to the director, who attempts to transfer it to the animator.... The animator then attempts to transfer it pictorially. He takes it out of the intangible, and places it in tangible form, in picture, for transference back to the mind of the audience...and picture presentation is clearer than any other means of transferring thought from one person to another.

When one looks at Disney films today, it is difficult to realize that he resented the limits of his imagination. If Walt Disney's vision did not arrive complete, it certainly grew over time.

To help him achieve his vision, Walt Disney attracted hundreds of people of diverse talents, including Leopold Stokowski and Salvador Dali. He treated his people well; if someone did not work out in one place, the person would be tried someplace else. Many people worked for him for twenty, thirty, forty years and more.

Disney hated to be told that something couldn't be done for technical reasons; it brought his creative drive to a halt. He wanted his people to think about what he was trying to do, and only later to concentrate on the mechanics of doing it. Indeed, no one with the title of engineer worked for Walt Disney. He felt that engineers designed only for themselves and were unconcerned about the eventual users of their products.

A typical Disney feature film would take three and a half years to make: six months of research; one year of work on story, styling, and experimenting; one and a half years of animation; and six months of follow-up to add color and music and to photograph the 460,000 drawings that make a finished film. The making of a Disney movie was a constant process of prototyping, revising, and rewriting, and the Disney organization was geared to this process.

The process starts with a story sketch. Woolie Reitherman explained it:

> A story sketch is not geography— it is not continuity— and it is not a diagram. Nor does it merely illustrate the dialogue for the sequence. Those are all the common mistakes of the beginning story sketch man. The story sketch should show character, attitude, feelings, entertainment, expression, type of action, as well as telling the story of what's happening. When you look at a board, it should reflect the feeling of the sequence so the viewer starts to pick up some excitement and stimulation.

Storyboards were springboards for new and better ideas at the story meetings, and the result was generally a complete revision of a sequence. The storyboards themselves, rough though they may have been, served as useful prototypes of the final film— everyone could see it and get a feeling for what the final film would be like as well as how it would affect their functional specialties.

When the story sketch was approved, the dialogue was added, and actors were found to record the voices of the various characters. But the storyboard lacked the element of time, and this affected everyone's judgment. Each image adds a small part to the larger picture that gradually grows in the audience's imagination. Because that is the picture that the animators must concentrate on, they made a film of the rough sketches, giving each sketch the time on the screen that its animated counterpart would have. The sound track, with voices, sound effects, and even music, was included. All this was still rough; the music, for example, would be some convenient music consistent with the desired mood. This was called the story reel. Everyone studied it: the layout people, the animators, the composer, the storymen. They asked what was good about it and what was bad. Each person could see so much better how his part fit into the whole. Of course they revised; these revisions were immediately inserted in the film. The story reel slowly changed into the finished film, just as metamorphosis changes a caterpillar into a butterfly.

Clicks were added where the music beat would be, so the animator could synchronize with them. When the rough animation for a scene was completed, it replaced its counterpart story sketches in the film. Temporary versions of the music were added, usually with a piano or organ. Animation scenes were added to the film when they were completed.

Throughout this whole process, everyone got to see a more and more complete version of the final film; they could relate what they had done to the whole and could better see what needed revision. They could see what worked and what didn't work:

> Many ideas that sounded great in those story meetings become sodden and lifeless when seen on the screen in relation to the rest of the business, and the sooner these elements can be discovered the sooner they can be corrected. Many other story ideas that were only "touches" will come to life in animation with so much entertainment that it is foolish not to get the full value from them, even if it means adding considerable footage.

This was not an entirely smooth process, but it was not supposed to be. Its purpose was to bring out what works and what doesn't work, the problems and the pleasant surprises, and to do it as early as possible. If the animation took too much time for the music, the composer might add another half measure. If a particular sequence did not work as expected, it would be redone or abandoned.

Disney kept his stories flexible well into the animation process. "Often a whole new character would appear from nowhere and take over the story. When we started *Snow White*, there was no Dopey in the cast, *Pinocchio* had no

Jiminy Cricket, and *Bambi* had no Thumper." Walt Disney said:

> The best things in many of our pictures have come after we thought the story was thoroughly prepared.
>
> It was never too late to make a change; nothing was ever set as long as the possibility existed that it could be made to relate better to the overall picture or communicate more strongly with the audience.

If a Disney picture was prototyped in the large as indicated above, it was also prototyped in the small. Norman Ferguson, who was the first to create the illusion of life in a cartoon in animating Pluto, made rough drawings for his first tests. Frequently, he merely drew a few circles and lines. If the basic concept animated well, he would proceed; if not, he could easily make changes. Any sequence, no matter how rough, could be quickly filmed to evaluate how well it was working. This encouraged experimentation and stimulated the animator's imagination. When the sequence felt right, assistant animators would fill in the details and turn it into a final crisp scene to be photographed.

While a final Disney film had about 460,000 finished cells, two million other drawings were needed to advance the film through its various stages. If a Disney film is a magnificent stone house, eighty percent of the stones fill the path to the house; twenty percent compose the house itself.

This approach was in sharp contrast to the other animation studios of the thirties. While he worked at another studio before becoming one of Disney's first animators, Bill Tytla saw his animation only by going down to the local theater after the film was released. When his boss at that studio heard about the prototyping and experimenting done at the Disney studios, his comment was, "When I hire a man to animate, I want him to know how."

Disney created a set of tools that helped him make a film, just as we have developed a great many tools to help us develop software. Some of Disney's tools were designed to help make a quality finished product; other management tools were designed to keep track of progress and ensure that all the details merged together correctly. But the main focus of these tools was to make it always possible for everyone to get a good feeling for the current "best guess" of what the audience's experience would be. Everyone could quickly adjust what they were doing to the reality, and see how well the adjustment worked. To develop quality software, we need a similar environment that will give us the current "best guess" of what the audience's experience will be.

So to the list of people who couldn't get things right the first time—Hemingway, Frank Lloyd Wright, Beethoven, and Picasso—we add Walt Disney. No one ever gets anything right the first time. Some of us realize it; others of us don't.

Finally, Disney and his artists faced the moment of truth that any communicator must face:

> As soon as the answer print of a new cartoon was received, the whole staff rushed over to the Alex Theater in Glendale to see how it would go with an audience…. Each director remembers at least one dismal evening out there under the streetlights, because these meetings made them face implacable reality. It was no longer the excitement of what might be but the undeniable harshness of what was…. It was a harsh way to learn a new profession, out there on the street at night, but it was positive, and it was definite. The audience reaction was always clear and strong and undeniable.

```
C6                                                    C1
                                                      17

    │     A          B          C          D
  1 │CHECK  #   PAYEE      AMOUNT     DEPOSIT
  2 │
  3 │             INITIAL   BALANCE    500.00
  4 │-------------------------------------------
  5 │ 101       RENT         360.00
  6 │           DEPOSIT                  250.00
  7 │ 105       TELEPHONE     65.15
  8 │ 103       VISA         120.65
  9 │ 104       LIFE INS      89.90
 10 │===========================================
 11 │TOTALS                  635.70    250.00
 12 │JANUARY       ENDING  BALANCE     114.30
 13 │-------------------------------------------
 14 │ 102       UTILITIES     23.45
 15 │===========================================
 16 │TOTALS                   23.45      0.00
 17 │FEBRUARY      ENDING  BALANCE      90.85

           PRESS SPACE BAR TO CONTINUE:
           PRESS Q TO RETURN TO MENU:
```

Figure 59: Software. VisiCalc, the most unexpected, and probably the most important software product for personal computers uses many techniques of effective communication. To be useful, computers must communicate effectively with their users, and writing software for people is an art and a craft just as much as writing, filmmaking, or any other communications craft.

CHAPTER THIRTEEN

Final Words

The profession of book writing makes horse racing seem like solid, stable business.

John Steinbeck

I have used VisiCalc and WordStar as examples in several places here, but they are not perfect designs. Indeed, they have both been superseded by better designs. When a product such as VisiCalc breaks new ground, everyone can find ways to improve it.

By concentrating on what has been good in the designs I discussed, I hope I gave you some insight into what works, and how to think. Things done well don't intrude, and thus frequently go unnoticed. Things done poorly are generally easy to see. Anyone can find fault in a good design; few can create one from scratch.

VisiCalc could be easier to use. It could have help screens and it could display the complete names of important commands and options, but these details should not blind one to the inherent quality of its design. VisiCalc was successful because its fundamental design was good, easy to use, and innovative.

If we look at Griffith's *Birth of a Nation* today, we can see that the picture quality is poor and the acting primitive. It is obviously dated. But given the constraints of the medium at the time, the editing of that film is first-rate, even by today's standards.

Similarly, when we evaluate VisiCalc or WordStar today, we tend to forget the constraints involved. VisiCalc was initially designed to work from a cassette tape, and had an elaborate help system that was not put in the first product release. WordStar was designed to work with low-bandwidth CRT terminals. When we evaluate these products in the context of the constraints they faced, and the quality of comparable software of their times, we see that their authors did excellent work.

I don't expect you to agree with everything I have said. But if this book makes you think differently about designing friendly software, our efforts—mine in writing this, and yours in reading it—will have been worthwhile.

Many people are concerned that they will be left out of the computer age. I don't think that is necessary or likely. I expect that as our software gets better, we will, by making them comfortable with computers, bring most people into the computer age. How we will do that over the next ten or twenty years is open to speculation. Personally, I believe that the most convenient and easy-to-use software will be developed by designers who approach their task with a communicator's eye and a determination to make life easy for their users.

Afterword

> *The Congress shall have the power to promote the progress of science and useful arts by securing for limited time to authors and inventors the exclusive right to their respective writings and discoveries.*
>
> **U.S. Constitution, Article 1, Section 8**

The professional communicator, be he writer or film-maker, is concerned with certain mundane matters. If imitation is the sincerest form of flattery, money is even more sincere. The communicator needs protection. Much of his work consists of simplification, and the effort expended in creating something is proportional to what he *leaves out,* rather than what he *puts into* his product. The simpler, and therefore the better, the result, the easier it is to copy. Furthermore, creative endeavors are inherently risky. Many attempts just don't work; when one finally succeeds at something, it seems only fair and just that the reward should be to the person who had the vision, took the risk, and made it work.

In film, writing, theater, painting, and other communications crafts, this is a recognized fact. When someone writes a book, no one can publish it without paying a royalty. Copyright protection for original work is easily obtained, and appropriating other people's original work is not only illegal, but is considered bad form. If someone wants to make a movie or play from a book, he must pay the author royalties. The courts willingly award significant sums when copyrights are violated. In August 1983 as I first wrote this, a major publisher was withdrawing a book from distribution because its author took the plot from another book.

Software writers have no such protection available to them, yet software is what makes computers useful. People don't buy TV sets, they buy the ability to watch TV programs; people don't buy hi-fi sets, they buy the ability to play records; and, except for hobbyists and some computer professionals, people don't buy personal computers, they buy the ability to run software that will get a useful task done. Predicting which software will be useful and which will work is not easy. As the marketing founder of Apple, Mike Markkula is one of the marketing geniuses in personal computers. When Bob Frankston offered to sell VisiCalc to Apple, Mike Markkula declined because he could not see VisiCalc as an important program.

Frankston and Bricklin produced and marketed VisiCalc anyway, and VisiCalc was responsible for at least half of Apple's sales during its period of greatest growth. However, since Apple computers retailed for at least ten times the price of VisiCalc, every VisiCalc sale generated about ten dollars in Apple profits for every dollar in profit that was split between VisiCalc (its marketers) and Software Arts (Frankston and Bricklin). Furthermore, VisiCalc's developers had no way to protect their product concept, and several other companies developed and marketed spreadsheet programs without paying royalties.

Developers of genuinely original products should be party to the financial benefits that flow from their work. The potential for profit did much to fuel the explosion of progress in industry. The holders of the early semiconductor patents, for example, made much of their money by licensing their patent rights to other companies. Technological advance comes when, to those who would advance the technology, previous advances are made available *at a price.* Whether he be a writer, a playwright, or an inventor, one thing that keeps the creative person going through successive failures is the expectation that when success is achieved, if someone wants what he has created, he must pay for it. It is not there for the taking.

When IBM wanted to use Charlie Chaplin to sell its personal computer, it paid for the right to do so. When the Disney organization told me that because of the number of text permissions they were giving us, they could not give us permission to have pictures of Disney characters in the animation chapter (in the first edition of this book), I had to use a blank page and your imagination. (I would not give the place that Walt Disney and his animators deserve to creators of lesser cartoon characters.)

Software is difficult to protect except against the most blatant kinds of theft. Most businessmen are realists who are willing to pay the going price for something. However, they see the going price for the intellectual property rights embodied in computer programs as "no charge." The inventor is provided with patent protection; the writer is provided with copyright protection; the software developer is provided with legal theories that lawyers will be happy to develop and litigate because they are both profitable and interesting. My own lawyer, who is one of the top experts on computers and intellectual property protection, says that this kind of law "is like going through the rapids on a raft; it is lots of fun, but you are probably going to get wet." (The lawyer gets wet; the client may drown.)

Recently, the Supreme Court has ruled that software is patentable subject matter; at QuickView we have applied for patents on both the Viewdex and the Viewcheck technology. Software patentability is such a new area that few people understand it. (I think we have the only patent lawyer in the United States who has both been a working programmer and has a degree in computer science.) Patentability is, however, useful in only some cases.

Conventional software copyrights give limited protection; they protect against someone copying a program's object or source code; they do not give the normal copyright protection against someone duplicating the work by starting from scratch but by referring to the original. If it was shown in court that someone read a book several times and tried to write the same book from scratch, it would be considered strong evidence of copyright infringement. If it can be shown in court that someone used a program regularly for several weeks and attempted to duplicate the program from scratch, shouldn't this be just as strong evidence of copyright infringement?

Should software be treated differently from the other communications crafts?

The thesis of this book is that writing friendly software is a communications craft. Consistent with this position, the software developer should get the same protection the writer, playwright, or other communicator gets. QuickView will apply for performance copyrights on its software products to see if the courts will give us the same protection for our work as other communicators get for their work. Since our position is a novel one, I suspect I will get to accompany my lawyer on one of her trips through the rapids.

A STATEMENT
FROM THE PUBLISHER

The material contained in the epilogue that follows we believe to be an honest attempt by one man to describe his experience from his point of view. So far as has been possible to ascertain, the events described actually took place, but any account presenting one person's view is by its very nature biased. Other interpretations of the events and other judgments from the facts are possible and even plausible.

From the point of view of the publisher, the primary question, beyond accuracy, is whether the narrative as set forth offers valid impressions and educational insights for the intended reader of this book. The answer to this question, in our considered opinion, is yes. Obviously, for those who are contemplating using patents to assert and protect their intellectual property rights in the real world of the U. S. software market, the account gives a vivid picture of what they might encounter. But also, for those who are vexed or bewildered to find their right to market or use certain ideas challenged by another party, the account supplies, if not a justification for such a challenge, at least a clue to what might be going on in the challenger's mind.

Representatives of one of the companies mentioned in this book, IBM, have indicated that the interpretation of their words and actions given in this epilogue is not a correct one. We have offered IBM space to include an unedited statement of their point of view.

R. S. Langer
Editor-in-Chief

Figure 60: Lawyering. Lawyers typify opposing aspects of communication. Persuading juries and judges, negotiating, and drafting contracts are one aspect; dissimulation, obfuscation, misrepresentation, and lying are another aspect. Watergate illustrates both with Attorney General John Mitchell (one of several Nixon lawyers who went to jail) on the right and Archibald Cox on the left.

AP/Wide World Photos.

The Wright Brothers and Software Invention

When a thing is new, people say, "It is not true." Later, when its truth becomes obvious, they say, "It is not important." Finally, when its importance cannot be denied, they say, "Anyway, it is not new."

William James

Verily, a pioneer has to get his justice in the same way that florists get bouquets from century plants.

Thomas Edison

You can get much further with a kind word and a gun than with a kind word alone.

Al Capone

George Bernard Shaw's play *St. Joan* is about how society treats visionaries. Joan of Arc hears voices and has a vision telling her how to force the English out of France. She acts on that vision. As long as this helps those in power, she is assisted. But once the English are pushed out of France, her ideas threaten the status quo of both Church and State and it is arranged to have her burned at the stake. Nothing personal, as Shaw makes plain; necessities of state. Centuries later, safely dead and no longer threatening, she is canonized. Any visionary threatens the status quo and thus risks the same fate. Inventors are visionaries. And they threaten the status quo. The successful ones are canonized. But first they are burned at the stake.

Let me tell you how this process works.

As I was writing the first edition of this book, I was developing Zoomracks. Zoomracks and its metaphor have consumed most of my time since I conceived the basic idea in 1981. From 1982 until 1986, when we introduced Zoomracks II, Chuck Clanton, my codesigner, and Tom Zimmer spent a considerable portion of their time on it as well. Two years after we introduced Zoomracks in 1985, Apple introduced HyperCard, a product with more sizzle, but with a more limited card and stack metaphor. Apple ignored us and our patents and we were forced to file suit. Eventually we settled, and Apple took out a license to our patents.

When I started out I hoped the metaphor would prove valuable, but, like any creative person, I had inner doubts. I felt that we would either succeed and make money or fail and go broke. What actually happened was more complex. Some of our ideas were accepted, but our rights to them were not. I did not want a fight, but when I asked that my rights be recognized, I was ignored and had to either fight for my rights or become a pancake under a corporate tank. Over time, I became more angry and more determined to have my rights respected.

In 1988, when things seemed most difficult, I read Fred Howard's biography of the Wright brothers, entitled *Wilbur and Orville.* Seeing that inventors as great as the Wright brothers suffered through experiences similar to mine was helpful. I now realize that my experience is typical of inventors, particularly independent inventors. I have identified 21 aspects of the invention process. Each is illustrated by at least two examples: one from the experience of the Wright brothers, and one from my own experience. Compared to the airplane, my invention may be a poor one, but it is my own. Now that I have been successful in getting my patents recognized, I would like to share my experience in the hope that others can learn from my experience and mistakes.

Most development consists of improvements on existing products, is done in established companies, and is incremental in nature. But fundamental ideas rarely come

Figure 61: *Information Scolaire,* Robert Doisneau, 1956. This exquisite photograph portrays what intellectual property rights are about. They are to reward the dreamer and frustrate the copier.

Photo R. Doisneau/Rapho.

from an established company (except as back-room projects) and are not incremental in nature, and as a result the road to their acceptance is more difficult. So the typical software developer will not face many of the problems I describe here. However, if you are developing a patentable idea and you don't have the protection of a large organization, you may want to know what the territory is like.

1. ATTACK A RECOGNIZED PROBLEM WHOSE SOLUTION WOULD BE USEFUL.

The value of solving the problem of manned flight was widely recognized, and several people attacked it before the Wright brothers. Augustus Herring was a fraud; Otto Lilienthal, Octave Chanute, and Samuel Langley made important contributions; Hiram Maxim, the inventor of the machine gun, and Alexander Graham Bell made honest but unsuccessful efforts.

If solving the problem of manned flight was considered important in the time of the Wrights, the problem of making computers more useful to users has been recognized for some years. While computers can run thousands of different applications, most people use computers for only one or two. Increasing the number of applications each user actually uses has long been recognized as desirable. We saw this problem as particularly relevant in software for small portable computers, as they will be used for a variety of applications such as address files, desk calendars, correspondence, to-do lists, etc. Since our initial objective was to develop software for portable computers, we felt we had to attack the problem of getting users to use many different applications head on.

2. THINK ABOUT HOW TO THINK ABOUT THE PROBLEM.

Our natural inclination is to think about the *problem* rather than *how to think* about the problem. Yet, great inventors step back and think about the thinking process itself, especially as it relates to what they are trying to invent. We see this in Wilbur Wright's letters. When one of his correspondents changed his mind and acknowledged that Wilbur was correct about an aspect of flight, Wilbur found him too ready to give in and replied:

> No truth is without some mixture of error, and no error so false but that it possesses some elements of truth. If a man is in too big a hurry to give up an error he is liable to give up some truth with it, and in accepting the arguments of the other man he is sure to get some error with it. Honest argument is merely a process of mutually picking the beams and motes out of each other's eyes so both can see clearly. Men become wise just as they become rich, more by what they *save* than by what they receive. After I get hold of a truth I hate to lose it again, and I like to sift all the truth out before I give up an error.

I find the passage stunning. Wilbur is able to provide clear and cogent thoughts about how hard it is to determine truth, how our reasoning process works, and how it is prone to error. He uses metaphors ("picking the beams and motes" and "men become wise just as they become rich") as much to help him formulate his own thoughts as to communicate them. Certainly a first-rate mind thinking about thinking.

Unless we identify our biases and blinders and how they affect our thought processes, we are unlikely to make an inventive breakthrough; the breakthrough is often the realization that what we assumed to be the case is not. In his book, *The Chip,* T.R. Ried devotes a chapter to how the inventor of the transistor, William Shockley, and the inventors of the integrated circuit, Robert Noyce and Jack Kilby, thought about the thought process in making their inventions. Shockley even wrote an essay entitled "Thinking about Thinking Improves Thinking."

My own thoughts about what was important to user interface design resulted in the first edition of this book. It was through this that I focused on the importance of metaphor to user interface design, and thus developed the card and rack metaphor.

Figure 62: Rarely can one see innovation in prospect— the completed innovation has changed what is in our minds, so we see with different eyes. This photograph gives us that rare opportunity. Can you recognize it? Can you see the potential in it? (See footnote.)

Figure 62 is *Golden Gate before the Bridge*, Ansel Adams, 1932. Now when you look at the photo, the image of the Golden Gate Bridge in your mind influences what you see and makes the image in the photo more obvious and natural.

3. FOCUS ON AN UNCONVENTIONAL, BUT ESSENTIAL, ASPECT OF THE INVENTION.

Early on, Wilbur Wright concluded that there were three essential problems to be solved in conquering flight: getting enough lift from the wings to keep off the ground; getting an engine powerful enough to sustain flight; and providing a means to control the aircraft once it was in flight.

Most airplane inventors focused on the first two problems, mounting expensive engines on the wings of planes, with little thought to controlling a plane in the turbulent air once it flew. The Wrights, however, focused their efforts on control. Early on, they conceived the basic idea of wingwarping: warping the wings in opposite directions on the right and left sides to regain stability or turn left or right. This concept of control informed all they did. They proved that the idea worked with a kite, then an unmanned glider, then a manned glider, and finally with powered flight. It is easier to solve problems early on a smaller scale; a crashed kite costs less money and takes less time to fix than a crashed airplane. And it is easiest to change ideas early on when the financial and ego investment in them is small.

The inventors of the integrated circuit likewise consciously took an unconventional approach to solving the interconnection problem: building all the components on silicon. Working independently, Noyce focused on solving the interconnection problem on the silicon chips, while Kilby focused on making resistors and capacitors with silicon. Since most people try the conventional approach, a conventional solution will be found if it exists, probably by several people at about the same time. While an unconventional approach is less likely to succeed, it is more likely to produce a breakthrough. If an inventor is going to make a significant contribution, it will more likely come from an approach that others are unlikely to pursue. Also, an unconventional

approach is more likely to produce a patentable invention—
something protectable. This may be less important to a large
company that has marketing clout, but it is crucial to the
small inventor if he expects to benefit financially from his
invention.

Making it possible for a computer user to use several different applications is usually treated as a technical problem of
switching between different applications, or a user interface
standards problem, or both. We focused on a third, less conventional problem: creating a rich metaphor that would encompass a wider class of applications. Users are reluctant to
learn new applications, but once a user becomes quite comfortable with one, he will use it for things it hasn't been
designed for. As was pointed out in Chapter 11, rather than
learn a new, more appropriate tool, spreadsheet users use
spreadsheets to write letters; word processor users use word
processors to keep a file of names and addresses; and dBASE
programmers use dBASE for budgeting.

Our objective was to design a more universal metaphor that would support a wide variety of applications. This
was the unconventional edge we would bring to portable
computers in particular, and personal computers in general.
VisiCalc had proven the value of computer metaphors, and
at about this time, Alan Kay, whose group at Xerox PARC invented what has been popularized as the Macintosh technology, independently said that we needed a new computer
metaphor.

Part of our unconventional approach was the display
technology described in Chapter 10. While it was crucial to
small screen displays, we knew it would be useful for larger
screens too. Our first product, Viewdex, was designed for an
Epson HX-20, which had a 4 by 20 display and displayed
one card from a stack of cards. We extended the metaphor
to a card and rack metaphor with Zoomracks. All along, we
attempted to push the boundaries of the card and rack
metaphor so it could support a variety of applications as
special cases while retaining its simplicity and similarity to
real-world analogues.

4. AVOID NONESSENTIAL PARTS OF THE INVENTION.

In deciding what is essential, one also decides what is not essential. The Wrights, for example, did not add wheels on their planes until very late. In 1908, five years after their Kitty Hawk flight, the Wrights first gave public flights and established their mastery of flight to the world. At the time, a French pilot, Earnest Archdeacon, insisted that the French machines were superior to the Wright Flyer because they had wheels and could start without the help of falling weights and rails. Wheels are essential to any commercial airplane; but they are not essential to solving the fundamental problems of flight. However, human nature is such that we are inclined to identify and work on solving the easy problems rather than addressing the difficult ones.

You probably have heard the story about a man who was observed searching under a lamp post. Asked what he was doing, he said he had lost his keys in the bushes. Asked why he was not searching in the bushes, the searcher said, "But this is where the light is." We likewise often search in the easy places and so put wheels on planes that cannot yet fly. It was probably with this in mind that Thomas Edison posted in all his shops the quotation of Sir Joshea Reynolds: "There is no expedient to which a man will not resort to avoid the real labor of thinking."

Getting distracted by the nonessential leads to the problem of feature creep, the adding of more features to a software product. Some of the early German planes had so many features added that they were too heavy to get off the ground. The Wrights focused on the essential. Frederick Lanchester, who had just published the pioneering study *Aerodynamics*, wrote after seeing the Wright machine in 1908:

> The Wright machine is astonishing in its simplicity— not to say apparent crudity of detail— it is almost a matter of surprise that it holds together.... [The Wright machine] appears not to

come to pieces but continues to fly day after day without showing any signs of weakness.

In the process of developing Zoomracks, we similarly left off the metaphorical wheels. The menus and word processor were not state of the art, and the graphics and our programming language were primitive. But these were not essential to the metaphor. Like the wheels of the airplane, they are easy to identify as necessary and easy to add, but adding them diverts attention from refining the central vision. Such details are best left until the central vision is refined, so that that vision better informs the design details. We tried to solve user interface problems in the conceptual model and visual domains rather than in the language domain. We designed Zoomracks features, such as its Help and macro facilities as an integral part of the metaphor, just as Louis Sullivan designed electric lights in his Chicago Amphitheater to be integral to its structure. I like to think of Zoomracks as being "astonishing in its simplicity," while I have to admit to its "crudity of detail."

5. USE METAPHORS
TO AID YOUR THINKING.

It may be obvious today that flying machines should look like birds, but it was not in 1900; other designs seemed just as likely. At that time, dirigibles seemed more promising than heavier-than-air flying machines; the Wrights' initial interest in flight came from a toy helicopter. The term *flying machine* invokes the image of a machine rather than of a bird, and early flying machines took on many forms. The Wrights observed birds to discover how they control flight, and invented wingwarping to do the same thing. But the value of metaphor is as an *aid* to thinking. The Wrights' first aircraft was a biplane, the design of which is not suggested by analogues in nature. Even those insects that do have two sets of wings have one set in back of the other, rather than one set above the other. Initially, the Wrights did not see how to implement wingwarping efficiently. Then another metaphor came to their rescue. One night, Wilbur found himself twisting a long, narrow, empty box from which he had just removed a bicycle inner tube to sell to a customer. He realized that the box could be easily twisted, yet remained rigid. It was the basic idea he needed to implement wingwarping and it necessitated two sets of wings, one above the other.

Similarly, metaphor is so influential to the Zoomracks design that Chapter 11 is devoted to the role of metaphor in software design.

6. INVENTION REQUIRES A TOTAL WORKING SYSTEM.

The Wright brothers' major focus may have been on control of flight, but they developed a total system: a heavier-than-air flying machine. In the process, they had to solve many detail problems: They found Langley's published experimental data on lift and drag to be in error, so they built one of the first wind tunnels and made their own measurements. They made advances in propellers, wing shape, and overall design that resulted in a complete working plane. Their plane flew because they kept solving problems until it could fly.

Thomas Edison also invented a total system. As mentioned in Chapter 11, his invention was less the electric light bulb than the invention of a system to generate, distribute, and use electricity, of which one important part was the light bulb. Edison used the metaphor of the gas distribution system to understand the electrical distribution system he needed. He even studied it to see how billing was done. Earlier inventors like Swan invented bulbs that worked at 10 volts without an understanding of the context in which they must work. Edison realized that for electric light to be reliable, bulbs had to run in parallel rather than in series. They also had to operate at a high voltage so that electricity could be distributed to them economically. The price of copper wire forced Edison to search for an electric light bulb that worked at 100 volts. The total vision of the distribution system informed the details of the light bulb.

In developing Zoomracks, we too had a total system we were trying to invent: a new computer metaphor. To work, it had to be embodied in a useful product. Much of the detail in Zoomracks was required to develop that product. We built a back-end database, a menu system, and a redisplay system to display the cards on the screen. Some of these details were innovative in themselves; others were not. But all were needed to make a total system, one that could work in the marketplace.

7. INVENTIONS ARE NOT DEVELOPED IN A VACUUM.

Isaac Newton said, "If I have seen further it is by standing on ye shoulders of giants." Progress is based on building on the work of others. If the Wrights were adamant in defending their own contribution to flight, they were ready to acknowledge their indebtedness to Lilienthal and others. The Wrights built on work going as far back as John Smeaton's 1759 equations for designing windmills.

The card and rack metaphor was not invented in a vacuum either. An important influence on my thinking was VisiCalc, the first spreadsheet. Alan Kay and his vision of Dynabook were an important influence. The Macintosh and other technology can be traced back to his pioneering work. D.W. Griffith and Walt Disney were influential in shaping my thinking about software design. Others, too, have influenced my thinking; one never knows all the sources.

8. PASSION
IS A MOTIVATING FORCE.

In an early letter, Wilbur Wright wrote, "For some years I have been afflicted with the belief that flight is possible to man. My disease has increased in severity and I feel that it will soon cost me an increased amount of money if not my life." The Wrights' interest in making money developed only later, when they realized that others were making money from their invention.

In my own case, I passionately believed that the rack metaphor had something important to offer computing and I continued to develop it over a long time. In developing HyperCard, Bill Atkinson was driven by a somewhat different passion— to make it easier to develop graphical Macintosh applications. While cooler, rational people make the incremental advances, those with a more passionate state of mind make the more fundamental ones.

9. MUCH OF
THE DEVELOPMENT IS
OUT OF THE CENTER OF ACTION.

For those working on the problem of flight, the Wrights were mysterious figures who did not let others observe their flights. While they avoided publicity as they developed their airplane, they arranged to be observed by reputable people such as the local banker and to have an account of their flight published in the obscure *Beekeepers' Journal* to establish priority. When the press wanted to see a flight, the Wrights invited them over but were unable to fly because of technical problems. The next day, when the press was no longer there, they fixed the problems and flew. Just chance?

We deliberately started small with limited financing from individual investors. New ideas are best pioneered without too much money and the pressures that come with it. The IBM PC market looked like it would have distracted us from the essential problem of working with users to develop a broad, unifying metaphor, so we ported Zoom-racks to the Atari ST and focused our primary marketing efforts there. We proved the metaphor on the Atari ST: A user survey completed the same month in which HyperCard was introduced showed that 91 Zoomracks users used it for a total of 125 different applications— an average of 5.2 applications each— at home, school, business, and government. Our plane might not have had wheels, but we knew it flew. If we had focused our early marketing efforts in the crowded PC marketplace, we think there would have been too many alternative solutions vying for users' attention for the card and rack metaphor to get a fair chance.

10. THE INVENTION
TAKES TIME TO BE RECOGNIZED.

The Wright brothers first demonstrated controlled flight in December 1903 at Kitty Hawk. Afterwards, the Wrights informed the local press; but dirigibles had flown for much longer times, so, according to Fred Howard, "A flight of less than a minute in North Carolina could not possibly be of interest to readers of the [Dayton] *Journal* or its city editor— or the Associated Press." The Wrights' accomplishment went virtually unnoticed for several years. At the time, few were sophisticated enough to understand what constituted a real flight.

There was a day— August 9, 1908— and a place— a racetrack near Le Mans, France— when the world recognized that the problem of flight had been conquered and that the Wrights had done it. By that time, flying exhibitions were common in Europe and flights of several miles had been made. But they were uncontrolled. A plane would take off, go in a straight line, or at least try to, and then land if it found a landing spot ahead. Any wind created serious problems.

Wilbur Wright took off, banked to the right, and headed for some trees. The crowd— used to the uncontrolled planes— gasped, expecting him to crash. Wilbur banked to the right again and circled the field twice and landed. Total flight time: one minute and forty-five seconds— a little less than twice the time of their 1903 flight, and five years later. The crowd went wild; the plane had flown like a bird; Wilbur had control. The observers could appreciate control because its absence was the norm, just as one can see white only with black for contrast.

The press pins events on the day's bulletin board; only later are they woven into the fabric of history. Just as the Kitty Hawk flight was not appreciated when it occurred, the trade press barely mentioned Texas Instruments' 1959 introduction of the integrated circuit. The opinion at the time was that three major problems would prevent the acceptance of the integrated

Figure 63: The Wright plane's first flight at Kitty Hawk in 1903.
Library of Congress.

circuit: First, silicon was inferior to Nichrome for resistors and inferior to Mylar for capacitors; second, transistor production was unreliable—only about ten percent of the transistors in an integrated circuit would work; third, integrated circuits would threaten the jobs of existing designers. These criticisms were, Jack Kilby, the inventor, observed, "difficult to overcome because they were true."

Similarly, the computer press did not treat Zoomracks' card and rack metaphor seriously. *PC Week,* the trade weekly for IBM and IBM-compatible computers, did not run a story even after being given a demonstration at their offices. Three years later, after we placed an advertisement advising HyperCard developers of our patents in *MacWeek,* a magazine for the Macintosh marketplace, *PC Week* ran *two* stories. It has been said that Zoomracks was "ugly," and it is a criticism that is difficult to overcome because—when judging by the visual standards of HyperCard—it is true. However, Zoomracks was not designed to be pretty, but to address deeper user interface design issues.

11. IT TAKES A LOT OF PERSISTENCE TO GET AN INVENTION ACCEPTED.

The Wrights tried to sell their plane to the U.S. government without success. Next, they approached foreign governments—again with little success. The Wrights were willing to demonstrate a working airplane, provided there was a commitment to purchase if they met benchmarks. But they were reluctant to demonstrate their plane without assurance that the buyer was real. Their discussions with the U.S. and foreign governments went on for years, but did not get serious until the Wrights' 1908 flights brought them public recognition as inventors of the airplane.

The card and rack metaphor also took time to get accepted. I conceived the initial ideas in 1981, and started our company in 1982. Our first product, Viewdex, was delivered into a management reorganization at one company in January 1984. The first version of Zoomracks was delivered into a reorganization at another company in December 1984 and was not accepted. We raised additional funds and introduced Zoomracks on the PC in September 1985. We then ported it to the just-introduced Atari ST. The Atari ST sales generated enough cash flow to fund one major upgrade, which we introduced in November 1986. HyperCard was introduced in August 1987, but it was not until December 1989 that Apple licensed our patents.

12. COMPETITORS, LACKING THE SAME VISION, WILL LIKELY MISS ESSENTIAL POINTS.

While the Wrights improved their plane from 1903, when they first flew at Kitty Hawk, to 1908, when they first gave public exhibitions, others flew planes for longer and longer distances. Octave Chanute tried to get the Wrights to enter contests lest they be left out, but the Wrights refused, knowing that their competitors' planes lacked control. Meanwhile, knowing that when the rest of the aviation pioneers saw how wingwarping worked they would modify their planes to use it, the Wrights refined and improved their own airplane. The Wrights were right; competitors quickly copied their ideas.

When HyperCard came out, we felt after talking to people about it that it missed on two fundamental points. The first point is a general one of vision, emphasis, and target audience. HyperCard and Zoomracks can be viewed as both productivity tools for end users and as tool boxes to build applications. HyperCard is more a toolbox for developing applications; Zoomracks is more a productivity tool. Except for canned applications, HyperCard's audience is mostly third-party developers and enthusiasts, rather than end users. Zoomracks was designed for end users and for the minds of those users in which we wanted to construct a mental model of a powerful unifying metaphor that they could take from one application to another.

HyperCard focused on capabilities that Zoomracks provided only in rudimentary form (graphics and a more sophisticated programming language) or capabilities that Zoomracks did not have (buttons and tear-off palettes). Zoomracks, in contrast, tried to to add capability within the metaphor itself. The results of the difference in emphasis are as follows.

HyperCard developers have to follow guidelines consciously to achieve consistency between applications, but the applications are more attractive; Zoomracks users are unconsciously constrained by the metaphor to enforce consistency between applications.

Additionally, HyperCard assists the user in building good-looking applications rather than applications that are easy to change; Zoomracks facilitates the building of applications that are easy to change rather than good looking.

Further, HyperCard is disk-based and requires substantial overhead to support its graphics, requires much larger files, and operates at a slower speed than Zoomracks, which is RAM-based.

Because it supports so many features, HyperCard has a more complex conceptual model. While the Zoomracks manual is 170 pages long, Apple has written a HyperCard user manual (258 pages), a HyperCard Script Language Guide (316 pages), and a HyperCard Stack Design Guidelines Manual (226 pages) to support HyperCard. The developer's edition of HyperCard 2.0 comes with five manuals totaling more than 1400 pages. This comparison is not entirely fair, as HyperCard supports many more features than Zoomracks and the HyperCard manuals duplicate information because they serve different purposes; but the disparity in size shows the cost of feature creep.

The second essential point that I think HyperCard misses on is specific. The rack metaphor, as opposed to the stack metaphor, provides a familiar, generic mechanism to unite the concept of cards and the concept of lists, letting the user view many cards at once. It provides a natural overview and navigation mechanism. With HyperCard, the user can see only one card at a time. Lists and navigation are not inherent in the metaphor, but must be created ad hoc for each application and will likely be done differently to suit the needs of the different applications.

There are good reasons to make the tradeoffs Hyper-Card made and to emphasize the visual aspects of the metaphor. Apple's market position is in graphical user interfaces. Still, as this is written, HyperCard's impact is not as strong as expected, given its early promise and substantial backing from Apple, which bundles it with every computer. Zoomracks was marketed with almost no funds on the ill-fated Atari computer and achieved a base of happy users who used it for a wide variety of applications. In my opinion, HyperCard lost its center, its unifying metaphor. As a result, it is difficult to learn and use as a productivity tool and inefficient as a development tool.

To users, the features and capabilities of a computer can be like a box of Christmas tree ornaments, wonderful to look at, but not yet organized or useful. In inventing the card and rack metaphor, we attempted to invent a Christmas tree as a structure to organize and present the ornaments. We spent most of our effort designing the tree, and with limited funds, we had to do with poorer ornaments— sort of like threading popcorn on a string or making chains of looped strips of colored paper. And then HyperCard comes out with a less well-designed tree, but with ornaments to dazzle the eye.

Of course, this is my own view. Software design involves making tradeoffs and every tradeoff has both its good and bad aspects. Bill Atkinson's vision was shaped by different pressures, different experiences, and a different context. If I differ with him on emphasis, I see his contribution to the genre as important.

13. ONCE BASIC IDEAS ARE PROVEN, COMPETITORS WILL USE THEM.

A patent is, in essence, a contract between the patentee and the government by which the patentee agrees to make his invention public and in return gets exclusive rights to its use for 17 years. This benefits society by disseminating new ideas, encouraging development of and investment in those ideas because they are now private property, and encouraging innovation by motivating competitors to invent around the patent. It also changes the nature of potential disputes from personal and hard-to-prove issues of theft of ideas to objective issues of whether something described and claimed in a patent was previously known.

If the test is an objective one based on the published patent, the usual case is that the earliest infringers of a patent have had exposure to the patented ideas. The Wrights showed and discussed their work with Augustus Herring and Glenn Curtiss, among others. Once people saw that wingwarping and other features worked, they modified their own planes accordingly. Most airplane designers copied from those who copied from the Wrights. Once an idea is proven to work, people who use it are often unaware of its origin.

Apple similarly had exposure to Zoomracks. Some of its ideas were described in Chapter 10 of this book, which was first published in 1984 and read by several people at Apple, including, I believe, Bill Atkinson. Apple signed a nondisclosure agreement to see Zoomracks in January 1985, two and a half years before HyperCard was introduced. We introduced Zoomracks and published an article describing it in October 1985. Bill Atkinson was told not to look at Zoomracks while developing HyperCard and did not do so until nine months before HyperCard was introduced. Though HyperCard was far along in its final form by then, he made changes that were material to one patent. All told, at least six people close to the HyperCard project saw Zoom-racks before HyperCard's introduction. When I showed Zoomracks to Alan Kay, he was kind enough to let me attribute the phrase "an important new metaphor by the author of the best book on user interface design" to him, and that phrase has appeared on our package since its 1985 introduction. So it is not surprising that the ideas of Zoom-racks were "in the air" at Apple Computer at the time Bill Atkinson was pursuing his vision in developing HyperCard.

I do not believe that Bill Atkinson or anyone else at Apple set out to copy Zoomracks (but I am not prepared to be so generous about others copying HyperCard). Bill Atkinson is driven to push the state of the art and his own vision, rather than clone what others have shown to be successful. His different vision accounts for the substantial differences between Zoomracks and HyperCard. These differences are what intellectual property laws are designed to foster: the laws promote diversity by motivating people to find diverse solutions. The user is better off because Hypercard and Zoomracks pushed the idea of the card and stack metaphor in different, albeit complementary, directions.

14. TO BENEFIT FINANCIALLY, PROTECT YOUR RIGHTS.

For an inventor, patents are the normal method of protecting one's rights. The basic problem an inventor has in defining his patent rights is that he must write a set of claims. Claims are rules that cannot be broken without the patent holder's permission. The problem of the patentee (and his patent lawyer) is to define rules so as to include what he did, what has not been done in the past, and what potential infringers will want to do. Since breaking the rules means paying the patent holder money, and since people are adept at avoiding rules (designing around the patent) or showing rules to be unfair (arguing that the rule includes things anticipated by the prior art), the patentee's job is tricky. Much of what the Wright brothers did, while it advanced the state of the art, was hard to patent. It was either easy to design around, arguably obvious given the prior art, or hard to make a rule about. The Wrights decided to patent wingwarping, the bending of the wings to control flight, as they believed it would be difficult to make an airplane that did not use that principle. They were right. Wingwarping is used in all fixed-wing aircraft since that time, usually manifested in ailerons, its modern equivalent.

The patent rules are not always easy for the inventor to work with, but it is the way the system works. Alexander Graham Bell, having done a poor job of documenting his invention of the telephone, spent years in court defending his rights. Stung by the experience, he kept detailed records of his every thought in his attempt to invent a flying machine, which failed dismally.

The ultimate question in deciding if a patent is valid and has been infringed is, "What would a jury find?" If you are the first to invent something, and patent your invention, you are doing what people expect. Juries expect this and focus less on the details of claim analysis than on the overall story of what happened. Who was first? Did the inventor work long and hard? Did the infringer develop independently or copy? If the inventor has a good story to tell, he will win his case. The Wrights won all of their cases.

We, too, resorted to patents for protection. We realized that developing new technologies is risky and takes lots of time. Since we were attacking a user interface problem, a solution, to be successful, would have to be simple and obvious, at least in retrospect. And if it is simple, it is easy to copy. So we protected ourselves with patents.

Like the Wrights, we found it difficult to protect our work. Patent claims are written in "patentese" and it took time to understand what the claims meant and what protection they actually provided. When I first saw HyperCard, I did not understand how to interpret patent claims and so I did not think it directly infringed our patents, but it seemed obvious that HyperCard was so close to Zoomracks that it presented, at minimum, a mine field for developers. It seemed at the very least that HyperCard was a Disneyland put down in the middle of my intellectual property. Only later, when I understood that patent claims should be interpreted as broadly as possible as long as they excluded the prior art, did I see that HyperCard directly infringed at least one patent. Only later did I understand the doctrine of equivalence and contributory infringement.

Arguments for and against patents and copyrights have been made many times and in many places since they were first granted in 1474 in Venice. Some people object to patents and copyrights, arguing that progress consists of standing on the shoulders of others and that to charge for those shoulders would retard progress. History shows, however, that inventors and writers are more likely to persist if they are fairly compensated for their work. The Constitutional Convention considered the matter and reached the verdict represented in Article 1, Section 8 of the Constitution, part of which reads:

> The Congress shall have a power to promote the progress of science and the useful arts by securing for a limited time to authors and inventors the exclusive right to their respective writings and discoveries.

The fact that almost all of the industrial world recognizes intellectual property rights in general and patents in particular speaks to the value of patents in practice.

15. SIMPLE CHANGES CAN MAKE A FUNDAMENTAL DIFFERENCE.

It was relatively easy to add the Wrights' control system to other airplanes once its value was recognized. Other work the Wrights did, such as determining the optimum shape of propellers and wings, was also easy to adopt in other aircraft. Yet these simple changes had fundamental effects on the aerodynamics of the aircraft. Once the basic idea is understood and proven, the resulting change in emphasis informs small changes to achieve a major effect.

One of Zoomracks' contributions was the use of the metaphorical framework of cards and racks to support a wide variety of applications, as described in Chapter 11. Once these fundamental ideas are exposed, implementing them is not that difficult, yet they result in a fundamentally different vision and can have a major effect on the product's success.

16. INVENTORS HAVE TO FIGHT TO HAVE THEIR RIGHTS RESPECTED.

Friends of the Wrights wanted them to enter competitions, and they could easily have won many. But they would have been competing against flyers who infringed their patents, so the Wrights refused, feeling that competing with the infringers would acknowledge them as equals. Wilbur wrote to a friend, "It is our view that morally the world owes its almost universal use of our system of lateral control entirely to us. It is also our opinion that legally it owes us." In a letter to Chanute, Wilbur wrote:

> You apparently concede to us no right to compensation for the solution of a problem ages old except such as is granted to persons who had no part in producing the invention. That is to say, we may compete with mountebanks for a chance to earn money in the mountebank business, but are entitled to nothing whatever for past work as inventors.

I understand what the Wrights went through. When you first see someone using your invention, you don't know what to do. Someone else might have invented it first, and you are not clear of the extent of your patent protection. So you try to track down prior art. In my own case, the more I looked for prior art and didn't find it, the more convinced I became that morally my invention included the card and stack metaphor. And the more I understood how to analyze patents and the protection they provide, the more I became convinced that I had legal rights as well.

Just as the Wrights were pressured to enter competitions, I was pressured to be just another HyperCard developer and not press for recognition of my rights. Like the Wrights, I insisted my rights be respected. As a result, I antagonized many. Early on, I brought my patents to the attention of Apple to no effect. Since Apple was unwilling to discuss the issue, I brought it to the attention of third-party developers who were investing time and money in developing HyperCard products and who could be liable for infringement penalties. I had based my business on the assumption that my patent rights would be respected, so when Apple would not discuss the patents with us, I put HyperCard developers on notice, lest our rights deteriorate. Since I empathized with the small developers, I offered royalty-free licenses to third-party developers if they would make their products compatible with HyperRacks, our HyperCard add-on. Most ignored me. Some got mad at me. They had enough problems without having to deal with my patents. Some thought I was trying to rip them off. Many were surprised that software is patentable. I understand their feelings.

The situation was similar to the one in football after Theodore Roosevelt forced the adoption of the forward pass. By 1913, it had been legal for a few years, but was not an important part of the game. The few times it was used, the receiver stopped and waited for the ball to be thrown to him and, standing still, he was immediately tackled. That summer, two players from a minor midwestern team practiced throwing and catching passes on the run. In October, they played Army and used the forward pass. Army lost 34 to 13. With that game, the forward pass, its receiver, Knute Rockne, and Notre Dame changed football and entered history. Army didn't say, "No fair. We didn't think you could catch a forward pass on the run." But software developers who complain when patents are brought to their attention are just saying, "No fair. We didn't think you could patent software." It may be understandable to complain halfway through a game when one realizes that he didn't understand the rules. But it is poor sportsmanship.

I have worked for several startups in my life. Most did not make it. I have developed many systems that never made it into the market. This is not unusual—risk and uncertainty are the nature of innovation. If you invest the time, money, and effort in playing a game and are lucky enough to have a winner, a patent lets you collect your winnings.

A patent is not without problems for the patentee. If a patent is invalid, someone need only show the relevant prior art; and it is illegal for the patent holder to attempt to enforce an invalid patent. I was concerned that Apple could have found prior art that would have invalidated my patents. I brought my patents to Apple's attention, but they did not show me any prior art, so I felt it was only reasonable to bring my patents to potential infringers so they could make their own evaluation and take appropriate steps. I wrote letters to the 114 largest Apple customers, advising them of my patents.

In *A Man for All Seasons,* Sir Thomas More is asked by King Henry VIII to declare that he believes the King's divorce and remarriage to be valid. The penalties provided by law for speaking his conscience will be severe. Treason is punishable by death. Thomas More therefore remains silent and is brought to trial. The prosecution points out that the world interprets his silence as meaning that he thinks the king's divorce is invalid. Thomas More replies, "The world may construe according to its wit, but the law must construe according to the law." The same is true of patents.

If a patent holder is circumspect and unwilling to directly accuse a product of infringement, but instead brings a patent to someone's attention, it is because he has concerns similar to Thomas More's. The penalties the law provides for speaking one's mind can be severe. Someone accused of infringement can file suit for a declaratory judgment to determine if infringement occurred, against which the patent holder would have to defend himself at considerable expense.

The situation is complex in that what the end user does affects whether infringement occurs. Patent cases are rarely open and shut; the existence of undiscovered prior art, the breadth of interpretation of the patent, the doctrine of equivalents in cases where literal infringement does not occur, and issues of contributory infringement and inducement to infringe all affect the location of the boundary between infringement and noninfringement. A patent holder will select his strongest case to pursue first, which might mean suing an end user who does something that much more clearly infringes and is simpler to prove in court. Meanwhile, it is both common courtesy and good legal tactics to place potential infringers on notice. It is not the patent holder's business to draw a bright line and tell others how to avoid infringing his patent. Avoiding infringement is the responsibility of the potential infringer, whose task is simpler. The potential infringer need not know where the line is, but merely that he has not crossed it.

Most patentees prefer to spend their time developing and selling products rather than suing people. Furthermore, it only makes sense to bring an infringement case when the damages are known to be substantial and there are assets to pay any judgment. Taking a patent case through trial costs at least one million dollars and can cost ten million dollars or more. A patent holder with shallow pockets is at a severe disadvantage in such a case. So patentholders bring their patents to the attention of potential infringers and let them draw their own conclusions and act appropriately. *The world may construe according to its wit, but the law must construe according to the law.*

Recent products such as ToolBook (a Windows-based product in the HyperCard genre) are seen as having been inspired by HyperCard and as using similar, though not identical, metaphors. As a small company having incurred the costs and risks of developing the original metaphor, and having proven it works, we now face competitors who have greater financial and marketing clout and who have products incorporating enhanced capabilities that HyperCard brought to the metaphor, while we lack the money to add these capabilities to Zoomracks. Without patents, we would be bankrupt. Our patents are a tool we can use to get our rights respected. We have the right to bring our patents to the attention of possible infringers. This puts infringers on notice so that liability will be accruing, with possible treble damages for egregious infringement. This can also have the effect of discouraging people from developing applications on platforms where the patent situation is unclear. In the case of my patents, potential users will want to answer the question, "If Apple needed a license to these patents, don't I need one too?"

17. INVENTORS BECOME AN OBJECT OF DERISION AND THEIR PATENTS ARE ATTACKED.

Many tried to design around the Wrights' patents on wingwarping. Ailerons, the modern equivalent, were one such attempt. One lawyer made a study of aeronautical patents and wrote an article concluding that ailerons did not infringe the patents and were "indisputably a public right."

The courts held that ailerons infringed.

One of the two reasons Fred Howard gives for writing *Wilbur and Orville* when so many other biographies exist is that they mention "next to nothing about the court battles over patents that caused the brothers to be vilified by many of their contemporaries as money-grubbing monopolists." Some quotes from this biography portray the climate they faced:

> [There was] the fear that the future development of aviation would be seriously impeded if Wilbur and Orville should seek to wring a profit from their basic patent by taking infringers to court.
>
> It was unthinkable that Wilbur and Orville should be allowed to collect royalties from aviators and manufacturers until their patent expired in

> 1923 just because they had been the first men in the world to maintain equilibrium in the air by warping the wings of their Flyer.
>
> Once the suits against infringers of the Wright patent were underway, Wilbur and Orville were fair game for vilifiers and detractors.

If we changed just a few words in the above quotations, they would describe the attitude of many about software patents today. At the time, Wilbur defended himself by saying:

> When a couple of flying machine inventors fish, metaphorically speaking, in waters where hundreds had previously fished...and spending years of time and thousands of dollars, finally succeed in making a catch, there are people who think it a pity that the courts should give orders that the rights of the inventors shall be respected and that those who wish to enjoy the feast shall contribute something to pay the fishers.

Whenever a fundamental patent spawns an industry, the claim arises that enforcing the patent will destroy the industry: millions for PR, millions for lawyers, but not one cent for the inventor.

It is not just patent rights, but other intellectual property rights that people are unwilling to recognize. In expecting my rights to be respected, I am only following the lead of Bill Gates of Microsoft who suffered from and called to account those who would "steal" his intellectual property rights in software. In the early days of personal computers, he wrote an open letter to computer hobbyists saying, "Most of you steal your software" and "The thing you do is theft." In his letter, shown below, you can see that he faced the problem so many software pioneers face.

Since Bill Gates wrote that letter, the software industry has matured to the point where we recognize that making copies of programs without paying for them is software piracy. But it has not yet matured to the point other

February 3, 1976

<u>An Open Letter to Hobbyists</u>

To me, the most critical thing in the hobby market right now is the lack of good software courses, books and software itself. Without good software and an owner who understands programming, a hobby computer is wasted. Will quality software be written for the hobby market?

Almost a year ago, Paul Allen and myself, expecting the hobby market to expand, hired Monte Davidoff and developed Altair BASIC. Though the initial work took only two months, the three of us have spent most of the last year documenting, improving and adding features to BASIC. Now we have 4K, 8K, EXTENDED, ROM and DISK BASIC. The value of the computer time we have used exceeds $40,000.

The feedback we have gotten from the hundreds of people who say they are using BASIC has all been positive. Two surprising things are apparent, however. 1) Most of these "users" never bought BASIC (less than 10% of all Altair owners have bought BASIC), and 2) The amount of royalties we have received from sales to hobbyists makes the time spent of Altair BASIC worth less than $2 an hour.

Why is this? As the majority of hobbyists must be aware, most of you steal your software. Hardware must be paid for, but software is something to share. Who cares if the people who worked on it get paid?

Is this fair? One thing you don't do by stealing software is get back at MITS for some problem you may have had. MITS doesn't make money selling software. The royalty paid to us, the manual, the tape and the overhead make it a break-even operation. One thing you do do is prevent good software from being written. Who can afford to do professional work for nothing? What hobbyist can put 3-man years into programming, finding all bugs, documenting his product and distribute for free? The fact is, no one besides us has invested a lot of money in hobby software. We have written 6800 BASIC, and are writing 8080 APL and 6800 APL, but there is very little incentive to make this software available to hobbyists. Most directly, the thing you do is theft.

What about the guys who re-sell Altair BASIC, aren't they making money on hobby software? Yes, but those who have been reported to us may lose in the end. They are the ones who give hobbyists a bad name, and should be kicked out of any club meeting they show up at.

I would appreciate letters from any one who wants to pay up, or has a suggestion or comment. Just write me at 1180 Alvarado SE, #114, Albuquerque, New Mexico, 87108. Nothing would please me more than being able to hire ten programmers and deluge the hobby market with good software.

Bill Gates

Bill Gates
General Partner, Micro-Soft

industries have in respecting patents. In our own case, people have derided our patent. One columnist headlined our royalty-free license for third-party developers as "Patently Obnoxious." I wonder what he would have said if we wanted money? Everyone is quick to say that there exists prior art that invalidates a patent, but slow to show it. Similarly, lawyers will be happy to write opinions of noninfringement. I am reminded of the exchange between Glendower and Hotspur in *Henry IV, Part I* with which we began Chapter 10:

> GLENDOWER. I can call spirits from the vasty
> deep.
>
> HOTSPUR. Why, so can I, or so can any man;
> But will they come when you do call
> for them?

When Eastman Kodak came out with an instant camera to compete with Polaroid's, it called the spirits from the vasty deep and obtained a legal opinion that their camera did not infringe Polaroid patents. Polaroid sued and got an injunction against future sales. Eastman Kodak has spent about 500 million dollars to buy back infringing cameras it sold to consumers, and must pay Polaroid 909 million dollars in damages. Total cost of patent infringement— 1.4 billion dollars. Plus legal fees.

A lawyer for ToolBook wrote me saying that they had a legal opinion that their product doesn't infringe our patents. I suggested that if they really believed that opinion they would be willing to warrant in writing that their product and applications built with it do not infringe our patents, or at least specify rules and hold harmless the developers of programs that follow the rules. I received no response.

The prior art Apple showed us as part of the settlement agreement was not close to our invention. And we were

Figure 64: Bill Gates's "Open Letter to Hobbyists."

Reprinted from the *Homebrew Computer Club Newsletter,* Robert R. Reiling, Editor.

not impressed with the infringement analysis Apple had prepared. I *was* impressed by the check that Apple wrote, especially considering the amount of corporate ego invested in "inventing" HyperCard.

I was not impressed either when the president of Mediagenics told me that Focal Point, one of the leading HyperCard products, didn't infringe. After I reached a settlement with Apple that covered third-party developers like Mediagenics, I was impressed to hear that Mediagenics was expecting to be sued and was prepared to settle. As every salesman knows, the reacting customer is the buying customer. As the patent holder knows, the more someone denigrates a patent, the more concerned he is about infringement.

Orville Wright said, "It is astonishing to what lengths propaganda will be used when financial interests are involved!" *The Wall Street Journal* and the *New York Times* ran stories saying patents are ruining the software industry. According to the *New York Times*, Ken Wasch, the Executive Director of the Software Publishers Associations (SPA), likened the licensing of software patents to "extortion" and said, "I can't think of a single software company that thinks the proliferation of patents is a good thing." The presidents of six software publishers who had patents, including SPA members, signed a pro-software patent letter to the editor in response to Mr. Wasch's comments.

Mr. Wasch's position may be useful for some of the larger SPA members who like the status quo and want to incorporate freely the innovations of smaller companies, but I cannot let his position go unchallenged.

The effect of patents is to increase the revenues and profitability of the software industry as a whole. Where a patented invention is valuable, software licenses will increase costs to publishers. But that cost is for something valuable to the end user, and so publishers can pass that cost on in their prices after adding a profit margin.

While Mr. Wasch has not explicitly said, "You don't have to respect software patents," in falsely saying that no software companies like software patents and in using the word "extortion," he gives aid, comfort, and respectability to those who would infringe software patents.

Has Mr. Wasch considered the implications of his position? The most that might happen is that Congress might pass a law eliminating software as patentable subject matter. Such a law would not take away existing patent rights; ex post facto laws are rarely passed. However, making software unpatentable is unlikely: historically, Congress has broadened, rather than narrowed, patentable subject matter. It is not the futility of Mr. Wasch's campaign that concerns me, but the cost to those who act on what he says.

Mr. Wasch's position reminds me of what happened to the South in the Civil War. The South fought the Civil War to preserve the status quo—the economic advantages of slavery. The large landowners were the major beneficiaries of slavery. The great masses had little to gain from slavery, but the issue was framed as "states' rights" and hundreds of thousands of people willingly fought and died for "states' rights." It was a rich man's war, but a poor man's fight.

Similarly, large software companies are concerned by the threat that software patents pose to the status quo. But when the issue is framed as "patents are bad for the small software developer," the mass of software developers who are naive about the practical realities of business, patents, and the legal system don't understand that they are being had. The problem for the small developer is not so much that he will innocently infringe patents; rather, it is that the small developer will fail to seek patent protection when he does something really innovative, or that he will blithely march through fields marked, "Warning: Mined with Patents."

Mr. Wasch called to tell me he was incensed at the letter I wrote to HyperCard developers that said, in effect, "Warning: Mined with Patents." He wanted me to send him a list of the people I sent it to. As he is the executive director of an organization founded to protect software as intellectual property and someone who makes himself available to the press to be quoted on software-intellectual property issues, I would expect that he would know I must assert my rights lest I lose them. I told him I would be glad to cooperate with the SPA to resolve the issue of my patent rights and would appreciate any help he could provide, and I sent him my mailing list. Nothing happened.

But the thing that most disturbs me about Mr. Wasch's position is that it can so easily be turned against SPA members. If the SPA will not acknowledge and respect the legitimate intellectual property rights of others, how can it expect others to acknowledge and respect its members' intellectual property rights? Doesn't Mr. Wasch's position give aid and comfort to anyone who wants to pirate a copy of software when he sees its price as "extortion"? Doesn't this undermine the SPA's very reason for existence— the prevention of software piracy? Whenever you see an SPA ad on software piracy, ask yourself what Mr. Wasch's position on patent piracy is and remember the Golden Rule.

Richard Stallman founded the League for Programming Freedom to make software unpatentable. This is not the first time an organization has used its influence to make software unpatentable. In the 1960s when IBM bundled software with their computers, the IBM party line at the time was that software should be freely available and not patentable. It would not have been in IBM's interest for a competitor to have the exclusive rights to a major software patent. J. W. Birkenstock, during his tenure as Vice President for Commercial Development at IBM, headed up a presidential commission to study the patent system. It issued a report in 1968 recommending that software not be patentable subject matter because *the paperwork on the patent office would be too burdensome.* The effect was to delay the practical patentability of software and deny the constitutional rights of patent protection to almost a generation of software developers. However, the Supreme Court in Diamond *vs* Diehr in 1981 ruled that software was patentable. The Stallman-IBM-Wasch position on software patents has been seriously considered, put into practical effect, and rejected by the courts.

18. MANY, INCLUDING FRIENDS AND MAJOR FIGURES IN THE INDUSTRY, ARE UNWILLING TO ACKNOWLEDGE THE INVENTOR'S RIGHTS.

Octave Chanute supported research into solving the problem of flight and had a long and helpful correspondence with the Wrights, yet later Chanute denied the significance of the Wrights' contribution and felt that they should not collect patent royalties. Wilbur Wright wrote him:

> It is rather amusing, after having been called fools and fakers for six or eight years, to find now that people knew exactly how to fly all the time. People who had not the least idea of flying until within the last year or two now attempt to write books stating what the situation of the flying problem was in 1900 and 1901, when we made our first experiments at Kitty Hawk. In view of our experiences in 1901 it is amusing to hear them tell that the science of aerodynamics had been reduced to a very exact basis, so that anyone could calculate without difficulty the lift and drift of aeroplane surfaces. After the real truth had been discovered, old experiments seemed to have an importance in value sometimes which they did not have at the time.

The Smithsonian Institution took 38 years to recognize that the Wrights were the first to achieve controlled flight. One of its directors, Langley, had built an early machine that never flew, although it did belly flop into the Potomac. Later, the Smithsonian hired Glenn Curtiss to reconstruct and fly Langley's plane to show that it could have flown before the Wrights' first flight. Curtiss, involved in patent litigation with the Wrights, was clearly biased and made several aerodynamically meaningful changes to the aircraft. Even so, it collapsed on takeoff.

EPILOGUE

In 1928, the Smithsonian still refused to acknowledge that the Wrights were the first to fly. Orville insisted that if the 1903 Kitty Hawk Flyer could not be displayed in the Smithsonian as the first airplane to achieve controlled flight, it would not be displayed at all in the United States. He sent it to a London Museum. Charles Lindbergh explained Orville's bitterness by saying that he had "encountered the narrow-mindedness of science and the dishonesty of commerce." Only in 1942 did the Smithsonian admit that the test results "did not warrant the statement published by the Smithsonian Institution that these tests proved that the Langley machine of 1903 was capable of sustained flight carrying a man." In 1948, the Wright Flyer recrossed the Atlantic and was given its current place of honor in the Smithsonian Museum as the first plane to achieve controlled flight.

Like the Wrights, I found that people were ready to criticize me for protecting my rights. One friend who was generally supportive called me after I had written letters to Apple users to warn them about my patents. He told me I had written a great book, but that no one would remember me for it. They would only remember me for that letter I wrote to Apple users. And no one would ever buy Hyper-Racks because I had antagonized all the Macintosh gatekeepers who determine what software to purchase. I found it ironic that having spent the better part of the last ten years trying to make software easier to use, I should be remembered as a knave for trying to protect my rights in a genre I originated. But I understand what is happening. Apple developers can't get mad at Apple, but they can get mad at me. It's like yelling at the kids after a bad day at the office. It's less risky than yelling at the boss.

I got a call from the president of a company that marketed a HyperCard-like product on the Macintosh. He complained that Rockwell wouldn't buy his product until the issue of my patents was resolved. He had started his company with a product similar to Apple's MacPaint, then marketed a product similar to HyperCard. Since his software ran on Apple computers, Apple was happy— his products helped sell Apple computers. He complained to me that with patents, software publishing "just wasn't fun anymore." Maybe not. A few months later he sold his company. His share was 19 million dollars. If anyone is interested in purchasing my share in my company for 19 million dollars, let's talk.

19. ULTIMATELY, ONE MUST SUE INFRINGERS.

The Wright brothers sued many companies, some more than once. Each time they won. But to sue for justice is to endure what the great Judge Learned Hand said he would dread more than "almost anything short of sickness and death." Indeed, Wilbur Wright suffered sickness and death. He became ill and died in March 1912 at the age of 45, an end Orville and others felt was brought on by the unwillingness of infringers to recognize their patents until forced to do so by the courts. But the general public took a broader view than those whose self-interest was at stake; Wilbur's death was front-page news throughout the world and a thousand telegrams of condolence and enough flowers to fill a boxcar were sent.

Protecting one's rights takes a toll on inventors: Bell and Edison spent much time in court. It even drives some to suicide. In 1954, after RCA refused to stop infringing his patents, Edwin Armstrong, the inventor of FM broadcasting, grew so frustrated with the long legal battles that he committed suicide, jumping out of the window of his New York apartment onto the pavement below. I expect the people at RCA, especially the lawyers, thought he took it too personally. His widow pursued the case in the courts and ultimately was awarded over 10 million dollars in damages for patent infringement.

Dr. B. I. Friedlander, a management professor, Director of the Center for Venture Management, and President-Elect of the Licensing Executives Society did an unpublished study on what large companies pay for intellectual property rights. He gave over 500 licensing executives a case study.

They were told that executives of General Motors were determining what royalty to pay for a new transmission system developed by General Electric. The new system would save 1000 dollars per car on several million cars a year. The typical royalties expected were one billion dollars a year. But in one half of the studies, he used "three guys from Alberta" as the developers instead of General Electric. The expected royalties were two to fifty million dollars in these cases.

It may be that the reason the "three guys from Alberta" got about one percent of what General Electric did was because of a bias against Canadians, but Dr. Friedlander's explanation has to do with the size of the licensor. Would General Motors or IBM or Apple say to an individual stockholder, "We are only going to pay you 1% of the dividend we pay to big banks, even though you both own the same number of shares"? Of course not. Why is intellectual property any different? The invention and rights don't change. The reason is that, as a practical matter, as Dr. Friedlander says, "The playing field is tilted in big companies' favor." This is the challenge small companies face. If Apple or IBM is like General Motors in my negotiations, I fit more in the "three guys from Alberta" category than in the "General Electric" category.

I, too, finally had to sue Apple Computer for patent infringement. I sued a five-billion-dollar company when I couldn't pay my phone bill. It costs over a million dollars to pursue a patent case all the way through trial. If you want to go first cabin, it costs more. I had to go steerage.

20. ONE MUST DEAL WITH LAWYERS.

Less than a month before Wilbur died, he wrote a letter to his lawyer that began, "Unnecessary delays by stipulation of counsel have already destroyed fully three fourths of the value of our patent." I have learned that the self-interest of lawyers is often a better predictor of how the lawyer will behave than the interest of their clients. They often make more by prolonging the agony than by curing the patient. This is what Wilbur was finding out.

And this is what I was to find out. About two months after we sent letters to third-party developers, Apple's patent lawyer called. I wanted to deal directly with Apple, but their lawyers insisted on staying in the middle. I, being naive, agreed. I spent time and money so my lawyer could talk to their lawyer without resolving the problem. Apple's lawyers served Apple's purpose by extracting information, draining our resources, and raising our hopes. Now I negotiate only with principals. It saves me a lot of time and money. If we reach an agreement, lawyers formalize it; if we don't, I don't have to pay any lawyers.

Apple had made what we thought was an offer to take out a license, but when we acknowledged their offer in writing, they said they had not made us an offer, but were asking us to make them an offer. (It's a clever tactic; they can tell us later that they couldn't sell management on "our" offer, and therefore what we thought was a minimum offer would then turn out to be a maximum.) When we made our offer, which was for substantially more than Apple suggested, Apple didn't respond.

I was not prepared for my next problem with lawyers. You expect their lawyer to make your life difficult. You don't expect your own to do so. Wrong; I told you I was naive. I discussed a contingency agreement with a litigation firm known for bankrupting A. H. Robins in the Dalkon Shield case. They told us they wanted to take the case on contingency and were used to dealing with arrogant Fortune 500 companies. Suddenly, we got a call from Apple after over a month of silence. Apple wanted to set up a meeting between me and "an officer of the company." By this time, I was so mad at Apple I couldn't think straight. I signed a deal with the lawyers on Monday. They sued Apple on Tuesday; it was very satisfying to walk into the meeting with Apple on Wednesday and drop a suit in their lap. But like most emotional decisions, it was dumb. I should have had the meeting with Apple, and made a deal with the lawyers later if necessary.

I had two lawyers, one of whom I'll call Silver Tongue. Neither had had much patent prosecution experience, but they were hired for expertise in litigation, not patents. Silver Tongue got his early experience in the Judge Advocate General Corps in the army defending murderers and the like. Apple countersued, using the same law firm it sued Microsoft with— big guns.

Apple Meeting One: Do I go? No! Later, Apple tells me that my lawyers made a settlement offer that Apple refused. I did not authorize any offer, nor was I informed of one. Be very careful about letting your lawyers attend meetings without you. It just presents a tempting opportunity for two sets of lawyers to plot against either or both clients.

I suggested bringing experienced patent lawyers to this meeting. Two patent lawyers had looked at my patents, at HyperCard, and at prior art like VisiCalc and other spreadsheets. Will Silver Tongue invite one of these lawyers to the meeting? No. What happens next? Apple's patent lawyers pull the wool over my lawyer's eyes on a technical point. I call both patent lawyers immediately after the meeting and they characterize Apple's objection as garbage. Meeting One: Silver Tongue looks the fool in front of Apple.

Apple Meeting Two: Apple tells us they will show us prior art and make an offer. Again, I suggest bringing a knowledgeable patent lawyer, without result. In the meeting, Apple shows us VisiCalc, the first spreadsheet, as prior art. My reaction: stifled laughter. Silver Tongue in front of the other lawyers says, "I'll really be worried if they can show scrolling a cell wider than the screen width." I expect they can, and Apple's lawyers tell Silver Tongue he "doesn't want to know." In private, Silver Tongue tells me their prior art "was impressive. We ought to settle." If either of the knowledgeable patent lawyers had been there, they, having analyzed it earlier, would have been able to refute Apple's analysis of VisiCalc. Meeting Two: Silver Tongue looks the fool in front of Apple.

Depositions are about to begin, which means my lawyers get a larger percentage of any settlement. I prefer to settle sooner. About this time, a businessman experienced in licensing software patents to large companies agrees to advise me. We decide to make an offer directly to Apple. My lawyers refuse to make the offer. I find I am fighting a two-front war. My lawyers are on one side, Apple is on the other side, I am in the middle. Granted, two important legal issues are involved: control of the client and fee enhancement. I can't say I know what Silver Tongue's intentions are, but I have a highly predictive model: Silver Tongue wants to move to the highest settlement percentage and then settle as quickly as possible. I call Silver Tongue with my advisor on the line to discuss the offer; Silver Tongue says this would be piercing the lawyer-client privilege, and insists my advisor hang up. Later, my advisor admiringly observes this to have been a clever negotiating tactic. I feel like a shark has bitten off my foot and is eating his way up my leg and I am supposed to admire the finesse with which he is doing it.

Figure 65: Tian'anmen Square, June 1989. At times, a patent holder has to take a stand alone against the forces powerful infringers can array against him. This picture also serves as a reminder that while patent holders have to fight to get respect, others have to fight for other more basic rights.

EPILOGUE

 I ask Silver Tongue, why not present my offer to Apple? Silver Tongue says he would lose credibility, but does not tell me why he would lose credibility. Later, Apple tells me that he made and Apple rejected an offer of less than half the offer I wanted to make. After much back and forth positioning, Silver Tongue tells me he will withdraw from the case rather than transmit the offer. I fax a request for a faxed letter of withdrawal. Silver Tongue decides not to withdraw. A meeting between me and Apple—client to client—is arranged instead.

 Apple repeats their offer and adds some extras. They point out the value of an Apple license. Apple tells me I have crummy lawyers. I defend them; they may be turkeys, but they are my turkeys. I make the offer that is over twice the amount that Apple already rejected and that Silver Tongue did not tell me about. Later, Apple tells me they were confused by this.

 Three meetings with Apple. Three times Silver Tongue looks the fool. And the third time he does it without being there.

 The next day, a process server serves me with some new papers. I tell him to put them on the pile with all the other legal papers. You have to admire the way that Apple gets the subtle details right.

 At first I decide to hold out. I am only fourteen months behind in the phone bill, five months behind in the rent. However, other than that, things are pretty bad. I write my resume. I will have to go job hunting. My adviser and I talk. We decide the value of an Apple settlement now is worth a lot. Apple is only ten percent of the market. With a settlement, I can develop software and market it to the other ninety percent of the market. I can eat. I can sleep. Perchance I might even dream.

 I call Apple: "Maybe we were both posturing at our last meeting; can we have another meeting?" "How about 2 p.m.?" I hang up. My phone rings. Silver Tongue's partner: "We have decided to withdraw from the case. We will file papers in court asking for a 60 to 90 day delay." Why did they withdraw then? Was it because they would actually have to wage the battle they contracted to fight? Was it because they had demonstrated a level of competence to Apple and that would make it difficult to conduct the lawsuit? Did that scare them? It sure scared me!

That afternoon I negotiated with Apple, knowing my lawyers were not behind me. Within a week we had signed a settlement agreement. It was for less than I thought was reasonable. But it was for a substantial amount and the credibility of Apple recognition.

I would like to believe my experience with lawyers is an exception. It may be an extreme example, but it is not unusual. A recent law review article found that "lying to clients is pervasive in the legal profession." Former Chief Justice Warren Burger said that "seventy-five to ninety percent of all American trial lawyers are incompetent, dishonest, or both." And if there are thousands of lawyer jokes, I suspect each one, like this article, is the fossilized remains of someone's deep, emotional experience with a lawyer. The next time you deal with a lawyer, remember the words of Steve Kumble, who built Finley Kumble into the second largest, but most powerful law firm in the world: "The client is the enemy."

It is easy to blame lawyers, but the problem is not that simple. More fundamental forces are operating. When you are small and being ignored but have something of value, you are seen as someone to be ignored by those whose interests you threaten, to be avoided by those who do not like to get involved, and as someone ripe for the plucking by those people (whatever their purported expertise is) whose actual expertise is in conning people. Examples of the first groups are businessmen and technical people who dismiss your contribution without serious consideration. Examples from the last group are the person who promises to sell your product, but whose only commitment is to taking exclusive marketing rights, and the person who says he can bring in major OEM sales, but whose only commitment is to receiving stock. You also find companies whose business is suing patent infringers after signing on frustrated inventors whose rights are ignored. Like bill collectors, such companies perform a useful social function.

When these or any situations develop to the point where serious money is involved, lawyers also become involved. George Bernard Shaw said that the reason that marriage was so popular was that it combined the maximum of temptation with the maximum of opportunity. The legal profession is popular for the same reason.

Some lawyers are honest; many are liars; others are more sophisticated, looking down on liars as "people who do not know how to deceive." If you are broke, you may find that an honest lawyer will give you a little time, knowing he might never get paid, but he cannot give you much. I am thankful to some lawyers here. Occasionally you might find, as I was fortunate to find, a lawyer at a point in his career when it is in his interest to invest a considerable, but still limited amount of time on your behalf. Such a lawyer can be a great help; but would you want to be some doctor's first open heart surgery, even Dr. Michael deBakey's? Unfortunately, if significant work is required and if both you and your adversary have lawyers, the frequent reality is that one lawyer will be competent, the other will be a shyster, and you get second choice. Thus, you will be spending a lot of time dealing with the ugly sides of two lawyers.

21. THE SECRET IN THE END IS OFTEN SIMPLE.

The secret of flight wingwarping was in essence simple. Orville referred to these lines from *Paradise Lost:* "So easy it seemed. Once found, which yet unfound most would have thought impossible...."

In our own case, the idea of using the metaphor of cards and racks as a basis for building different computer applications is simple in concept and seemingly obvious in retrospect, but it takes time to make that idea a reality and for its value to be appreciated.

ON REFLECTION

The controversy about software patents that is raging is understandable when put into perspective. It is similar to what has recently happened in Eastern Europe. Eastern Europeans realize that communism doesn't work, and, having little experience with private property, are nervous about it and think it unfair for speculators to make exorbitant profits. Capitalism works, and communism does not work, because private property gives the owners of the property the incentive to invest in and improve it. Intellectual property is no different from other property: Whoever creates property has the right to keep, sell, rent, or otherwise control what is done with it. The average software developer has little experience with patents, just as the average Eastern European has little experience with private property. Both fear the unknown and are concerned about hypothetical problems.

Legions of intelligent people have been seduced by communism. But the value of private property is shown by the success of capitalism. Experience shows that communism is the rose, capitalism the cabbage, to use the metaphor in the title of Chapter 11. Since software is a new and immature technology, it is not surprising that its practitioners have little experience with patents and so have a second- or third-world mentality about intellectual property rights. The arguments against such rights, like the arguments in favor of communism, are intellectually appealing and are advanced by intelligent and well-meaning people, yet on inspection they are based on the rose of intellectualism, rather than the cabbage of reality.

We will advance software design as we make all advances—by looking for cabbages, things that have proved to work in practice, rather than by looking for rosy intellectual arguments. The place to look for cabbages is in history, nature, what people use, and how people act, not in academic theories. D. W. Griffith did not create the art of film from scratch, but built on his knowledge and experience of the stage and what writers like Charles Dickens did. Louis Sullivan rejected intellectual theories of architecture and looked to nature. Nature is the ultimate cabbage; it is the record of what works—ninety-nine percent of the species that ever existed have died out. Even the Constitution was written by men who had knowledge of history and experience with people in everyday affairs, not by men who acted on ideas they found intellectually attractive. Few were lawyers or academics. The result is a cabbage, if there ever was one; or as Churchill put it, "Democracy is the worst form of government except for all the others that have been tried from time to time."

Since 1981, my work has been woven from three intertwining themes, all of which seek to make use of the cabbages of what has been proven to work outside of computer science. First, designing user-oriented software is best thought of as a communications craft, letting us graft onto the experience of thousands of years of people's communicating. Second, software user interfaces are intellectual property, letting us graft onto the experience of 500 years of intellectual property law. Third, a large family of computing applications can be transported into the metaphor of cards and racks, letting us graft onto people's experience in using cards and stacks of paper. In each case, we have taken a sprout from computer science and grafted it onto the strong rootstock of existing experience.

A CASE STUDY IN DEFENDING ONE'S RIGHTS: NEGOTIATING WITH IBM

As this book goes to press, we are negotiating with IBM to get our rights respected. These negotiations provide a unique and useful opportunity to show you how a small company negotiates with a large company and how to analyze, act on, and take advantage of what happens.

IBM licensed the image of the Little Tramp from Charlie Chaplin's widow Oona Chaplin, who owns and has the resources to protect those rights. Were the Little Tramp himself to approach IBM and ask that his rights be respected, how would IBM treat him? Picture the Little Tramp standing by the side of the road when a big truck with "IBM" on the side passes by and splashes him from head to foot with mud. Now picture the Little Tramp going into IBM world headquarters in Armonk, New York, showing people the mud all over his clothes, and asking for money to pay the cleaning bill. To put that question into the perspective of Dr. Friedlander's research mentioned under point 19 above: Would IBM (General Motors) treat the Little Tramp (three guys from Alberta) any differently from Oona Chaplin (General Electric)? You be the judge.

As I write this, IBM bundles ToolBook with PS/2s on some systems that it markets in the higher education market. The higher education marketplace has always been important to IBM because schools are where people's computer preferences are first shaped. IBM is fighting Apple tooth and nail in this market— HyperCard, which is bundled with the Macintosh, is popular here and IBM likely wants ToolBook as an equivalent product.

In 1988, we called around IBM to find the right person to speak with to see if IBM was interested in this genre. I was given the name of someone in Software Vendor Operations as the appropriate person, and we wrote to him. The response we got was a form to fill out for submitting existing programs, so we felt we struck out. We rented booths at the two trade shows where HyperCard was a major focus to demonstrate Zoomracks, in part to be visible to IBM or others interested in the genre. The shows were small, so the booth space was inexpensive, and our booths looked like what the Little Tramp would have had.

In the first show in June of 1988, we had the only MS-DOS product in a trade show of Apple and HyperCard products. Our letters to HyperCard developers and Apple users made us visible in the Apple marketplace; anyone who was knowledgeable about the HyperCard marketplace would know about our patents. We wrote IBM again in 1989 and, just before we settled with Apple, we got a letter in return saying that IBM was not interested in acquiring a license to our patents. If IBM had shown interest in our patents at that time, we would have been in a better position to negotiate with Apple. I don't see how IBM could have properly researched this genre without being aware of us. I am not suggesting that IBM deliberately ignored our patents any more than I am suggesting an IBM truck deliberately splashed mud on the Little Tramp.

Under these circumstances, I was surprised to read in the trade press that IBM was bundling ToolBook into the higher education marketplace. I can understand why IBM might not want to approach Apple for a license on Hyper-Card. But I would have thought that they would have approached us as the inventors of the genre at least to get information.

In any case, I purchased a copy of ToolBook. It seemed to have the same infringement issues as HyperCard. So in July 1990, I wrote letters to Asymetrix (who manufactures ToolBook), to Microsoft (who bundles a ToolBook runtime version) and to the two companies I knew that bundled the developer's edition of ToolBook: Zenith and IBM. This has the legal effect of putting them on notice. In response, Microsoft wrote me a letter saying talk to Asymetrix (cc: Asymetrix). A lawyer representing Asymetrix wrote me a letter telling me that Asymetrix had a legal opinion that Tool-Book did not infringe, and held me personally liable for false and defamatory statements to Asymetrix customers or potential customers (cc: Zenith). Aha! Touched a nerve! I am happy to accept personal responsibility for any false and defamatory statements I make. Will they do the same? If you use ToolBook, you might consider asking Asymetrix if the lawyer who did the patent analysis or Paul Allen, its owner, will accept personal liability and hold you harmless if you infringe our patents when using ToolBook, or what rules you should follow to be indemnified.

We replied that if Asymetrix were interested in a license to our patents they should contact us directly, as we deal only with principals. No one contacted us. When one side approaches the other in negotiations, it shows weakness in one's negotiating position. So it is always better if the other side approaches you. Your job in these negotiations is to figure out how to get the other side to want to approach you, rather than how to approach them.

Only IBM responded. Now from a strategic point of view, it might seem that IBM, being so large and powerful, is a poor choice of an early target. It has massive resources that it can use to try to invalidate our patents. Realistically, however, if my patents are to be invalidated, it is better that it happen sooner rather than later. IBM has a policy of respecting intellectual property rights, so those responsible must address the issue and document its resolution. Our patents are hardly a core issue for IBM. But the issue is important for IBM both in the short term (since they want an equivalent to HyperCard to compete with Apple) and in the long term (because they have to consider the strategic impact of the Apple platform's having a license to our card and rack metaphor patents if the metaphor develops into an important genre). Also, I don't have to worry about getting sued; IBM believes it can negotiate its way out of anything, and so the only way they will sue me is if they see me being obviously unreasonable.

My strategic objective is to value my patents by having IBM show us the best prior art they can find. Or in terms of IBM's needs, how does IBM intend to conform to its stated policy of respecting intellectual property rights with respect to our patents? When I have their answer, I can make my business plans for non-Apple platforms. If I like the answer, the fact that it carries IBM's credibility is useful to us. Tactically, I must be tenacious in getting IBM to answer that question no matter what tactics IBM uses to divert me. The combination of Apple and IBM respecting our patents gives us tremendous credibility.

While it is important to put developers of products inspired by HyperCard on notice, strategically they are a poor target choice. They are inexperienced with patents and, thus, are at a disadvantage in making objective business judgments with regards to them. Our patents are a core issue for them. Such developers are more likely to want to fight a legal battle from the advantage of a better financial position than mine. Given the anti-patent feeling in the software community, a decision to fight could be cloaked in righteous indignation. After I address the issue with IBM, I can go back to others I have placed on notice.

In August, I got a call from someone at IBM who said he was responsible for handling this matter. He told me IBM would respond within two or three weeks. In early September, he wrote saying that things were more complicated and that IBM would respond by the end of October, but that IBM wanted to resolve the matter. In the middle of October, he was in the Silicon Valley on other business and we met. I told him our story and gave him information, including copies of my prior correspondence with IBM, my book, and our user survey—all of which seemed to come as news to him. He seemed particularly surprised because, he said, he had checked out our patent numbers on IBM's patent database and had not found them. I pointed out that as a patent holder I had the right and responsibility to assert my patents and bring them to the attention of possible infringers, and that included writing letters to Fortune 500 companies who are perforce IBM's customers. He agreed I had that right. I said that we were not in the licensing business, but were a software publisher and developer. I was open to a business arrangement whereby IBM might help to fund software development. He mentioned that IBM had made an investment in Metaphor, a local company, and said IBM would respond by the middle of November.

The most important thing to understand in any negotiation is BATNA: Best Alternative to a Negotiated Agreement. The other side will ask themselves what you will do if they don't negotiate a peace settlement, and they will calculate (or if you are lucky, miscalculate) the consequences to them. What you want to do is develop and improve your BATNA, because that is your leverage. My BATNA is to survive in the Macintosh market while trying to create a climate for business opportunities to develop on non-Apple platforms. Specifically, I will: a) keep my overhead low; b) sell

HyperRacks on the Macintosh to, among other things, create expectations for what the card and rack metaphor should do, thus enhancing the value of our patents; c) promulgate our rights in the genre through, for example, this book; and d) do what I can to increase the discrepancy between what can be done on the Apple and non-Apple platforms as represented by our intellectual property.

Notice that there is a weakness in my strategic plan that I will have to address later. An IBM license achieves the objective of increasing the credibility of our patents, but at the cost of decreasing the discrepancy between the Apple and non-Apple platforms.

At the beginning of November, my IBM contact called to tell me he had a proposal shaping up that he wanted to pass by me and offered to set up a meeting at Comdex, the big computer trade show. But just as we were about to set up the meeting, he said it would be better if he could get back to me the following week, the third week of November. At the end of November, with no response, I wrote him a letter pointing out IBM's repeated delays, the fact that I was due to deliver the manuscript of this book by December 10, and that I would assert my patent rights in this book and in letters to Fortune 500 companies later. I called him shortly before December 10 to see if IBM would respond. I explained, "I'm just a small guy trying to protect my rights." "Yes," he said, "I know." He also told me, "We don't know who is liable, Microsoft, IBM, or Asymetrix. This has turned out to be a real can of worms." I think he was referring to the question of who was liable if someone ran an infringing ToolBook application using the ToolBook runtime included with Windows 3.0 on any IBM computer.

If the possible infringer asks for more time early on, it means they haven't found prior art and have to look harder and have to study the ramifications of the matter. If a big company says it will get back to you in three weeks to resolve the situation and does, the news will be bad. Probably a brief letter saying something like, "We don't really have anything to talk about; by the way, enclosed is some prior art that you might find of interest."

On December 10, my contact got back to me to give me IBM's official response. In patent negotiations, you have to listen carefully and analyze what the other side says. It's like Watergate; is it a real denial or a non-denial denial? People want to be very careful of what they say lest their words be used against them in later negotiations or future court proceedings. For example, you will generally hear something much more like "We are still studying the ramifications of your patents," rather than "We don't know who is liable, Microsoft, IBM, or Asymetrix. This has turned out to be a real can of worms." So you have to try and build up models of what might be happening and test them on the basis of the evidence. It is like debugging a program. After each conversational point below, I give my analysis of what may be happening. It may be wrong, but be very careful of acting on what you are told without solid evidence to back it up.

IBM tells me they spent a lot of time on this. *Analysis:* This is a standard negotiating tactic designed to make you feel guilty for wasting IBM's time on a frivolous matter.

IBM's position is that it does not infringe our patents. *Analysis:* IBM's patent lawyer has been able to write a good-faith opinion that IBM does not infringe our patents. Note particularly the use of the word "position." It means, "We are less than certain." If they had high confidence they would tell us why, on the record. Getting such an opinion on file helps avoid treble damages should they be found infringing.

IBM is willing to listen to us tell them why we think IBM infringes. *Analysis:* The patent lawyer feels his analysis will not give IBM the protection it needs and has recommended that IBM negotiate a license if one is available at a reasonable price. (You may remember that Eastman Kodak did an analysis on the Polaroid patents that did not hold up.) Also, the analysis might not consider contributory infringement. IBM's willingness to keep talking is evidence that the problem is not resolved.

IBM would not show us any prior art because, "Why should we help you make your patents stronger?" *Analysis:* IBM, whose expertise and prior art libraries on software patents are second to none, came up with poor prior art in their patent search. Since we understand that IBM's usual tactic is to show prior art to scare patent holders, we suspect that they can't find any prior art good enough to give us a scare.

Even if IBM does infringe, IBM is indemnified by its contracts. *Analysis:* IBM is concerned about infringement. Why else be concerned about indemnification?

IBM wants us to talk to Asymetrix and Microsoft instead of IBM. *Analysis:* IBM would like to get rid of this hot potato by tossing it to Asymetrix and Microsoft. IBM may also want to begin to lay the groundwork for claiming that the liability lies with Asymetrix and Microsoft. IBM would like this problem to go away, giving them a resolution to this problem consistent with their policy on recognizing intellectual property.

I tell my IBM contact that I wrote letters to Asymetrix and Microsoft and that they know how to contact us if they want to discuss acquiring a patent license. If IBM wants them to license patent rights from us, IBM should ask them to contact us. If someone wants to buy, they can call us. Our BATNA strategy lets us do this. Meanwhile, potential liability accrues.

IBM is interested in looking at the '308 patent when it reissues. (You have two years after a patent issues to ask for broader claims. We reviewed the patent description for features that we anticipated and that are in HyperCard, and filed for new claims. Our objective is to make it difficult, if not impossible, to provide HyperCard functionality on non-Apple platforms without infringing our patents.) *Analysis:* IBM sees possible problems with the '308 patent, but this might be just a delaying tactic.

In the same phone call, my IBM contact told me that IBM did not bundle ToolBook into the higher education marketplace. I suggested that he check, and pointed out that that was the reason given when I wrote IBM originally. He said, "Why should I find out, so I can tell you, so you can tell me?" So I made a few calls, culminating in one to the appropriate businessperson in Academic Information

Systems at IBM, who said he would have a member of his staff call me. The next morning, less than 48 hours after I was told that IBM didn't bundle ToolBook, my IBM contact called to tell me that IBM bundled ToolBook and that he would send me a brochure listing it. My IBM contact had also told me that IBM had talked to Apple's outside patent counsel, whom I called and who said he did not talk to anyone at IBM about our patents.

To the inexperienced in such negotiations, it might seem I am being lied to. This is not the case. These are negotiating positions or tactics designed to influence you. Always check out the other side's negotiating positions; it helps calibrate statements that you can't check out directly. Until now, delay was probably caused by the bureaucratic process of examining the patents and getting the business people involved to make a decision. At this time, my analysis is that IBM wants to license our patents but wants to get them as cheaply as possible. IBM seems to be trying to drag things out. I think I am beginning to get *sandpapered*, as wearing down the other party in negotiations is sometimes called. Treat it as a game. It is fun to play, especially if you have a good BATNA and prepare three or four good moves of your own.

I am beginning to feel that IBM screwed up and did not consider our patents in making the decision to bundle ToolBook. If this is true and our patents are strong, then IBM must consider what its BATNA is in case a license is not available on acceptable terms. Here are some possibilities: a) Stop bundling ToolBook. *Analysis:* IBM doesn't like to change corporate strategy in midstream. b) Modify ToolBook so it doesn't infringe. *Analysis:* It is not easy to go out and take capability away from a programming environment that has users developing for it. c) Take the position that Tool-Book doesn't directly infringe, but some applications do. *Analysis:* If so, will IBM agree to indemnify customers creating uncertain future exposure, or will IBM expose its customers to getting sued for using software bundled with an IBM computer? IBM charges its customers top dollar, in part because they don't have to worry about such problems.

d) Pay us to upgrade Zoomracks to be competitive with HyperCard. *Analysis:* This means that during the two or three years we would spend doing this there would be no products with HyperCard-like capability on the IBM platform without the legal cloud of our patents. Big companies like IBM do patent analyses just so they don't have to negotiate from positions like this. It is particularly true since, until the issue is resolved, the legal cloud of our patents will likely inhibit application development on these platforms. All of these would seem to be unattractive to IBM, which suggests they should be willing to pay a high price to resolve the problem. Of course, IBM might have a better BATNA or good prior art that would make us settle cheaply, but the only way to get benefit from it is to show it to us.

When, as just happened, the other side's position ("We don't bundle ToolBook") does not bear up when the facts are checked, a good tactic is to call them on it. It gives the other side a chance to move forward or to dig themselves in deeper. I ask my contact, "What are the rules? Are we trying to make things as difficult as possible for each other, or to resolve the situation?" "The latter," my IBM contact replies. Plucky little fellow that I am, like the Little Tramp, I will act on what I hear—provisionally. I mail a copy of the "Roses and Cabbages" chapter to IBM and suggest that porting HyperRacks as a ToolBook add-on to the IBM platform might be an appropriate approach to solving the problem, but IBM shows little interest. However, we do set up a telephone meeting to discuss our patents with two IBM patent attorneys in Boca Raton, my IBM contact in New York, and myself and one of my patent attorneys in San Francisco.

The two major sources of possible infringement liability are a) using the full version of ToolBook as bundled by IBM and b) the secondary issues of using an infringing application with the runtime version of ToolBook that ships as part of Microsoft Windows. We bring up the primary issues of infringement and one IBM patent lawyer says, "We only looked at infringement problems in the runtime; we haven't looked at the developer's edition. We don't even have a copy and it will take two weeks to get a copy." I am being told that IBM has not looked at the most basic thing to look at. It seems strange, but it is possible. The IBM attorneys could be hung up on the issues of the ToolBook runtime shipped with Windows 3.0 because the potential liability was so much larger and the issue of who was liable was so much more complicated and interesting. Or IBM could be sandpapering me. So, as in debugging a program, it is time to try a test case.

The next day, I phone my IBM contact to tell him I am angry that after almost six months, IBM has not even looked at the relevant software. I point out that I expect to have the galleys of this book in a few weeks and that IBM might want to consider what is on the record. My contact tells me to be careful of what I say lest IBM sue me for tortious interference with business. Aha! I hit a nerve. IBM wants me to make decisions from fear. Obviously, you should be careful about what you write or say and have it reviewed by lawyers. But you can assert your rights. And you can tell the truth, which is what common decency and the law demand. I bring up the issue of IBM not having looked at ToolBook. My contact says, "Do not assume that just because we said that we have not looked at the developer's version of ToolBook, that we have not in fact done so." So, along with Ron Nessen's "Previous statements are inoperative" during Watergate, we have another euphemism for "position." Sandpaper, sandpaper. But I am getting better; I reduced the time it took to get IBM to eat its words from 48 hours to 24 hours.

My contact tells me IBM has prior art "in manuals for old IBM products." If IBM has prior art, I am skeptical that it is in IBM manuals—I suspect that that is just a prefabricated phrase used in these situations. When I first asked for prior art, my contact said, "Why should I send you prior art so you can make your patents stronger?" Now he says, "If we show you the prior art, your patents will be worthless." I think this is less a 180-degree shift in position than my IBM contact reaching into his prefabricated phrase box and pulling out a phrase that didn't match—rather like getting one black sock and one brown. However, my contact indicates that IBM will consider a nuisance license. This is a good sign. No infringer has ever paid real money for a valid license. Infringers always buy nuisance licenses. They must devalue your property as worthless so you will be grateful for the few cents they deign to give you for your miserable rights. This is the time to note Heckel's Principle of Big-Company Negotiation: *There is no such thing as a free lunch—unless you're the lunch.*

IBM makes other arguments. ToolBook is a loss leader, and they can stop bundling ToolBook or design around my patents. *Analysis:* Great. Tell the world that ToolBook presents infringement problems. I win.

IBM tells me only a small proportion of applications might infringe our patents. We do cover capability that people might not use at first, but that proves to be valuable later. Focal Point II, for example, included infringing capability that the original version of Focal Point didn't have. *Analysis:* We are not selling. IBM might be a buyer. Remember your BATNA. We can always sell our technology later when the market values it higher.

IBM tells me they only pay one-time fees and can't pay royalties because they don't have any way to account for it. *Analysis:* If a big company licenses a patent, they normally want a one-time fee and usually freedom of action. Normally, IBM is licensing patents at a point in time when they can design their products around the patents if they have to, so you are selling your licensed technology to IBM in competition with alternative technologies and will accept this condition because of the legitimacy an IBM deal provides. If, however, IBM is already using the technology or it is a standard (like, for example, the RSA cryptographic patent), you can generally set the terms. Still, you have to evaluate your respective BATNAs.

IBM suggests an absurdly low conditioning number, assuming I wanted to give them a license. A conditioning number is an offer, or suggestion of an offer, designed to lower your expectations. IBM points out to me how valuable an IBM license is and says I should go after all the other companies that sell IBM clones and ship Microsoft Windows with a ToolBook runtime. This is a standard big-company tactic to get a sweetheart license. "We give you legitimacy; now go and work hard at making our competitor's life miserable by licensing them." The first licensee always gets a better deal because it provides legitimacy. We were happy to give IBM a sweetheart license in 1989, but they wrote us saying that they were not interested. Apple was. No more first licenses are available. Apple popularized the genre with HyperCard, and thus are the ones who can bestow and have bestowed legitimacy on our patents.

Why would IBM take negotiating positions that so quickly crumble on examination? Is it because they thought I was naive? Is it because they needed some way to stall for time? Is it just part of the sandpapering process? Is it because they were covering up their not having dealt with the problem before bundling ToolBook? Whatever the reason, I think it means weakness.

It is understandable that a big company like IBM doesn't like anyone, especially someone dressed like the Little Tramp, standing there with mud-spattered clothes telling them what to do. However, whatever surface empathy I had for IBM's position has quickly came off with the sandpapering.

IBM might feel they are negotiating with the gun of my patents to its head. If so, I didn't put the gun to IBM's head. I wrote and told them about the gun. Twice. Still, they took the gun, purchased bullets, put them in the chamber, and pointed it at their own head (or at the heads of their customers). Of course, IBM says that only some uses of Tool-Book might infringe. Maybe so. Maybe we are talking Russian roulette. I'm not even threatening to pull the trigger at this time. I am only pointing out that the gun might go off and someone might get hurt. I am just asking IBM: Please, put down the gun.

To be fair to IBM's users, IBM should draw the infringement line. IBM should tell its users what rules to follow to avoid infringing our patents. If IBM is infringing our patents with ToolBook, then they should stop bundling it. All I ask is that IBM conform to IBM policy on intellectual property rights. If IBM wants to use our intellectual property, it should negotiate from the point where they acknowledge our rights, which is, I suspect, how they negotiated with Oona Chaplin for the rights to the Little Tramp.

I have a doll of the Little Tramp (properly licensed) that Hamilton Gifts markets. How, I ask, would the Little Tramp respond to being sandpapered? I expect the plucky little fellow would come alive, wipe the sawdust from his eyes, and find his creative juices flowing. If you accept your opponent's metaphor, he wins. As a small company, you should reject the metaphor of sandpapering; you are playing by their rules. When a big company stonewalls you, your task is to get the big company to deal with you on a fair basis. Sandpaper does not work on stone walls. Dynamite does. If the other side wants to play games, make it a spectator sport. The stonewalling in Watergate turned it into the great spectator sport of the middle 1970s.

The dynamite I have been preparing is this Epilogue. In a negotiation with a large company, you should imagine the final resolution being tried in front of a judge and jury. You have to position yourself to be the one in the white hat if things go to trial. If you can do this and the other side finds it is wearing a black hat, it won't likely get to trial. I am prepared to be able to show that I have been wearing the white hat. First, I kept record of events so I can document what happened. I also wrote letters to IBM. Second, I tried both to be, and to give the appearance of being, fair and reasonable all along. Many jury issues come down to what a reasonable person would do. Third, I have been persistent. Fourth, I have informed IBM of the pertinent facts: I invented the genre, I am adding new material for the new edition of this book, and I have every right to assert my patent rights. This both builds credibility and prevents the big company from later claiming that you sandbagged them. Fifth, I didn't tell everything; for example, I did not tell them what new material would be in the book. It is tempting to try to sell the value of your technology, but the people you are dealing with are often negotiators who can't appreciate your technology and whose only job is to get rid of a problem as cheaply as possible; and the only thing they will do with the information you give them is use it against you.

EPILOGUE

Information is power. Giving your enemy information only serves to help them fight you better. Give it out slowly for some useful purpose such as rewarding a positive move on their part, or to have an appropriate psychological effect. Carl von Clausewitz in his classic *On War* said, "If you want to overcome your enemy, you must match your effort against his power of resistance, which can be expressed as the product of two inseparable factors...the total means at his disposal and the strength of his will." In a little guy *vs* big company fight, the little guy must attack the big company's strength of will. If the big company's troops (others in the company) or civilians (its customers and the public) don't want the company fighting the war, it won't fight, and you can negotiate peace on your terms. I kept this Epilogue in reserve for the psychological moment when the book was within a decent warning time of going to press. In it, I would say, "If you want to use our patents, a license goes with Apple computers. There are no licenses on non-Apple platforms." But before sending it to them, I asked what would Charlie Chaplin have done to strengthen it? He would probably make a movie illustrating what happened to the Little Tramp. So I wrote up this case study and added it to this Epilogue.

On January 22, just as I was about to mail this Epilogue to IBM, I got a call from my IBM contact. It would seem that resolving this problem is on his task list. He said our patents had "no value" to IBM, but that IBM would give me a nuisance license— $5,000 or $10,000 for a fully paid up license on both patents: (IBM called me up to tell me it wants to pay me money for something of no value to IBM?!) He also told me I could write in my book that IBM had taken a license. (IBM might like me telling the world that IBM had a license to our patents just as Apple did, but I would not. My strategy is to emphasize and increase the differences between Apple and non-Apple platforms.) I asked my contact for prior art and was told that I could have it as part of the settlement. I insisted on seeing the prior art before the settlement so I could evaluate their offer and was told that if I wanted to see the prior art before licensing IBM, it would be "in court." "If you want to see it, sue us," he said. That day, I sent through courier an earlier version of this Epilogue to IBM's Director of Licensing, my contact's boss. He called me two days later. He had read all 80 pages of material—both the Epilogue and the "Roses and Cabbages" chapter, and he set up a meeting in San Francisco for February 5, which he would come to with my IBM contact and an IBM patent lawyer responsible for the analysis of our patents. If IBM is willing to fly three people from the east coast to the west coast for a meeting on less than two weeks' notice, it suggests that they take our patents or this Epilogue or both seriously.

IBM's Director of Licensing is more polished than my regular contact. I am now dealing with Number 600 fine sandpaper. He told me that IBM does not "incinerate" people, referring, I assume, to St. Joan. He assures me that IBM treats everyone the same, whether they are big companies or widows and orphans. Such smooth sandpaper. I'm sure he is right. IBM lays the mine fields, digs moats, and puts up barbed wire, and big companies and widows and orphans have to get through them just the same. He tells me how my IBM contact was "anguished" when he saw this Epilogue and how he is a good Catholic boy and a former FBI agent. A tactic to gain sympathy; I almost started to feel sorry for him.

In the late 1960s, J. Edgar Hoover was coming under fire for making statements that were not helpful to the administration, and President Johnson was asked why he didn't fire Hoover. He replied, "I'd rather have him inside the tent pissing out, than outside the tent pissing in." Some of my readers may feel that the use of this earthy term has no more place here than it does at the luncheon table. And they are, in a sense, right. This is because we all understand that when it comes to eating and drinking, what goes in one end goes out the other, but we don't normally discuss it. Those of you who are software developers and who look with disdain on protecting one's intellectual property take a position that makes as much sense as building a house without a bathroom. The companies you work for handle these realities in a different department, giving you the luxury of ignoring them. If, however, you are an entrepreneur you must make sure your house has a bathroom. Intellectual property lets you mark your territory just as animals do. When Apple set up a tent inside our territory, we began marking it. And Apple analyzed the situation in the same way President Johnson did and decided they would rather have us marking our territory after we were made welcome in their tent. Having been made welcome inside Apple's tent, we looked to find the bigger tents in our territory. And, as you can see by this book, we are busy marking our territory.

In the phone conversation, IBM's Director of Licensing tells me that what I wrote suggests that IBM was "unethical" (his term, not mine). In this case study, as in any case study, or in any business situation, one should objectively look at reality and not characterize behavior in terms of ethics. It is not useful. As Michael Corleone says in *The Godfather, Part III*, "Don't hate your enemy; it only clouds your judgment." IBM's Director of Licensing tells me he will be sending me a letter, which he does. In it, he says, "I am convinced that you were treated in a fair and professional manner" and "We adhere to the highest principles of integrity and fair dealing in all of our discussions and negotiations." He also says of the Epilogue, "We find that it is inaccurate and conveys false impressions of IBM's motives and tactics. Accordingly, this Epilogue, as it currently stands, is unfair to IBM...." (This Epilogue has been rewritten, but only in the normal manner of rewriting.)

IBM has not identified any specific inaccuracies, even though I asked them to in two letters. I stand by what I reported. I am not trying to embarrass or extort IBM. I am trying to understand and report what is happening, in part for my own education and understanding, and in part to help others who are faced with similar negotiating situations. I interpret the letter to mean that IBM wants to resolve the situation and that this letter is not being written to me, but for the record, which some future lawyer might use to argue from in front of a judge or jury if the matter is not resolved. At this point in time (funny how Watergate expressions keep popping up), I am prepared to believe that what I have seen so far is not representative of IBM's normal negotiating style.

In preparing for the meeting with IBM, I assess the situation. IBM told us they will show us prior art and discuss the infringement. I have every right to publish the case study. However, threatening to publish it unless IBM does something might be considered extortion. Remember, you want to do everything to wear the white hat. I want to avoid not just extortion, but the appearance of extortion. After discussions with my advisors, and considering the fact that IBM has told us that they will show us prior art, and since I am prepared to believe that what I reported, while accurate, is not representative of IBM's normal practices, I make a decision to tell IBM that I will not publish this case study. I feel this shows good faith on my part and indicates I am not trying to extort them. But it is risky; if IBM has "right on" prior art that invalidates my patents, I have both surrendered my negotiation leverage and given up the ability to publish something that has real value in helping small companies negotiate with large ones. As I do this, I picture myself as the Little Tramp dressing for the meeting by putting a sign around my neck that says "Sucker." But I decide to take the risk.

We have the meeting in my lawyer's office in San Francisco. Three of us; three of them. Early on, IBM's Director of Licensing brings up my case study, and I tell him of my decision not to publish it, and that ends that subject. Over the day (we met from 10 a.m. until 5 p.m.), there is much discussion, but little of it is fruitful. IBM says it has prior art, which will invalidate the patent, but that it is concerned that if that prior art is sent to the patent office for reexamination, the patent will survive reexamination because the patent office might make an error. IBM, the Director says, has had some recent bad experiences where it had prior art, which it claimed invalidated patents. When it gave the art to patent holders, they went back to the patent office and had the patents successfully reexamined over the prior art. IBM did suggest that they let an impartial third party examine the prior art and provide us with an evaluation. However, we have never heard of such a procedure and thought it would only serve to provide further delay. The bottom line is that IBM proposes a deal of the form, IBM will give me $10,000, a PS/2, and show us the prior art for a fully paid up license on both patents. They argue that I should take this deal because "I will be able to make my patents stronger."

(If you are a clonemaker approached by IBM to license IBM's Microchannel patents, you might consider finding some prior art and telling IBM that you have some "right on" prior art that invalidates IBM patents, but that you will give IBM $10,000 for a fully paid up license. Tell them you are concerned that if you give it to IBM, the patent office will make a mistake and IBM's patents will survive reexamination. Tell IBM, "Trust me; it's really good art." If they go for it and give you the $10,000, you might offer them a real good deal on a bridge, since they have the money to spend. You might even get your $10,000 back. My IBM contact licenses IBM's Microchannel patents, so you will likely be talking to someone who sees the merit in your argument.)

Let's analyze this. First, how can the prior art be "right on" if when we get it we can go back to the patent office and possibly make our patents stronger? An inconsistency. I think IBM's biggest secret is that they don't have any secrets—at least not with respect to prior art on our patent. It may be true that the patent office will make a mistake and our patents will survive reexamination in error and that would make it much harder for IBM with its limited legal resources to fight the patent in court. It just wouldn't be fair to IBM. Does anyone who has gotten this far in this Epilogue still believe that life is fair? Is IBM telling us they don't know what life in the big city is like? It is more likely that the patent office will do its job and the reexamined patent will issue over the prior art without change, or the claims will be further limited because of the prior art. We are willing to take that chance. If we expect to live by the validity of our patents, we should be willing to die by it. We understand life in the big city.

IBM even offered to include a cross-license to all the patents in their patent portfolio. This has little value to us unless we want to go into the clone-making business or be bought out by a clonemaker. As a large company who has to worry about anti-trust, IBM has to have a consistent patent licensing policy. The bottom line is that we can license individual patents from IBM for 1% of my sales and their whole patent portfolio for 3%. As a practical business matter, I am not worried about infringing IBM patents.

But look at the deal from IBM's point of view. IBM gets me to tell my readers that a license goes with IBM computers. And, of course, IBM gets me to spend my time licensing IBM competitors. All I have to give up is my business strategy, which is to increase the gap between the licensed Apple and unlicensed non-Apple platforms. I guess I am wearing that sign saying "Sucker." IBM gets everything and gives $10,000 in return. If I am really stupid, I'll take the PS/2 and spend my time developing for the IBM platform instead of the Macintosh.

Of course, if my patents are worthless, it is a good deal. So I ask IBM if it will indemnify customers who use ToolBook from infringing our patents. "No." What will IBM say to its customers about our patents? "We will say, 'No problem'." IBM won't, it would seem, put its money where its mouth is.

The most interesting thing IBM wanted as part of the deal was for us to agree to license Asymetrix if our patents survived reexamination in the patent office. In the words of IBM's Director of Licensing, "We don't want you to nuke one of our vendors." I interpret this as a concern that we might get an injunction against Asymetrix preventing future sales of ToolBook.

Picture the Little Tramp sitting there with a sign that says "Sucker" around his neck and being told that he might have the status of a nuclear power. I don't want to speak to our intentions, but if you are using ToolBook, be aware that IBM's Director of Licensing says we might be able to "nuke" Asymetrix. If we can "nuke" Asymetrix, we might also be able to "nuke" IBM (if getting an injunction against IBM's bundling of ToolBook can be considered "nuking").

IBM repeatedly told me to go to Asymetrix and get them to take a license. This tactic is generally known as "Let's you and him fight." Actually, it's more like "Little boy, why don't you go fight that big guy over there, since Paul Allen, Asymetrix's founder, is worth about 1.5 billion dollars?" Two can play this game: If I were Asymetrix, I would be furious that IBM's Director of Licensing said that tiny HyperRacks might have the capability to "nuke" Asymetrix. On the other hand, if I were IBM, I would be furious that one of my vendors sold me a product that a company like tiny HyperRacks could "nuke" them on. And if I had built strategic marketing plans based on that product, I would consider suing that vendor for any consequential damages. Oh yes, if I were a software company developing ToolBook applications, I would be furious at both IBM and Asymetrix for getting me to spend time and money developing for a platform that had the cloud of our being able to "nuke" the vendor hanging over it. And if I were Spinnaker, who makes Plus, or Brightbill-Roberts, who makes HyperPad, I would be furious that IBM was prepared to demand protections for their competitors, but not for them. If you are concerned about getting caught in the middle of a real donnybrook, might I suggest you consider working on the Apple Macintosh with us, where all is peaceful with regards to our patents?

At one point in the meeting, we tentatively and reluctantly suggested a number in the low six figures as being part of some deal, to have it rejected out of hand as being off by an order of magnitude.

IBM's Director of Licensing said he had read the 80 pages I had sent him. Twice. I was impressed. We writers can be a little vain at times. The subject of Silver Tongue came up and I asked him what he thought of that appellation. "I didn't like it." "Why?" I asked. "I think of myself as 'Silver Tongue'," he replied. I have to give him a few points there. He certainly outtalked our team at the meeting. And I didn't think of the metaphor "nuke" for what you can do with my patents. And I'm pretty good with metaphors.

The meeting broke up and our side was really down. Our risky opening gambit of telling them we would not publish this case study seemed to have backfired. In analyzing the meeting, we came up with two possible (and speculative) explanations. First, IBM's Director of Licensing's ego might have been such that he felt he could talk us into a cheap license. His seeing himself as "Silver Tongue" supports this possibility. Second, IBM had dropped the ball in evaluating our patents when they decided to bundle Tool-Book. And for IBM to pay what the patents are worth could only be justified by exposing an embarrassing error at a higher level: Our patents should have been considered as part of the decision to bundle ToolBook. After all, IBM is not supposed to get into situations where they can be nuked.

In a sense, we lost another battle— one of many— in that we did not resolve the matter. But as Clausewitz said, a bad outcome may be "merely a transitory evil, for which a remedy may still be found." Or to put it another way, it doesn't matter if you lose all the battles. What is important is to win the war. In losing the battles, you can build a record, gaining strength in your defeats and ultimately sapping your opponent's energy and will to fight.

After reviewing the meeting, we realized two things. First, IBM had led us to believe that it would provide us with prior art. For example, IBM's Director of Licensing had said in his letter to me:

> We have arranged to meet with you...to answer any questions you may still have on our position regarding your patents, including a discussion of prior art, and to hear any additional points of concern you wish to express. At this meeting, we will be happy to go the "extra mile" to explain to you that IBM's study of your patents was complete and the findings of non-infringement compelling.

We felt that IBM's refusal to show us their prior art was not in the spirit of this statement. Since IBM did not seem to feel bound to act on its statement with regards to showing us the prior art, I did not feel I had to be bound by my voluntary statement that I would not publish the record of our interactions. So I am publishing it and bringing it up to date. This decision was just reinforced in that all on our team felt that IBM's behavior in that meeting was consistent with their earlier behavior.

As we step back and get an appreciation of the big picture, it seems we are well positioned for the future. IBM, after spending considerable time analyzing our patents, has probably found the best prior art to use to try to invalidate our patents. IBM has asserted that they have prior art that invalidates our patents, but they are unwilling to show it to us or to the patent office for reexamination. It is only fair and reasonable to point out to users of products like ToolBook on non-Apple platforms that the Director of Licensing for IBM has told us that if the patent office sees IBM's prior art, our patents could survive reexamination and we could "nuke" an IBM vendor with the reexamined patent. So, there is some uncertainty in using ToolBook and similar products on non-Apple platforms. Of course, there is an easy solution for end users. Use the Apple Macintosh as your platform. We license our patents on a case-by-case basis, and deal only with principals.

Our licensing IBM on unfavorable terms has negative value to us, as it eviscerates our strategy of increasing the disparity between platforms represented by our intellectual property. As long as our patents create a cloud of uncertainty over unlicensed platforms, our strategy is working. It doesn't bother me that publishing this will make me unpopular with IBM. Indeed, we place value in being perceived as the irritant that produced the pearl of IBM's predicament: It will help sell this book, increase our credibility in the industry, and deflect people's hostility engendered by our patents from us to IBM. Having been reviled in the Apple marketplace when we asserted our patent rights, I expect to be welcomed back, making it easier to develop and sell HyperRacks there. Of course, I still risk losing my patent if IBM actually has good prior art and shows it to the patent office. But I have been living with that risk for years.

Our major objectives were to get credibility for our patents and to emphasize the difference between the Apple and non-Apple platforms. We think we have achieved those objectives.

In reviewing what has happened, I don't for a minute believe it was because I was smarter than IBM or planned the outcome to be what it was. Indeed, IBM's array of tactics was impressive and if I, rather than IBM, had made the last mistake, the results might have been different. Indeed, the final outcome is still in doubt as I write this. But if I succeeded in attaining my present position, it was because I stuck to fundamentals: developing my BATNA, keeping my options open, and tenaciously insisting that IBM deal with the issue and show us the prior art as part of negotiating any agreement. When all of IBM's tactics came to naught, I found myself to have been lucky. But chance and luck are what business is about. You must create the opportunity for lucky things to happen, and exploit that luck when and if it occurs.

In order to be fair to IBM, we provided them with copies of this Epilogue and offered them the opportunity to bring any information to our attention. We also offered to print a two-page letter so that IBM could present its position on what I reported, including issues such as what kind of problems, if any, users of ToolBook on IBM computers might have with respect to our patents; our potential ability to "nuke" Asymetrix; and other issues it wishes to address. IBM did not take advantage of our offer.

I like to think that up there somewhere, the Little Tramp is smiling because once again he has played a role in deflating the rich and powerful.

ABOUT THE FUTURE

HyperRacks, our HyperCard add-on, brings the rack metaphor and other capabilities to HyperCard. We want to advance our vision of the card and rack metaphor on the

Apple Macintosh, where our patents have been recognized and licensed. Since Apple has always been a leader in bringing new technology to personal computer users, this is a good place to develop and refine our vision of what the metaphor should be; sooner or later, ideas that first take root on Apple computers are grafted into the IBM and other computer markets. When we have the resources, we will upgrade Zoomracks to bring our vision of the card and rack metaphor to the market on IBM and compatible computers.

If you are thinking of using ToolBook or another product similar to HyperCard on non-Apple computers, ask the question, "If Apple provides a license to our patents for its users, do I need a license?" Since IBM's Director of Licensing has said we might be able to "nuke" Asymetrix with our reissued patents, you may wish to ask the program's publisher to indemnify you against infringing our patents, or at least to specify rules that you must follow to be indemnified from infringement. You may wish to ensure that the indemnification holds you harmless and includes consequential damages in case you are enjoined from using your application. IBM has a patent indemnification clause in their contracts. Why should you settle for less? Better yet, just use Apple Computers. A license to our patents goes with an Apple computer no matter which software you use on it, so it is a completely risk-free environment as far as our patents are concerned.

Louis Sullivan and D. W. Griffith who, more than anyone, shaped their professions into their modern forms, did not acquire intellectual property rights to their contributions, were unable to play a significant role in their professions in their last years, and died in financial difficulties, suffering the fate of Saint Joan of Arc. Other pioneers who acquired ownership rights to the intellectual property they created were able to avoid the fate of Saint Joan. Charlie Chaplin sued infringers and continued to develop the Little Tramp through many films. That character established a position in people's minds so effectively that IBM licensed its use to introduce and sell IBM computers. In his early days, Walt Disney created Oswald the Rabbit, but his distributor owned the copyright. Faced with demands for control from the distributor, Disney walked out, determined never again to create anything he did not own. He went on to create Mickey Mouse and build the Disney organization on intellectual property rights. The same is true of patents. Xerox was built on the technical vision of Chester Carlson and the business vision of Joe Wilson. Polaroid was built on the vision of Edwin Land. Intellectual property rights not only compensate those who create new ideas and put them into practice, but provide them with the means and opportunity to develop the visions they originated. Society is the ultimate beneficiary.

If I have tried to involve you, my readers, in this cause, I suppose I am like the woman whose daughter was killed by a drunk driver and who founded MADD, Mothers Against Drunk Driving. When it happens to your neighbor, it's unfortunate; when it happens to you, it's a tragedy; when it happens to you and you see it's been happening to others, it becomes a cause.

As I look back, I see I was lucky to get some fundamentals right, but I got a lot of the details wrong. I thought the portable computer market would develop faster than it did; I thought our software would take less time to develop than it did; and I thought Atari could sell computers. Wrong. Wrong. Wrong.

Al Alcorn, an inventor of Pong and one of the founders of the original Atari, suggests that all progress is due to people who do not know what they are doing, because if they did, they would never take the risks. There is some truth to what he says.

As inventors, we are skeptics. Our job is to find illusions: to identify the papier-mâché bricks in the wall of accepted knowledge. And our experience is to have our illusions destroyed: to find, among other things, that the intellectual property rights written into the granite of the Constitution are rocks to be kicked out of the way or run over with a tank by big companies, or are something to complain about by journalists with 5 p.m. deadlines. It is not surprising then that most inventors believe God is just another illusion. The Wrights were the sons of a bishop, but were unbelievers. Edison boasted that he was a heathen. Nevertheless, we inventors do have a patron saint— someone who had visions and pursued them— Saint Joan of Arc.

I had expected that big companies would seek to have me concentrate my energy and creativity on developing my invention to mutual benefit, rather than on my fighting them. I did not seek the role of defender of software patents or fights with Apple and IBM. But I fight for my rights. Successful inventors have to. To be a successful inventor, you have to be innocent like a baby so that you see things in a fresh way, but not so innocent that you let people take your candy.

BIBLIOGRAPHY

ADVERTISING

Ogilvy, David. *Confessions of an Advertising Man.* New York: Dell, 1963.

A good book on advertising.

————. *Ogilvy on Advertising.* New York: Crown, 1983.

A more recent and better book on advertising by the same author.

O'Toole, John. *The Trouble with Advertising.* New York: Chelsea House, 1981.

A good book on advertising written by the chairman of a major advertising firm.

Ries, Al and Jack Trout. *Positioning: The Battle for Your Mind.* New York: Warner Books, 1981.

ARCHITECTURE

Alexander, Christopher. *Notes on the Synthesis of Form.* Cambridge: Harvard University Press, 1964.

This book's insightful examination of the problems of architectural design is just as relevant to software design.

Blake, Peter. *Form Follows Fiasco.* Boston: Atlantic-Little, Brown, 1977.

An intriguing book describing the failures of modern architecture.

Wright, Frank Lloyd. *Writings and Building.* New York: Meridian, 1960.

ART

Edwards, Betty. *Drawing on the Right Side of the Brain.* Los Angeles: J. P. Tarcher, 1979.

I recommend the upside-down drawing exercise.

DESIGN AND CREATIVITY

Adams, James L. *Conceptual Blockbusting.* New York: Norton Publishing, 1980.

A good book on creativity in design written from an engineering perspective.

Hanks, Belliston. *Design Yourself.* William Kaufmann, 1977.

A visual book on design and creative thought written from the point of view of graphic art and industrial design. Read the article on Einstein entitled "Visual Thinking— An Attribute of Genius."

Kim, Scott. *Inversions.* New York: Byte Books, 1981.

Scott Kim designs words that communicate the same right-side up as upside down, and talks about the perceptual problems involved.

McKim, Robert H. *Experiences in Visual Thinking.* Monterey, CA: Brooks/Cole, 1980.

A good book on visual thinking and design written from the perspective of a mechanical engineer.

FILMMAKING

Brady, John. *The Craft of the Screenwriter.* New York: Touchstone, 1982.

An interesting book that consists of interviews in which six top screenwriters discuss screenwriting.

Brownlow, Kevin. *The Parade's Gone By.* New York: Ballantine, 1968.

An excellent book on the age of silent films.

Eisenstein, Sergei. *Film Form: Essays in Film Theory.* New York: Harcourt Brace Jovanovich, 1949.

Gish, Lillian. *The Movies, Mr. Griffith & Me.* New York: Avon, 1969.

Lillian Gish worked with Griffith on many of his films. Here, she tells what it was like to be present at the creation.

Goldman, William. *Adventures in the Screen Trade.* New York: Warner, 1983.

This book describes making films from the perspective of the Hollywood screenwriter. Every artist must take risks, and to demonstrate this, several times Goldman climbs a tree, goes out on a limb, and then invites his friends to the party.

MacCann, Richard Dyer, ed. *Film: A Montage of Theories.* New York: E. P. Dutton, 1966.

Recommended in this collection of essays on film are those by Dudley Nichols, Pudovkin, Alfred Hitchcock, Ingmar Bergman, and Alexander Knox.

Rosenblum, Ralph and Karen Robert. *When the Shooting Stops the Cutting Begins.* New York: Penguin, 1980.

An excellent description of filmmaking from the perspective of the film editor for *The Pawnbroker, A Thousand Clowns,* and *Annie Hall.*

Talbot, Daniel, ed. *Film: An Anthology.* Berkeley: University of California Press, 1967.

A collection of essays on film. The essays by Lewis Jacobs on D. W. Griffith and by Ben Hecht on Hollywood are both interesting and well written.

Thomas, Frank and Ollie Johnston. *Disney Animation: The Illusion of Life.* New York: Abbeville, 1981.

This book is must reading for anyone seriously interested in designing friendly software.

Truffaut, Francois. *Hitchcock.* New York: Simon and Schuster, 1966.

INDUSTRIAL DESIGN

Caplan, Ralph. *By Design.* New York: St. Martin's, 1982.

Dreyfuss, Henry. *Designing for People.* New York: Viking, 1955.

I first read this book five years ago. Rereading it recently, I was surprised to see how much it affected my thinking about designing programs for people.

Nelson, George. *Problems in Design.* New York: The Whitney Library of Design, 1965.

A collection of essays on design by an industrial designer.

MAGIC

Fischer, David. *Jasper Maskelyne: The War Magician.* New York: Coward-McCann, 1983.

This book describes how a stage magician thinks by describing how Jasper Maskelyne created some of his better illusions. (He moved Alexandria harbor ten miles to the west, thus causing the Nazis to drop their bombs uselessly in the desert.)

Hay, Henry. *The Amateur Magician's Handbook.* New York: Crowell, 1950.

A good beginning book on magic. It discusses briefly the importance of the psychology of magic.

PSYCHOLOGY

Arnheim, Rudolf. *Art and Visual Perception* (new version). Berkeley: University of California Press, 1954, 1974.

This is not light reading, but it gives interesting and useful information on how people perceive things and how art uses these perceptual factors.

Arnheim, Rudolf. *Visual Thinking.* Berkeley: University of California Press, 1969.

This book argues convincingly that most thinking is visual. Difficult reading at times, but the chapters entitled "Words in Their Place" and "Art and Thought" are interesting reading.

Gibb, Jack R. "Defensive Communication": essay in Leavitt, Harold J. and Louis R. Pondy, *Readings in Managerial Psychology.* Chicago: University of Chicago Press, 1964.

Gombrich, E. H. *Art and Illusion: A Study in the Psychology of Pictorial Representation.* Princeton, NJ: Princeton University Press, 1977.

Hunt, Morton. *The Universe Within.* New York: Simon and Schuster, 1982.

Cognitive psychology for lay audiences; cognitive psychology is probably the branch of psychology that is most relevant to user interface design.

Koestler, Arthur. *The Act of Creation: A Study of the Conscious and Unconscious in Science and Art.* New York: Macmillan, 1964.

Lakoff, George and Mark Johnson. *Metaphors We Live By.* Chicago: University of Chicago Press, 1981.

A linguist and a philosopher show the importance of experience and metaphor in thought and communication.

SALES

Macali, Paul J. *The Lacy Techniques of Salesmanship.* New York: Hawthorne, 1982.

Unfortunately, most books on sales are written by insurance salesmen of the work-hard-and-talk-fast school. This book treats selling on a more sophisticated level. It is recommended by a former president of IBM, T. Vincent Learson.

Richardson, Jerry and Joel Margulis. *The Magic of Rapport.* San Francisco: Harbor, 1981.

An interesting look at an important aspect of interpersonal communication.

SOFTWARE

Brooks, Fred. *The Mythical Man-Month.* Boston: Addison Wesley, 1975.

A classic book on managing programming projects and a joy to read. We can learn as much from how it communicates as from what it says.

Heckel, Paul. "Designing Translator Software." *Datamation* magazine, February 1980.

The Craig language translator development is used as a case study in prototyping a product.

Heckel, Paul and Richard Schroeppel. "Software Techniques Cram Functions and Data into Pocket-Sized Microprocessor Application." *Electronic Design*, April 12, 1980.

A discussion of the software technology used to make the Craig language translator.

Kerningham and Plauger. *Elements of Programming Style.* New York: McGraw-Hill, 1974.

This book describes how programmers can simultaneously communicate software implementations to both computers and other programmers.

Hoare, C. A. R. "The Emperor's Old Clothes." 1980 ACM Turing Award Lecture. *Communications of the ACM,* February 1981.

Smith, David Canfield; Charles Irby; Ralph Kimball; Bill Verplank; and Eric Harslem. "Designing the Star User Interface." *Byte* magazine, April 1982.

A good description of what went into designing the Xerox Star—a signal product in friendly software design.

Tesler, Larry. "The Smalltalk Environment." *Byte* magazine, August 1981.

Thomas, J. C. and J. M. Carroll, "Human Factors in Communication." *IBM Systems Journal,* Volume 20, Number 2, 1981.

An article that describes friendly design as a problem in design of a communication process.

WRITING

Fugate, Francis L. and Roberta B. *Secrets of the World's Best-selling Writer: The Story-Telling Techniques of Erle Stanley Gardner.* New York: William Morrow, 1980.

The chapters entitled "The Readers' Servant" and "Luring Readers" are of particular interest.

van Leuwen, Mary-Claire. *A Handbook for Scholars.* New York: Alfred A. Knopf, 1979.

Orwell, George. *Collected Essays.* New York: Harcourt Brace Jovanovich, 1971.

The essay "Politics and the English Language" is the best essay on clear writing and thinking. All his essays are models of effective communication and a joy to read.

Strunk, William, Jr., and E. B. White. *Elements of Style.* New York: Macmillan, 1979.

Trimble, John R. *Writing in Style.* Englewood Cliffs, NJ: Prentice-Hall, 1975.

The chapter entitled "Thinking Well" is particularly recommended. This excellent book on writing deserves a much wider audience than the college students for whom it was intended.

Watt, Ian. *The Rise of the Novel.* Berkeley: University of California Press, 1957.

This book describes the birth of an art form— the modern novel that was developed in the eighteenth century.

MISCELLANEOUS

Kuhn, Thomas S. *The Structure of Scientific Revolutions.* Chicago: University of Chicago Press, 1970.

This book shows how strongly perception— in the sense of paradigm— has influenced the development of science.

Rogers, Everett with F. Floyd Schoemaker. *Communication of Innovations.* New York: Free Press, 1971.

Schon, Donald. *Technology and Change.* New York: Delacorte Press, 1967.

ROSES AND CABBAGES: FAMILIARIZING AND TRANSPORTING USER INTERFACE METAPHORS

Apple Computer. *Human Interface Guidelines.* New York: Addison-Wesley, 1987.

Dawkins, Christopher. *The Blind Watchmaker.* New York: Norton Publishing, 1987.

Derganc, Christopher S. "Thomas Edison and His Electric Lighting System." *IEEE Spectrum*, February 1979.

Heckel, Paul. "Zoomracks: Designing a New Metaphor." *Dr. Dobbs Journal*, November 1985.

Hughes, Thomas. *American Genesis.* New York: Viking, 1989.

Liddle, David. "Challenge of the Real World." *MacWeek*, December 6, 1988.

McPherson, James M. "How Lincoln Won the War with Metaphors." *Abraham Lincoln and the Second American Revolution.* New York: Oxford University Press, 1990.

Minsky, Marvin. *Society of Mind.* New York: Simon and Schuster, 1988.

Morrison, Hugh. *Louis Sullivan: Prophet of Modern Architecture.* New York: Norton Publishing, 1935.

Norman, Donald A. *The Psychology of Everyday Things.* New York: Basic Books, 1988.

Pardo and Landau. *U. S. Patent Number 4,398,249.*

Quickview Systems. *Zoomracks User Survey.* Los Altos, CA: Quickview Systems, 1987.

Quickview Systems. *U. S. Patent Numbers 4,486,857 and 4,736,308.*

Rahenkamp, Robert. *U. S. Patent Number 3,610,902.*

Sculley, John. *Odyssey.* New York: Harper and Row, 1987.

Shneiderman, Ben. *Designing the User Interface: Strategies for Effective Human-Computer Interaction.* Boston: Addison Wesley, 1987.

Sullivan, Louis. *The Public Papers.* Chicago: University of Chicago Press, 1988.

Wright, Frank Lloyd. *In the Realm of Ideas.* Carbondale, IL: Southern Illinois University Press, 1988.

EPILOGUE: THE WRIGHT BROTHERS AND SOFTWARE INVENTION

Berger, Bill and Ricardo Martinez. *What to Do with a Dead Lawyer.* Berkeley: Ten Speed Press, 1988.

Bolt, Robert. *A Man for All Seasons.* New York: Samuel French, Inc., 1960.

Conot, Robert. *Thomas A. Edison: A Streak of Luck.* New York: Da Capo Press, Inc., 1986.

A biography of Thomas Edison.

Crouch, Tom. *The Bishop's Boys.* New York: Norton Publishing, 1989.

A biography of the Wright brothers.

Grutman, Roy. *Lawyers and Thieves.* New York: Simon and Schuster, 1990.

Howard, Fred. *Wilbur and Orville.* New York: Alfred A. Knopf, 1988.

Hughes, Thomas. *American Genesis.* New York: Viking, 1989.

Josephson, Matthew. *Edison, a Biography.* New York: Mc-Graw-Hill, 1959.

Lerman, Lisa G. "Lying to Clients." *The University of Pennsylvania Law Review,* January 1990.

Lotus Development *vs* Paperback Software, *et al.,* 740 F. Supp 37:15 *USPQ* 2nd 1577 (D. Mas 1990).

McCormick, Mark. *The Terrible Truth about Lawyers.* New York: Beech Tree Books, 1987.

A lawyer turned businessman gives useful advice on dealing with lawyers.

Ried, T. R. *The Chip.* New York: Simon and Schuster, 1984.

Tells the story of the invention of the integrated circuit.

Shneiderman, Ben. "Protecting Rights in User Interface Designs." *SIG CHI Bulletin,* October 1990.

BIBLIOGRAPHY

"Software Industry in Uproar over Recent Rush of Patents." *The New York Times*, May 11, 1989.

See also "Letters to the Editor," June 8, 1989.

Stein, Sol. *A Feast for Lawyers*. New York: Evans and Company, 1989.

Sullivan, Louis. *Autobiography of an Idea*. New York: Press of the American Institute of Architecture, Inc., 1924.

"Will Software Patents Cramp Creativity?" *The Wall Street Journal*, March 14, 1989.

Index

314

INDEX

M

Machiavelli, Niccolò, 91
Macintosh computers, 157
McPherson, James, 155
macros (in Zoomracks),
     178–179
magic as illusion, 82
manuals. *See also* users
     deficiencies of, 45, 55–56
     good writing and, 119–122
marketing versus software
     engineering, 125–126
Markkula, Mike, 218
Maskelyne, Jasper, 80
Maugham, W. Somerset, 83
mechanics of tasks,
     transparency of, 60–62
Mediagenics, 254
Méliès, Georges, 8
Mencken, H. L., 155
mental models, 163–164
menus, 63, 71
     in rack metaphor, 189
     standardization of, 158
messages. *See also* commands
     informative, 42–43, 57–59
     judgmental, 15, 46–48
     respectful, 3
metaphors. *See also* rack
     metaphor
     communicating with,
          36–39, 41, 155–156,
          161–163, 190–198, 201
     gene, 194–201
     power of, 155–156,
          165–168, 232–233
     scrolling, 191
     transporting,
     paper-based, 190–194
     versus familiar, 162, 168
Michener, James, 20, 112

Minsky, Marvin, 160, 161, 164
movies. *See* film
Murphy's Law, 40
*Mustard Seed Garden Manual
     of Painting,* 107 (Fig.)
The Mythical Man-Month, 37,
     41, 62–63, 125

N

negotiations
     with Apple, 239, 253–254,
          260, 261–266
     with IBM, 268–291
Nichols, Dudley, 86, 125, 131
*Notes on the Synthesis of
     Form,* 56, 101
Noyce, Robert, 227, 229

O

observability of software, 94
observation, importance of,
     105–109
orientation of users, 68–69
Ortega y Gasset, José, 203
Orwell, George, 27, 29, 65,
     100–101
O'Toole, John, 77, 105
output forms in Zoomracks,
     180–181

P

PageMaker, 157, 192
paper-based transporting
     metaphors, 37, 190–194

V

W

Whorf, Benjamin, 161
Wilbur and Orville, 224
windowing systems (in
   paper-based transporting
   metaphors), 190–191
Wittgenstein, Ludwig, 43
word processors. *See also*
   WordStar
   conceptual models of, 159
   evaluations of, 44–46
   in HyperCard and
   Zoomracks, 179
   in paper-based
   transporting metaphors,
   191
   "what you see is what you
   get" principle, 59–60
WordStar
   for experienced and novice
   users, 75–76
   friendliness of, 10
   help command in, 58
   informative messages of,
   43, 48
   orientation of users by, 69
   reinforcing intent of
   commands in, 41–42
   relative simplicity of, 93
   success of, xxvi–xxvii,
   215–216
   user-oriented nature of, 25,
   71–72, 117
   users' attention focus in, 40
   wait states in, 56
Wright brothers, 224, 233,
   235, 236–237, 238, 239,
   246, 250
Wright, Frank Lloyd, 85–86,
   111, 130, 157, 160

Wright, Wilbur, 227, 229, 233,
   235, 237, 246, 257
writers. *See also* patents on
   software; software design
   as communicators, 1,
   126–127
   learning process for,
   119–121
writing friendly software. *See*
   software; software design

X

Xerox Star, 30, 37–38, 52, 69,
   158

Z

Zimmer, Tom, xxvii
Zoomracks, 170, 172, 174
   (Fig.)
   criticism of, 238
   demo rack for, 181
   file system in, 180
   future of, 292
   help system in, 180, 181
   macros in, 178–179
   metaphorical basis of, 169,
   230, 234
   output forms in, 180–181
   patents on, xxvii
   success of, xxviii
   user feedback on, 182–183,
   236
   versus HyperCard,
   183–185, 239–241, 243